Note to the second edition

Over the past four years I have been gratified, and at times surprised, by the success of *The Project Manager*. I have had lots of encouragement, discussion and some critical feedback. I am particularly grateful for the detailed comments from one anonymous reviewer (whoever you are – thanks!). In this edition I have utilised some of the feedback I have received to make this a better text.

I have updated the book in line with current project management thinking and research, included a number of diagrams, and generally tried to improve the text. Finally, there is a new chapter concerned with the wider context of project management. There are several topics that are not really project management, e.g. portfolio management, benefits management and change management, which all project managers need some familiarity with. Chapter 12 discusses these.

The goals and target audience of the book remain unchanged.

Richard Newton
March 2009

Introduction

The secret art

How do you consistently manage complex projects successfully?

There are people who are very successful at running projects. They have a track record in continuously meeting the objectives of complicated developments. When brought into conversation, and if they are being open, they will often query why people value what they do so highly – not because the things delivered in projects are not highly valuable, but because they think what they do is not that difficult. A regular comment is 'it's really just common sense, isn't it'. They work hard, but they do not get into that maniacal stress and overload that is often a feature of less well-run projects. They seem to be calmly in control. On the other hand, there is a huge number of people, including many project managers, for whom delivery of projects is at best a hard fought struggle and at worst a complete mystery – a secret art that they have not mastered. They somehow do not have the same type of common sense referred to by their more successful peers. So what is this black magic that is so simple to some and yet impossibly hard to others?

It's time to share some of the secrets.

Why read this book?

Project management is a skill set greatly in demand within both the public and private sectors – a skill set that a few decades ago would probably not have been formally recognised in any consistent way. Now it exists internationally both as an established profession in its own right, and as a competence that forms a part of many managers' general toolkit of capabilities. The demand for experienced project management professionals is a reflection of its success.

And yet for all its success and demand, there is something wrong. Ask a cross-section of managers in any large organisation whether they have absolute, or even high, confidence in their organisation's ability to deliver projects and you will get a resounding 'no'. There have been countless studies of the low percentage of projects that are delivered to time and budget, or the high percentage that are late or even never completed, and the figures are usually depressing. For all the processes, training and methodologies there is a gap between the hype and expectations and the actual experience. In contrast to this, most organisations have or know of a few people, 'safe pairs of hands', who can consistently manage to deliver exceptional projects to time and budget. What causes this gap, and what is it that these individual safe pairs of hands do that is different?

> so what is this black magic that is so simple to some and yet impossibly hard to others

To many people outside the project management profession it can seem at one extreme an almost mystically valuable black art and at the other a set of bureaucratic pomposity. At times the latter can be true, but project management is never magical. It is of tremendous value when well applied. The problem actually lies with those last three words of the previous sentence, 'when well applied'. Applying things well is hard enough, but there is little common consensus in the case of project management about what good application looks like.

At one level good application can be seen as the use of a quality project management approach. The profession is supported by a set of processes and methodologies which attempt to define 'how' to run a project. However, ask an experienced project manager what makes a good project manager and they will rarely mention understanding of the formal methodologies. The open secret among project managers is that good project management is about how you work, interact and communicate with people. So where can you start?

The place to start is with some definitions. There are many definitions of what a project is, and what project managers do. And even if you never intend to manage a project in your life it is essential for every manager to at least know the meaning and purpose of project management. You are most likely in any business career to find yourself involved in or needing a project. Having at least rudimentary project terminology is therefore useful. This book is not a glossary of terms, but in Chapter 1 the basic definitions are reviewed. This is mainly to give context to the rest of the text, and to provide a minimum common level of knowledge to build from.

Once some definitions are in place you can start to learn more about project management practice. In becoming a recognised profession, with commonly defined processes and working methods (such as PRINCE 2 or MSP), associated widely recognised accreditations (such as PRINCE 2 practitioner, or IPMA level B), professional institutions to belong to (such as the Association of Project Managers or the Project Management Institute), and even chartered status, much work has been put into defining good project management practice. The development of systematic methods has raised the standards and given consistency to project management. This defined approach can be referenced on many training courses and in literally hundreds of textbooks. They are variable in quality, but there are excellent reference texts and trainers out there. The aim of this book is not to add to these processes and methodologies, although they are referred to as necessary.

So if this book does set out to define project management roles, processes or methodologies, what is its purpose? It is a reference book, a set of observations from my personal experiences of what differentiates the great project manager from the merely average. This is not a normal project management primer. There are many excellent books and courses that can teach you the ABC of project management. It answers the question: what is it that you need to do to be a *consistently* good project manager?

The reason you should read this book is that it provides a set of experience-based lessons to consistently deliver results. If you are a project manager, have project managers on your team or recruit project management staff, it will provide you with a valuable addition to your core skills.

It is fair to ask at this point, what is my qualification to do this? It is simply that I have worked as everything from a junior project manager to a senior programme director within companies and international consultancies. I have successfully delivered everything from consultancy projects with budgets of a few tens of thousands through to major programmes launching new products and business changes with budgets in the hundreds of millions. I have also learnt from the experiences of recovering messed-up projects and messing up a few of my own. I have run project management teams, have taught and coached project managers, and have employed both permanent and contract project managers. I have operated up to director level in large companies as the customer or sponsors of projects being run by project managers. I have been involved in the development of delivery methodologies and project management approaches for consultancies. I have set up project management teams and project management centres of excellence in large companies. I have built competency-based assessment and standard career definitions for project management teams. In doing this I have worked extensively in the UK, mainland Europe (including France, Italy and Germany), the USA, Singapore, Kazakhstan and Australia. During this time I have deliberately observed and noted my impressions as well as managed delivery. What I have mainly observed is that even with the strengths of good process and training the difference between the results achieved by an average and the consistently good project manager are huge. Yet when I have analysed the reasons for this difference, as I have now been doing for a number of years, they are not so complex, and do not usually come down to basic project management knowledge. This book defines what those differentiating factors are. They are not a black art!

Will this book help you? It is true that some people are born to be project managers and intuitively know what to do, in the same way that some people are born to be accountants, lawyers or successful entrepreneurs. Yet all of these people, at least the really good ones, are willing to pick up lessons here and there, and there will be some valuable lessons here for you if you are lucky enough to be in this category. Then there is the much larger group of people who have the ability to be good or even great in their chosen profession but need a little guidance on the way. This book will help you too if you are in this category. Finally, there are project managers who feel that it is time for them to step up the project management ladder, make that move from junior to senior, cross the chasm from managing projects to managing programmes, or simply move from occasional project management roles to being a full-time project manager. That step will be assisted by this book.

The primary hypothesis of this book is that learning the core project management processes and following good standard project management practice is an important skill for a project manager, but that there is a host of hard and soft skills that are needed in addition. Taking that hypothesis, this book defines what those things are. Some of them are really good practice for any manager, others are specific to this profession.

This book is not a tick list or a process. Tick lists and processes are great when you get started and helpful in kick starting your thinking, but as things get more complex they do not provide everything a project manager needs. In fact, over-strenuous application of project management processes can be detrimental as it can make something that is best done with skill and experienced-based judgement into an unproductive mechanical application of bureaucracy. You will not find too much mention of terms like 'Gantt', 'PERT' and 'critical path analysis'. There is no talk of risk assessment methodologies or earned value analysis. There is little reference to the design of management forms, or how best to structure timesheets. It is not that these things do not have value; a good project manager has a wide toolkit of such capabilities that he often applies. It is simply that there are hundreds of good books, courses and people you can refer to, to understand these elements. What is frequently missing is the thing that says, 'So, OK, now you know all the processes. You have read all the books, done the courses and even implemented them on live projects. You have seen their value, and sometimes the difficulty of actually implementing them. But so have many other equally qualified project managers. And yet among this group are some who constantly deliver results and some who struggle.' Why is this? Well, here it is.

It is aimed at the experienced project manager, but will have lessons for the novice too. The sooner these are learnt the sooner you will be on your way to being a great project manager. What you will find is that many of these lessons appear simple, straightforward, and even obvious. Maybe, but like common sense, they do not actually appear to be in common usage.

A brief word on job titles

We seem to have entered an age of what I call job title escalation. We have all seen the term 'consultant' move from being used by top doctors and specialists to being used by all and sundry. We have watched as the job title director migrates from being reserved for people on the board to becoming an attribute of the middle manager. We have looked at the organisation chart for financial services companies where everyone seems to be a VP. This phenomenon is equally true when it comes to being a project manager. There are project coordinators, project managers, project directors, programme managers, programme directors and

> 66 we seem to have entered an age of what I call job title escalation 99

portfolio managers to name a few. Next to these titles may be a qualifying adjective like junior, senior, associate, executive and so on. To add to this complexity there are also professional project managers whose job title and permanent role is to be a project manager, and there are people who, for a period of time, take up the role of project manager while holding down a different job and having a different job title.

For the sake of sanity I will bundle this lot under the title 'project manager'. A project manager comprises a recognised professional skill set and is a job title that can be held with pride by those who really know what it means.

This makes life easy for me in writing this text, but obviously hides much detail about various levels of skills. There is value in the different role titles in some situations, and there can, for example, be a significant difference between a true programme manager and a junior project manager. But I do not intend to go into that in detail, as it will not help with the content or focus of this book. In practice I always take the job title of any individual with a pinch of salt. To use an old expression, the proof of the pudding is in the eating, and the same is true of the various types of project manager. Sometimes the titles reflect real skills and experience, occasionally a formal difference in role, and there are, as I intimated above, separate methodologies for programme managers in addition to those for project managers. However, all too often these different job titles are simply a reflection of over-inflated egos and positioning within organisational hierarchies. This unfortunately has had the effect of devaluing the titles and leads people to seek ever grander, and in some cases ridiculous titles. Bring on the senior executive consulting programme director!

To avoid any risk of bias I have intermittently swapped between the pronouns 'he' and 'she' throughout the book.

Work-streams, projects, programmes and portfolios

As well as having a hierarchy of job titles, the project world has a hierarchy of chunks of project work. A component of a specific project with a particular focus may be called a work-stream or work-package; a large or complex project or a set of interrelated projects may be called a programme (or for the USA, program); many projects together, whether related or unrelated but within some common area of responsibility, may be called a portfolio. In Chapter 1 I will define a project. The categorisation of projects of different scales, or the sub-categorisation of components of a project into chunks of work, can be useful but is often applied in a bogus or over-emphasised manner.

I avoid the distinction in most of this book as it is about better project management. To me this is about managing better, not necessarily bigger.

“ whatever the scale of the projects you manage you can do it better ”

Whatever the scale of the projects you manage you can do it better. If this was a general text on being a good manager I would not differentiate between a team leader, a manager and a department head; the principles of good management are the same. The skills here will help you to manage bigger projects and programmes if that is what is important to you, but they will also help you to manage your work-stream better. So, for now, forget the hierarchy – I will focus simply on the principles of great project management.

(For those who insist on understanding the difference, there is a short section in Chapter 12 which describes the role of a programme manager.)

A short overview of the contents

The contents of this book are structured to achieve two results. Firstly, it is written so you can read it easily from end to end. It is not an overly long book, but it is packed with value. Whether you diligently sit down and read it in one session, go through a little every night before you go to bed, or use it to fill your commuting time, you will find it easy to consume. Secondly, it is written so that you can call upon specific parts of its advice in an easy manner. Carry it around with you and use it on a daily basis. At the end of the book (page 278) a quick reference guide provides a chapter-by-chapter summary of key points for easy future reference.

The book is divided into thirteen chapters. Each can be read on its own or in sequence. In the following table I note the chapters and have tried to give them a priority rating out of 3 (3 being the highest priority). You will get the most benefit from reading the whole book in the order it is written, but if you are short of time and must prioritise, start with those chapters with the highest priority rating. (The ratings for Chapters 5, 7 and 10 are a reflection of how important these topics are to this book, rather than how absolutely important they are.)

Chapter	Title	Overview of chapter contents	Rating
1	Some basics	Review of basic terminology – project, project manager, customer, success.	1
2	Listening and talking	Core communication skills for project managers – the basis of good project management.	3
3	What actually is your project?	Really understanding what is wanted from the project you are delivering.	3
4	Some key traits	Personality traits needed by the project manager.	3
5	Getting your project started	Setting up your project taking account of practical realities. You understand the theory, but what does it all mean in practice?	2
6	Personal styles	Personal styles to avoid and to encourage in project managers.	2
7	Managing your project	A rapid overview of the mechanics of managing your project.	2
8	The team	How to manage your project team and get the best from them.	3
9	The limits of knowledge	Tasks project managers regularly get involved in that they should really avoid.	2
10	The mechanics of project management	Project management process basics that get forgotten.	2
11	Knowing when to say 'no'	When and how to avoid involvement in a project.	1
12	The wider context	An overview of supporting disciplines related to project management and useful to the project manager.	2
13	Closing thoughts	Round-up for the book.	2
	Quick reference guide – summary contents	Chapter-by-chapter summary of key points for easy future reference.	2

The structural logic of the book is as follows: I start by defining its objective and key terminology (Introduction and Chapter 1), then there are two interwoven threads. The first takes the reader through a project life-cycle, what must be done at each stage, and the tools you have to manage (Chapters 1, 3, 5, 7, 8, 10 and 12). In these I put project management processes in context and provide some practical and implementable advice. In parallel with this I weave a description of the human side of project management that is core to success but that is normally forgotten about (Chapters 2, 4, 6, 8, 9 and 11). I finish with my closing thoughts (Chapter 13) and the Quick reference guide.

For each topic I start by identifying the issues associated with it. Where possible I provide good practical answers and approaches to these issues. In some situations there are no single answers, and here I provide a framework of questions for the reader to use to work out an answer in the specific context she is working in. It is an intelligent guide to project management that does not say it is a purely mechanistic topic, but is one that requires the project manager to think and make judgement-based decisions.

Some basics

You must understand and be able to define the key terms used within your project. This must include a clear definition of your role as the project manager, a definition of the customer, and a common understanding of success for your project.

An assumption about readers of this book is that not only are you interested in project management, but you may already know something or even quite a lot about it. However, as a starting point, and to ensure we are working from the same knowledge set, it is worth having a common definition of some basic concepts. The starting point for us is to have a common view of **what is a project**, and **what is a project manager**. (If you know all about these things then you can feel free to skip the first two sub-sections of this chapter.)

As well as ensuring that you can follow and absorb the contents of the book, it is important to be able to define these terms. You will regularly need to use them yourself on projects and when communicating about projects. Being able to define these terms easily when required shows competence; struggling to define them looks like incompetence.

Having defined what a project is and what a project manager does, it is sensible next to think about who drives you to do a project. A project is undertaken because someone or some group of people want it done and want something achieved. This person or people are the customers. The next sub-section quickly runs through the concept of a customer for a project. This is not so simple or clear cut as project managers often think and 'who is the customer?' is a good question to keep asking yourself when running a project.

With these basic definitions understood, and given that one of the core aims of this book is to articulate the differentiating factors between the average and the really successful project manager, you had better also have a view of what success means in this context. This is discussed in the fourth and final sub-section of the chapter. Even if you think you are an expert it is worth running through this sub-section.

All the definitions given in this section are my own.

What is a project? What is project management?

A project is essentially a way of working, a way of organising people, and a way to manage tasks. It is a style of coordinating and managing work. What differentiates it from other styles of management is that it is totally focused on a specific outcome, and when this outcome is achieved the project ceases to be necessary and the project is stopped. Contrast this, say, with running a production line, or managing some company operations – these are tasks that run continuously and have no one single end point.

> what differentiates it from other styles of management is that it is totally focused on a specific outcome

A project starts at a defined point in time, ends at a specific point in time, and is complete when the outcome (normally as agreed at the beginning of the project, and normally defined in terms of specific tangible deliverables) is achieved. Typically, there are limited resources, most commonly money and people's time, to deliver the outcome. When the outcome is delivered something will have changed. Although different projects may have some common features, each project is unique, with a specific one-off set of activities.

However, just because a project starts does not mean it will complete successfully. History is full of examples of failed projects. Projects are typified by uncertainty, ambiguity, unknowns and assumptions. This lack of certainty is related to all aspects of projects, and is known in project management terminology as *risk*. Although various projects have significantly different levels of risk, they are all inherently risky, and achievement of the desired outcome is often far from certain.

Project management is a formal discipline that has been developed to manage projects. A wide range of activities can benefit from project management, from building a ship, constructing a house, developing an IT system, designing, building and launching a new product, to running a cost reduction exercise. The types of skills necessary to perform each of these activities vary immensely, but they can all be delivered by a project and managed by the project management approach. They all meet the criteria of having a clear and definable outcome or result.

As one of the primary characteristics of projects is that they are risky, project management can be considered as a way of overcoming the uncertainties and ambiguities inherent in projects. Project management is concerned with the bounding of risk through clear definition, detailing and ensuring understanding, and controlled management and overcoming of the remaining risk through risk management.

Project management tools, techniques and processes can be a powerful means of achieving a desired outcome, or in project manager parlance of 'delivering'. I have a very strong faith in the capability of this approach, but it does have its limits. These are useful to understand, as it helps to scope the boundaries of projects. Great as this approach is for achieving a specific set of deliverables, it is not a helpful technique if it is applied to continuous activities such as running a railway line or a production plant. I have experience of project mindsets being applied to operational situations and in all cases the results have been sub-optimal. Project management also is not helpful in situations of continuous change, when there is an ongoing stream of minor adjustments to processes or working practices.

What is a project manager?

A project manager is a person who has the responsibility for delivering all the components of a project. This can be a full-time job or a role in a given situation. The work a project manager does varies from project to project, but in essence the project manager is responsible for scoping out the work (see Chapters 2 and 3), planning it and determining what resources are required (see Chapter 5), getting the resources allocated (see Chapter 5), and then managing the completion of the tasks required and ensuring any risks or problems that may cause the completion of tasks to be delayed or stopped are resolved (see Chapter 7). A project manager works according to a project management approach (see Chapter 10). (In addition a project manager needs to apply a set of communications and people skills as discussed in Chapters 2, 4, 6 and 8.)

Sometimes there can be hierarchies of project managers. Each project manager then has a specific area of the project she is fully responsible for, and she in turn reports to a more senior project manager, often called a programme manager. As we have discussed in the Introduction, the job titles and scope of roles can vary, but the fundamental responsibilities of the job do not. (There is more to being a programme manager than simply being a more senior project manager. This is discussed in Chapter 12.) If you are working in a situation in which there are multiple project managers, you must be able to define your own specific role; the best way to do this is to be able to show which part of a project plan you are responsible for managing, and which deliverables you are responsible for ensuring are delivered.

A professional project manager is someone whose full-time job is to be a project manager and who is usually trained in project management processes and tools. This can be differentiated from someone who takes the role of a project manager on a specific project but who normally fulfils a different function.

The key point is that for any one scoped piece of work the project manager is the one person fully responsible for its delivery.

Who are projects for?

Every project is done for someone, or some group of people. These are the customers. At first glance this seems a simple concept and theoretically it is. The relationship between a project manager and their customer should be clear and explicit. In practice, it can be obscure and full of various levels of intrigue and politics (I do not exaggerate). Unless there is a specific need to differentiate between various customer groups, for simplicity's sake throughout the rest of this book I shall generally refer to the person or group of people a project is done for as 'the customer'. However, as a project manager you do need to understand fully the concept of customer in each and every project you are involved in.

> **the relationship between a project manager and their customer should be clear and explicit**

My definition of a customer is someone who has any of the following three characteristics:

1 She will legitimately put objectives or requirements upon the project.
2 She will enjoy the benefits of the project once it is complete.
3 She has a formal role in judging the success of a project once it is complete.

It is critical for the project manager to understand that:

- The customer has objectives and requirements which must be understood, as these are what the project must fulfil.
- There is often more than one customer.
- Different customers or customer groups may have different (and potentially conflicting) objectives, requirements and measures of success.
- The project needs to have a common set of objectives and requirements documented and agreed with the customer(s), noting those which must be considered and those which can be ignored.
- The customer's views and needs may change through the life of the project.

So far what I have stated is elementary. In reality, the ability to identify and understand the needs of varied customer groups is a complex subject in its own right. For most projects the customer can be broken down into various categories, and all have some interest in its being undertaken. The most common categories are:

- The sponsor
- The financer
- The beneficiary
- The end user
- The end customer
- The stakeholders (which is a broader group than customers).

These groups are defined and described in some detail in Chapter 2.

When you start a project it is worth thinking through each of these categories of customer and determining whether they exist, and, if you need to, to interact with them and manage their input to the project. Ideally there is a single person who acts as the overriding customer, or customer representative on a project. This person is often the project sponsor and they are critically important to a project's success, but it is a foolhardy project manager who assumes that the sponsor really represents all needs and does not review these other groupings, even informally, when kicking a project off. The dangers of not understanding fully who has objectives and requirements on a project are essentially:

- **Incomplete or incorrect plans** – and hence the project does not deliver all that is required.
- **Unsatisfied customers** – which can result in a lack of support or even active obstruction during the life of a project. It can also result in the project manager not being seen and treated at the end of a project as a successful manager.
- **Poor understanding of success** – customers may assess success in many ways, and unless you understand these your project may well fail. (This is described in more detail below.)

What is success?

If this book is to lay out a debate about what makes a successful project manager, I had better define what success is. Without this baseline it is possible to argue forever about whether the factors I have described in this book are really the basis for success; without agreeing this, success can become like beauty, its measure being in the eye of the beholder.

I need to start therefore, like a good project manager, by scoping out what I mean by success in this context. Every individual has their own definition of success, whether that is to have a great family life, hold down a good job, be able to retire at 45, have a new Porsche on your drive, or feel spiritually fulfilled on a daily basis. These are about 'personal success' and, as this is not a self-help manual, I am not intending to say too much about this beyond the few words in the next sub-section. In this book, when I talk about success I generally mean success in terms of what constitutes *project success*. If I am the customer, sponsor, stakeholder, or person paying for a project, how do I define project success?

Personal success as a project manager

There is an almost infinite number of ways of defining personal success, but these definitions lie beyond the remit of this text. However, in the limited context of the career of a project manager, how would he or she define success? Typically, to a project manager the definition of success is the successful completion of the project, to such an extent that they are able to go on to run other projects and are sought after to run the projects of their choice. What makes such projects worth doing to any individual typically falls into one or more of three categories:

- **The project content** – personal success driven by the ability to choose the projects working in the most interesting areas. Some project managers are driven by the desire to manage projects which relate to specific areas such as new technology or organisational change, or in particular industries or geographic locations.

- **The project complexity** – this relates to either the riskiness of the project, or the fact that the project is working in novel areas. Some project managers specialise in intellectually complex projects, or those that have a high risk or need recovering from seemingly intractable problems.

- **The project scale** – the size of the project or programme. There is a significant difference between running a £50k, 50-man/day project and a £5000m, 500-man/year programme, and the latter requires a variety of more advanced skills.

All of these are valid and interesting options for project managers, and in many cases it is a combination of these factors that excites or interests project managers. The key point I would make to any project manager is that the ability to select between the types of project you are involved in as a project manager will be driven over time by people's expectations and experiences of your delivery of projects. In other words, your personal success is directly related to your perceived project success.

> **your personal success is directly related to your perceived project success**

Project success

Every project will have a set of things that can be used to measure success. These may be formally laid out as critical success factors, or may simply be implied between the project manager and whoever is driving or sponsoring the project. In fact, one of the first tasks, and key skills, of a good project manager running a well-run project is to get clarity around the explicit success factors and tease out the implicit or hidden ones. In some projects the results will be a simple set of deliverables; in others they may be a very complex set of interrelated factors. In some cases these may even be contradictory, leaving the project manager to perform a balancing act, trading one off against the other.

The theory is that at the end of a project the person who wanted it done can simply compare what she or he has been given with the success criteria and decide whether a successful outcome has been achieved. Every project manager balances this against a list of caveats and reasons that can limit the ability to achieve the successful outcome (for example: this is enough money and time for the project as long as nothing changes; or, I will get it done as long as I get these resources; or, the end results will be achieved as long as this risk does not occur).

Unless it is a very simple or very clear cut project, defining the absolute measure of success can be hard and the definition is usually subject to ambiguity and change. However, in simple terms all types of success measures can be boiled down into the following three high-level categories:

- **Deliver the deliverables** – this may seem blindingly obvious, and for many projects, especially the non-complex ones, success is simply the achievement of the deliverables planned at the start of the work. Such deliverables will take many shapes and may be documents, IT systems, other technology and infrastructure, buildings or, more subtly, some kind of business change. The list of possible deliverables is endless; a project and a project structure can be used to deliver almost anything.

- **Achievement of associated benefits** – typically someone or an organisation who has initiated a project wanted the deliverables for some reason that gives them benefits. A common business example would be to deliver a new IT system, which in turn results in the benefit of lower costs or higher quality somewhere else in the business. So, using this example, success is then measured by checking that the lower costs and higher quality have been achieved.

(I will discuss this last point more in Chapter 12, but it is worth pointing out that there are three problems with knowing exactly what benefits have been achieved. Firstly, they are often difficult to measure. Secondly, it is usually difficult to be sure that it was the project that delivered them and not some other change. Finally, they typically arise only after the project has been completed and the project manager is working on something else. But I will ignore this for now and assume that they can be measured.)

Hence success can be measured first against a pile of deliverables, and a stack of achieved benefits. But success is not simply a matter of delivering deliverables and achieving business benefits; there is a specific caveat: they must be delivered within the time and cost agreed at the outset of the project, and to the agreed scope and quality. It is no good delivering deliverables and achieving benefits if the cost is too high (or more generally the amount of resources used was too high), it took too long, the quality is not good enough, or the end results are somehow less than originally perceived or planned.

But let's assume that success is achieved. We have got to the end of the project. We did not spend all the money or use up all the time. The deliverables are wonderful and the benefits are now rolling in. Is that enough? Well, almost, but not quite. There is one more factor:

■ **Customer satisfaction** – this is the third category of success measures, associated with the deliverables and benefits but not synonymous with them. Every project has a customer of one form or another. This may simply be the person asking for or paying for a project. Or it may be a host of people with a complex set of relationships. Understanding who the various stakeholders in projects are is a skill project managers should acquire, and the degree of success will depend on these people being happy with the outcome of the project. Some project managers may baulk at this final category, on the basis that it is not often specified as an explicit requirement of the project and may simplistically be seen as an outcome of providing the customer with the deliverables originally requested and achieving the follow-on business benefits. Another reason for discounting it is that it is often intangible and difficult to measure. These things are true, but then no-one ever said being successful was easy. Success is more complex than handing over deliverables and waiting for benefits to roll in. Being truly successful is not always about doing simply what you were asked to do. If a project manager wants to be successful, he must be successful not only in his own eyes but also in the eyes of his customers. Happiness, satisfaction or delight on the customer's behalf is core to being a successful project manager.

So, if that is what success is, what is a successful project manager? It is simply someone who consistently completes projects and meets these three goals: he gets the deliverables completed and handed over, he sees the business benefits arising, and he leaves the customers with smiles on their faces. If you can do this consistently, then you have every right to feel you are good – and I can pretty much guarantee you will stay in demand.

As a final note, in the remaining chapters I will show how this is not always absolutely true, as the key to success is really about meeting *expectations* about deliverables, benefits and satisfaction. This is related to achieving it, but subtly different. Reality is reality, but expectations and perceptions can be managed to change! This too is part of the project manager's art that will be discussed in the following chapters.

Listening and talking

Think about, plan and execute your communications with care, effort and impact. Your communications must be based on an understanding of your customer that goes beyond the requirements specification and sharing periodic reports. Your communications with the project team must go beyond sharing the project plan and having sporadic updates.

The most important chapter in the book

If you are just getting started in your career as a project manager and are taking time to learn the trade then this chapter is a very good place to begin. Alternatively, if you are an experienced and very busy project manager with only the time to read one chapter of the book, read this one. The other chapters all have valuable insights that will improve your project management and it would be a shame not to read them now you have a copy of this book, but this chapter contains the essence. All else is about advancing skills and finesse; this chapter is about getting the basics right.

Although the topics in this chapter are rarely covered in any project management course, they can be considered as even more fundamental than learning the various disciplines and processes that make up a project manager's toolkit. They may be missed because they are obvious, or because they are thought of as rudimentary rather than fundamental. My experience is that the communication skills I describe are the core differentiator between great project managers and the average, and yet are rarely analysed or taught in the specific context of managing projects.

This chapter aims to make you think about whom you should communicate with, what you need to listen to, and how you should respond. It does have some specific answers, but it also poses questions that you need to answer yourself, and which may have different answers in different situations. It is focused as much on how you communicate as on what you communicate, as to be successful you not only need to communicate the right information you need to do it in the right way. If you take only one lesson away from this chapter it should be to think about, plan and execute your communications with care, effort and impact. Do not forget it because it seems so self-evident.

The chapter is broken into three sections. I first look at understanding the audience you are meant to communicate with, then I look at the things you need to listen to from your customer, and finally I cover the key communication skills a project manager should possess. Some of the project management concepts that involve communications will not be dealt with in detail until later chapters, but I have decided to cover communications first as it is the framework that underpins and surrounds everything else. Without adequate communication skills you will never succeed.

Your audience – whom you must listen and talk to

Key lesson

Identify and assess your audience's information needs. Identify who is your customer and plan your interaction with them.

This section briefly looks at whom you need to communicate with and why. All too frequently project managers regard communications as a painful overhead and not as the core task that it is. 'I am so busy talking to people that I do not have time to get on with my day job' is a familiar complaint that misses the point that talking to people is *the* central part of a project manager's workload.

In most situations either we communicate with whoever we intuitively feel we need to communicate with, or we respond to a specific stimulus to talk. We do not often sit down and independently ask ourselves *so who is it that I need to be in dialogue with now*? It is true that much of good communications needs to be intuitive to project managers, and any good project manager will have built up from experience mental triggers to begin communications when starting out on a new piece of work. You may even now be thinking *isn't it obvious who I need to talk to*? The purpose of this section is not to confirm what is already clear to you, but to make you think and plan your communications explicitly. The truth is that intuition is usually at best incomplete, and at worst flawed. Some key communications will be missed if you wait for external triggers. You need to plan them out. Frequently project managers rely too heavily on their reflexes. Good project managers are often great instinctive communicators, but they also plan through and make sure they have covered all their bases when it comes to communications. On a big project, thinking through and planning whom to communicate with is a worthwhile use of significant amounts of project management time.

> 6 6 thinking through and planning whom to communicate with is a worthwhile use of significant amounts of project management time 9 9

The dangers of not adequately identifying your audience are a risk to the project. If you do not enter into dialogue with all the people you need to, the level of risk will increase. Risk that you will miss the point that a customer wants you to understand. Risk that you will not be told something you need to know. Risk that you will miss out some vital task in your plans. Risk that your customer will want to change something and you will remain unaware. Risk that some group of people you have not spoken to will actively oppose your work. The list is endless. The misunderstanding of what is wanted and what is happening, and the incomplete explanation of what you want and what should be happening, lies at the core of most project failures.

So let us start by considering what basic groups of people you need to communicate with. All project managers have a set of people they must talk to in both informal and formal ways on a regular basis. This audience can be split into three broad categories:

1 People directly involved in the project – this can be the project team, but will also include suppliers and other third parties responsible for delivery and delivery-related activities.

2 Customers of the project – the person or group of people for whom a project is being delivered.

3 Other stakeholders – a wide group that can include anyone else impacted by, or able to impact the outcome of, the project.

Next, let us briefly think through – who are these people, how important is each of these three groups we have identified, and what must the project manager consider in each case? Table 2.1, at the end of this section, summarises the key communication actions a project manager should undertake for each of these groups.

The project team

The main day-to-day communications of the project manager will be with the project team. It should not need to be said, but without these the project will not even get off the starting blocks. As far as the team goes, the project manager obviously needs to communicate with them to explain what needs to be done, and to direct their work. In addition, the project manager needs to:

- Explain and continually update understanding on the plan and scope as they change through the life of the project
- Provide specific instructions as to which tasks are to be performed by which team members
- Motivate the team to complete their work in an effective and efficient manner
- Understand the team member's progress relative to the plan
- Support the team to keep progress going
- Understand issues and risks as they arise
- Understand the team and personal dynamics so any management intervention that is required can be planned and implemented
- Listen to the team, as they are a source of critical information, good ideas and suggestions.

In doing this the project manager must learn to understand what information is relevant to the project team, and what approach to communicating with them is best.

Who is on the project team is probably obvious, but think through who else needs to be brought into your regular communications process. Do you have any third-party suppliers delivering key activities into the project? Do you have any specialists who contribute for only short periods to the project? Groups like this need to be directed as much as any core project team members.

Unless you can be sure that everyone on the project knows everything they need to do their work, and to do the correct work, then more communication is required.

Customers

In business the phrase 'the customer is king' has become such a well-worn mantra that it rarely needs saying, and when it is said it feels like a cliché. As we discussed in Chapter 1 all projects have a customer, and yet rare is the project manager who really thinks in terms of a customer–supplier relationship. How customer-focused are you when managing your projects? There is usually a gap between the theory of customer focus on projects and the reality. One reason for this gap is that it is often taken for granted that the project is customer-focused as the customer has normally defined and documented some requirements. The other reason is that the whole concept of 'the customer' can be complex on a major project.

Unless you are continuously and consciously focused on your customer's needs and achieving them (or at least managing expectations about them), customer satisfaction will decline and your project will not be the 100% success that it might be. This is not only about giving good news or doing only what the customer wants, but also having an open trusting relationship in which you have empathy for and understanding of their needs.

The customer can be broken down into several distinct categories:

- **The sponsor** – the role of the sponsor varies from project to project. Most project managers know them as the person they must send their periodic status reports to. The sponsor should be the person driving the work, acting as the senior interface point for the project manager. This person may or may not be the beneficiary of the work, but is often ultimately accountable for its completion. He or she will direct the project manager and act on a day-to-day basis as if they were the primary customer. The relationship with the sponsor should be two-way: they need to direct the project manager, but he or she is also a resource the project manager can call on for help. An example might be a project to build a new production line for a company. In this case the sponsor may well be the operations director; she is the person who is accountable for ensuring there is enough production capacity and so will sponsor a project to build the new production line. She will provide the overall scope for the work, and will help resolve problems the project manager cannot sort out on his own.

- **The financer** – the person paying for the project. This is quite often the sponsor, but in some organisations it may be someone different, with more or less interest in the outcome of the work. For a major programme of work, it may, for example, be the finance director. The finance director (FD) or chief financial officer (CFO) needs to be kept on board as he or she may be able to cut the flow of funds at any time, but otherwise may have limited interest in the work. In the example of the project to deliver a new production line, the FD or CFO will be very interested in how much it costs and that it is completed but, unlike the operations director, will normally not be too interested in the daily details of the project's progress.

- **The beneficiary** – the person or group who will realise the benefits from the project if and when they are achieved. This may be the sponsor but can be quite a different set of people. While on a day-to-day basis they may have limited involvement and interest in a project, if the beneficiaries are not satisfied with the end results the project will not have succeeded. In the case of a company building a new production line to expand capacity, the beneficiaries are really the company's owners who will receive greater profits as a result. If the new production line does not deliver the profits expected they will be unhappy and will take appropriate action.

- **The end user** – the person who will end up using the deliverables from the project. For many projects these are the staff of the organisation involved. These people are not really the beneficiaries as they do not personally benefit from the results, but if they are unhappy or unable to use the deliverables the project will not be a full success. In the example given, the end users are the people who work in the production plant. They are customers who need to be considered, as any production facility must be usable by the staff involved.

- **The end customer** – the final customer. For example, a different project may be delivering a new product to a supermarket chain. From the project's perspective, during the life of the project the supermarket chain is the customer. However, the supermarket is doing this in turn to sell to its customers – the end customer. Do these people matter? Typically, on a day-to-day basis on a project, individually they do not. But they do matter to the overall project's success: if the end customers do not like the supermarket's new product they will not buy it, and the project will have been a failure. Their views and needs must be understood, either directly or indirectly through a specialist like a marketing department.

Project managers do need to talk and listen to the relevant members of the customer community on a regular basis. The relevant customer in any specific situation will vary and you must take time to work out which customer is appropriate.

Overall, the project manager therefore has to:

- **Identify who the customers are** – when you think through the list above you can see that this is not necessarily as straightforward as it might trivially seem to be. Go through the list above for every project you are involved in and make sure you know how critical these groups are to the success of your project.

- **Identify relative criticality and importance** – not all customers are as important as others: you have limited time and you will not be able to communicate fully with everyone. Do not use this as an excuse for poor customer management, but focus the majority of your time on the most important.

- **Determine what information is relevant to them** – each of these customer groups has different information needs. A financer will typically be worried about how much you have spent relative to how far through the project you are, the end customer will be more concerned with how the end result matches their needs.

- **Determine what is the best timing, media and approach to use in passing information** – some customer groups will need very regular, perhaps even daily communications. Others will be quite satisfied with more infrequent information. I have seen very successful projects having only quarterly brief communications to certain customer groups. Some need very detailed reports, others short e-mails.

- **Determine what you need in return from the customer** – information flow is a two-way process. Project managers often dump information on their customers without thinking what they can get in return, whether this is some more requirements or a commitment to do something that will help the project or project manager.

I talk more about each of these later in the chapter.

Stakeholders

I introduced the concept of stakeholders in the previous chapter. The importance of these stakeholder groups varies immensely from project to project. On small projects, or those with deliverables that have impact in a limited domain, they can largely be forgotten. At the other extreme with large business-change programmes, or things that have a significant impact on large numbers of people such as a major road-building programme, communicating with stakeholders may be one of the main tasks on the programme. As far as the stakeholders are concerned the project manager needs to:

- **Identify who the stakeholders are** – who can impact or is impacted by the project?
- **Assess their relevance to the project** – are they only marginally relevant, or is their support critical to the project?
- **Target those with significant impact on the project's success** – anyone who can stop you delivering is likely to need to be managed.
- **Target those significantly impacted by the project's outcome** – should this be a goal of the project. For example, on a project to build a new road there may be a large number of people affected by the road – some positively with faster journey times, some negatively by suddenly finding themselves living by a noisy road. These people may not be able to impact the project's success and so you may feel you can ignore them. Your sponsor may still require you to take their views into account and to minimise the impact upon them. Taking people with you is often a success factor for large projects.
- **Determine appropriate communication** – the goal of the communication is to understand the stakeholders' viewpoints, to encourage those in favour of the project to support it, and to mitigate the responses of anyone opposed to the project.

I discuss stakeholder identification and management processes in more detail in Chapter 10.

The audience needs are summarised in Table 2.1.

table 2.1 Communication actions by audience type

Project team	Customer	Stakeholder
Communicate what needs to be done by when.	Identify who the customers are.	Identify who the stakeholders are.
Explain and update understanding on the plan and scope through the life of the project.	Identify relative criticality and importance.	Assess their relevance to the project.
Provide instructions – which tasks are to be performed by which team members.	Determine what information is relevant.	Target those with significant impact on the project's success, and
Motivate to complete work in an effective and efficient manner.	Determine what is the best timing, media and approach to use in	those significantly impacted by the project's outcome.
Understand the team member's progress relative to the plan.	passing information.	Determine appropriate communication.
Support the team to keep progress going.	Determine what you need in return from the customer.	
Understand issues and risks as they arise.		
Understand the team and personnel.		
Listen to the team for information, ideas and suggestions.		

Listening – learning to understand what the customer wants

Key lesson

There is much more to understanding your customer's needs than is written in the requirement specification. As project manager you must understand all the requirements at a high level, and specifically understand fully the scope of the project. Real understanding requires a constant two-way dialogue.

It will seem clear to most project managers that to deliver a project successfully you have to start by knowing what your customer wants. After all, it is self-evident – if you do not know what the customer wants you would not start on a project. Without understanding what the customer wants, how would you know what to do? Without understanding what the customer wants, would it be worth even considering starting a project? Logically the answer to these questions is 'no', but in practice it often happens that a project starts without fully understanding customer needs. This happens for a number of reasons, such as:

- **The customer does not know what they want** – or to put it more accurately, they know they want something, but they do not really know what it is. I have frequently seen even senior executives coming up with the answer 'we need a project', without knowing quite what question it is trying to answer.

- **The customer cannot define what they want** – they know roughly what they want but need help in expressing it in a useful format. Communicating what is wanted in an unambiguous way is often hard. Don't you ever find yourself being quite clear about your need for something but having difficulty communicating this to others?

- **The customer thinks that you understand what he wants** – without needing to explain it. This is a very common problem for in-house project managers who can be faced with line managers who think by common experience with day-to-day issues nothing ever needs to be fully explained. I am sure I have even met a few senior executives who believed in telepathy!

- **The customer's thinking about what they want is not stable** – they are quite clear about what they want until they see it starting to form at which point they decide they need something else. This something else may be a minor tweak on the original idea or it can be substantially different. (There are some specific development techniques such as prototyping to help resolve this type of problem.)

- **The customer is impatient for results** – to some people work such as collecting requirements and planning activities seems like wasted time, and they want to get on with achieving tangible results. Although with any degree of thinking this is obviously nonsense, it is a common viewpoint.

It is worth being prepared for the fact that you may find yourself in any of these situations, and also being explicitly aware of them when you do find yourself there. In fact, the most productive mindset to take is to assume that the customer does not exactly know what he wants and needs some help getting it scoped out. The project will not be a success unless at some stage, and preferably reasonably early on, the requirements and reason for the project are commonly shared and understood.

> ❝ I am sure I have even met a few senior executives who believed in telepathy ❞

Requirements exist in various forms, whether it is an architectural plan for a building, a requirements specification document for an IT project, or a bill of materials for a complex procurement project. Whatever format the requirements exist in, they are the basis for the output of the project.

Approaches to collecting requirements, especially in technology-led work, have evolved over time. Initial structured approaches relied on completing a full and detailed requirements capture at the start of the project. No development was done until all the requirements were complete. Such approaches have been given the general title of 'waterfall' as they require full completion of a step of a project in its entirety before cascading on to the next step in unidirectional processes through the life of the project. Like a flow of water, the project progresses in only one direction. The alternatives are many, but they can be lumped together under the title of 'iterative' development approaches. These rely on enough requirements being captured before moving on to the next step when some deliverable, or a prototype, is produced, which in turn generates more thinking on the requirements and hence an iteration back into requirements capture. Such iterative approaches may flow between requirements capture and delivery several times before completion. The different approaches suit different types of project and different technologies. However, the overall point is that whatever the approaches towards requirements capture and development are, requirements are at the core.

What the customer wants is normally encompassed within a number of key documents on a project and, depending on the industry or organisation in which the project is being carried out, these documents may have different names. The size, level of detail and richness of these documents is usually a function of the scale of the project and complexity of the deliverables. What can be said in generic terms is that there are several essentials the project manager needs to know before she can say she understands what the customer wants. They are:

- **The objectives of the project** – defining why it is being pursued. This is normally presented as a part of the scope.
- **The scope of the project** – defining what counts as 'inside' and equally important what counts as 'outside' the project. This is usually held in some kind of project definition or brief.
- **The measures of success** – defining the things that can be measured at the end of a project to see if success has been achieved. This is usually also held in some kind of project brief.

- **The detailed requirements** – defining all the particular things the customer wants from the project. This is normally held in a specific document, typically referred to as the requirements specification or requirements catalogue. Development of detailed requirements can often be a stage of the project rather than a prerequisite of the project.

Teasing out, refining, documenting and checking requirements is a skill in its own right. On more complex projects this is not even the role of the project manager, but is a specialist skill set typically called 'business analysis' (this is discussed more in Chapter 9). However, even if doing all the detailed requirements capture is not the job of the project manager, she does need to be sure that it is complete. In addition, the task of capturing some particular sorts of requirements – 'scoping requirements' – is specifically the role of the project manager. (This is outlined more fully below.) Another way to look at it is that scoping is really the last step before the project can begin, while requirements capture is normally an activity carried out during the project's lifetime.

Any basic course in project management will teach that project managers need to collect and document what the customer wants in one way or another, and will stress the importance of understanding scope. Many project managers carry template project scoping and project definition documents around with them. They start each project by essentially filling in the blanks. This can be both effective and efficient. The problem comes not in knowing what to capture in general, but in understanding how to go about capturing it and the ability to judge when sufficient detail is available and when more is needed. All too often project managers are guilty of not putting enough effort into this process of understanding customer needs, and taking what is initially said to them at face value.

     ❝ it is your customer's project, not yours ❞

Although there are specific times when listening is critically important, listening to understand the customer is something that project managers need to learn to do throughout the life of a project. Without writing a treatise on business analysis, there are seven lessons for the project manager when it comes to understanding customer needs:

- **Make assumptions explicit** – minimise the number of assumptions, and, if you must assume, get the assumptions clear and shared.
- **Derive a clear understanding of scope** – and make sure you can write it down in words meaningful to both you and your customer. If

you cannot write the scope down you probably do not fully understand it, and will almost certainly have difficulty communicating the scope to other team members.

- **Make sure you understand the customer requirements and how they relate to the project you are running** – expect differences of opinion over requirements between different customers, and put in place some mechanism for resolving them.
- **Keep checking and enhancing your understanding** – things change and being sure last week is not the same as being sure today.
- **Understanding the customer** – this is not simply about understanding the things documented in the requirements specification.
- **It is your customer's project, not yours** – the attitude you take to your customer's input is important.
- **Listening is probably your biggest task** – you will probably spend more time listening than any other activity. It is essential to be good at listening, and if you are not, learning how to get better.

Let's think about each of these in turn.

Listening lesson 1 – Make assumptions explicit

The golden rule is: check your understanding, do not assume anything.

Managing assumptions is a core project management activity that is often forgotten. In every conversation and communication there are lots of embedded ideas and implicit information. However, there is absolutely no guarantee that what is clearly implied within the words of one person is also clearly implied in the understanding or interpretation of those words by the person listening. This becomes especially true when people are firmly lodged within an organisational culture (I'm sure you will have been involved in those 'why do you do it this way? – because we always have' conversations), or when specialists in one field or another talk to each other, passing what is very clear information to one another, but is not clear to anyone without their background. What you need to do as a project manager is to make these assumptions clear; at the very least, other people in the project need to know them. In addition they must be checked, as often they may undermine the project if they are not true.

Poor understanding of assumptions is one of the major sources of risk on projects. (In Chapter 4 I look at when it is reasonable to make assumptions, and in Chapter 10 I describe more about the process of managing assumptions.)

Whenever you are collecting information on the project, keep asking yourself the questions 'are there any assumptions within that statement?' and 'that does not make sense unless something else is assumed ... what is it?' – and if it seems that these are valid questions then ask the person to make the assumptions explicit.

Listening lesson 2 – Understand the scope

Detailed requirements capture is best done by a trained business analyst, and as this book is not a primer in business analysis I will not go through everything business analysts must do. However, there is some key information which it is the responsibility of the project manager to capture, refine, understand and document. This is what I will call 'scoping requirements'. They are the requirements which define the fundamental shape, size, purpose and range of the project and are critical to understanding what the customer really wants.

Understanding scope is the first thing a project manager must start to do when appointed to a project. For a project manager a full understanding of what is within, and almost as important what is not within, the scope of a project is essential. An inability to understand and communicate the scope of a project is as close to a cardinal sin as it is possible to get in project management.

When you have talked with your customer to understand a project's scope, the next thing to do is to write it down. The reason for writing it down is firstly obvious, because it means it will not get forgotten and it can easily be shared. Also important is that the practice of writing down the scope in a coherent manner is a good test of whether you really understand it or not. If you cannot write it down you probably do not fully understand it, and will almost certainly have difficulty communicating it to other team members.

Understanding the scope of a project is so fundamental that I have broken it into a separate chapter. Chapter 3 expands on this subject and defines a set of key questions that you can use to be sure that you have really scoped out the project.

Listening lesson 3 – Understand customer requirements and how they convert into a project

The whole of this section of the chapter has been about listening to customers and prompting them with the right questions at the right time.

When you have done this you will have a full set of customer requirements. The next thing you have to do is to convert these into a project. That is what project managers do.

That sounds straightforward. In doing this you need to have a good grasp of what the requirements are, why the requirements exist, and how this converts into a project plan. Without this understanding you will have difficulty shaping and running the project, and you will find it very difficult to manage a team – the team will need their work explained and put in context.

The test for you is the ability to answer the questions in Table 2.2. The answer to all of these questions must be 'yes'. This is not a demand that you analyse, memorise and understand each and every line of the requirements specification, and each and every line of every plan within your project. It is a demand that someone on the project has done this, and that you have a logical understanding of how it all comes together. When you look at every major activity within the project you must know why it is being done and what the impact of its failure will be. (I always read the whole requirements specification, even if it is often long and tedious. I do this to ensure I understand what will be required in the project and to make sure there are no surprises hidden away in the details.)

table 2.2 Checking project requirements

Key requirements questions	Yes	No
Do you have an overall grasp of the customer requirements, and how they relate together to give the overall customer solution?	☐	☐
Do you understand why the customer has included these requirements?	☐	☐
Has the customer included only requirements which relate to achieving the agreed scope and objectives of the project? (If the answer is no, you have two choices: reject the requirement, or revise the scope of the project.)	☐	☐
Do you understand how these requirements will translate into blocks of work that the project will deliver?	☐	☐
Do you understand how these blocks of work hang together?	☐	☐
Can you visualise and explain this?	☐	☐
Will the combined set of requirements achieve the customer's desired outcome and expectations?	☐	☐
Is each requirement clear, unambiguous, traceable (i.e. do you know its source?), and testable (i.e. do you have a way of being certain you have achieved it?).	☐	☐

Without this knowledge you cannot plan, manage or deliver the project. If you are on a project and you cannot answer 'yes' to each of the questions in Table 2.2, do some more work so you can answer 'yes' (or find someone else to run it). In practice, on a project with any complexity you will be reliant on other specialists to build components of the plan for each specialist area. However, you still must integrate the components into the overall plan, and you own and are accountable for that plan.

When requirements are captured, expect differences of opinion about both what requirements there are, and what their relative importance is. Only the very simplest of projects clearly have one customer who gives all requirements and therefore you must have some mechanism for agreeing what counts legitimately as a requirement. This can be as simple as the sponsor having the decision, or can entail setting up a requirements committee which can resolve any requirements conflicts. Make this mechanism as simple as possible, or you risk never completing the requirements capture stage of a project. (People can generate and discuss requirements for ever. One of your early tasks is to get control over this process and see that it is completed in a timely fashion.) In the last question in Table 2.2, I note the need for requirements to be traceable. This is because when there are conflicts you need to know who to involve in any discussion, and who to inform if their requirements are rejected from the project.

Listening lesson 4 – Keep checking

The first point I noted here in capturing requirements was to assume nothing. Once you have documented requirements and agreed them with the customer, assuming they will never change is a poor assumption. Regularly go back to the customer and check the basic scoping requirements; when key decisions are being made based on these that will alter or shape major parts of the project, test them with your customer. Being posed with a statement of the format 'we are doing x, because of your requirement y' is a powerful way for people to be forced to see the implications of their requirements and from that to decide whether they really were needed and whether they need to be changed.

Do not simply do this once; keep checking with the customer. You should be constantly vigilant to the question yourself – *have requirements changed, have assumptions changed?* All good projects have a change control process which can be used when requirements change to manage the assessment and impact of that change upon the project and to get agreement to that when it happens. However, the change control process is merely a mechanism to handle the change; it will not generate the changes itself.

At this stage some project managers may well be thinking 'but I don't want changes'. A project without changes is a more straightforward thing to deliver than one that keeps changing. That is true, and one key reason why it is worth putting in the effort to get the requirements as right as possible up front. But however comprehensive the requirements capture, however long you spend in conversation with your customer on your scoping requirements, people are fallible, people cannot predict the future with any accuracy, and even the most senior customer is not in control of or aware of everything. A project that successfully delivers yesterday's needs cannot be guaranteed to be considered a success today. Make sure it is controlled, but be open to change.

Whenever you need to check your understanding, don't be afraid to ask the apparently stupid question. Occasionally, asking a stupid question can make you look as if you don't understand, but this is rare. More often than not, asking the really basic questions can generate a much deeper understanding and can highlight hidden assumptions. It's a trick that successful senior executives know very well. Watch them; they will often ask apparently naive questions and through them find out things that the clever question never does.

Listening lesson 5 – Customer needs go beyond requirements specification

Remember that no matter how good your requirements capture process, it will not capture all of your customer needs. Your customer will have needs about the way you work with her, the style of interaction you adopt and various other factors. We are all imperfect, we work in a political and social world that has needs beyond pure functional requirements, and finally we are all human and how we interact is important to us. It is your job as a project manager to see not just that the project delivers the requirements specified, but also that it does so in a way that is acceptable to the customer.

Listening lesson 6 – Remember it's not your project

As project manager your job is to ensure the project meets its objectives, but in the end it is not your project. You are the agent of your customer, and this must be reflected in the way you listen to your customer and think about the project, and in your behaviour. The high-level guidance is that your customer owns the 'what' of the project, and you own the 'how'. In this situation 'what' refers to the scope and requirements, 'how' to the way in which it is managed and delivered.

This does not mean you should not have views, or even be opinionated, but you must know who has the last say in what situation. A constructive relationship is one in which you can challenge the customer about requirements, but the choices are hers; similarly she may challenge you about how you plan to deliver the project, but the final choice is yours.

Two good examples of where this is often forgotten are in defining requirements and in making changes to scope. Project managers must avoid the temptation to add or remove requirements that seem obvious to them; if you think something is missing or should not be included, advise your customer, but let her make the decision. With customer-driven changes the problem can be more insidious. Project managers often develop an attachment to a project and a passion to complete it, and can resent it when people try to change things that make their lives more complex. It is worth remembering that the project does not exist for the project manager's benefit, and as long as the customer understands the impact of a change, it's her decision to make.

The project belongs to the customer and the customer needs to know how it is going and has the right to change it or stop it when they want to. When you listen to your customer, listen openly, hear what they say, by all means debate and challenge their needs, questions and suggestions – but don't forget who has the last say.

Listening lesson 7 – Listening is probably your biggest task

There are no average projects, and there can be no absolute rules about what listening is required. But typically, 50–75% of your communication time is in listening rather than transmitting. I know very successful project managers who spend 90% or more of their time communicating. The maths is not complex, and it means that they are spending something like 45–68% of their time listening. Of course, this is not just to project customers, but to the project team and to other stakeholders.

For something you are going to spend possibly two-thirds of your time doing, don't you think it's worth making sure you are good at it? We think of listening as an innate skill we are all good at. We also tend not to think of listening as something we can learn to do and improve. Yet we are often unaware of how poor we are at listening. It is possible to improve your listening skills. Get some feedback on your listening skills and work at improving them.

Communicating with your audience

Key lesson

Talk, talk and talk again – the weekly report will not do it all. Practise and learn the eighteen communication lessons to ensure you communicate fully and continuously with your customer and project team.

So, you have now got a great and comprehensive set of requirements that everyone on the project understands. You know that there are a few assumptions, but they are clear and explicit and you know what will happen if they turn out to be false. You have also put in place efficient mechanisms for regularly going back to your customer and checking that nothing has changed. The project is up and running and things are starting to happen.

" talk, talk and talk again " Project management does not operate in a black box. Even when you know everything that you do, you need to go back and talk to the customer and talk continuously with the project team. One of the absolutely fundamental differences between the good and the great project manager is often the amount of regular communications.

It should be obvious why you need to communicate with your project team. Given that you have a documented scope and set of requirements, it may be less obvious why you need to talk to your customer. Rather than shrugging this point off as being too simple, it really is worth putting yourself in your customer's shoes as it drives understanding and the opportunity for comprehensive empathetic engagement.

The key reasons why you need to communicate with your customer throughout the life of the project are as follows:

- It's not usually your money you are spending or your resource you are using, and resource owners have a right to understand how things are going and whether resources are being used well. In most organisations, resources of one form or another are scarce or limited, and it is worth remembering as a project manager that people have the option of allocating them elsewhere at any time. The most common resources of money and people's time can easily be shifted to other work, and managers must make an active and ongoing choice to allocate them to a project. For a project to continue to be a success it needs continuing access to resources. Managers will continue to allocate people only if they see that the project is worthwhile and it is working. You not only need to deliver results, you need to be seen to be delivering them and to do this you must tell your customers!

■ Success as a project manager requires trust. You do not have an inalienable right to be trusted and it is not automatically achieved; trust must be gained and you can improve on trust by good regular communications. If you disappear for six months, telling your customer you will come back when everything is done, you are likely to find that your customer is not impressed and does not believe you (and he or she should not accept this).

■ Things change and you need to talk them through; you cannot assume that changes you need to make, whether of cost, time, resource usage, scope or whatever else, will be acceptable to customers. On the other hand you also cannot assume that the customer will not want to make changes himself. The world customers operate in is dynamic: even though a few weeks ago your project may have been their number one priority, it may not be today.

■ You may need or want the customer or sponsor of a project to do something for you. Passing things up or along the management chain, when done in a constructive manner, can be an extremely powerful way of getting things done.

■ We are all human and human beings like to be talked to, and they base their judgements of others largely on their interactions. This sounds trite, but a project manager who diligently hides in a corner while managing a project is less likely to be seen as a safe pair of hands. This may be unfair, but it is human nature.

■ It's good to have to report on progress – it keeps project managers on their toes! Be honest with yourself – don't you work harder when someone is measuring your performance?

■ Managing a project is all about having the right information. If you don't seek it out, listen and ask the right questions, you will never deliver a successful project.

The basic mechanism for a project manager's communications is usually some form of regular reporting, be it weekly or monthly (though in some cases daily or quarterly). The rest of this section will describe how, while this is essential, it is not enough on its own. There are eighteen additional communication lessons the project manager should learn. They are structured into three main groupings:

1   Your planning and approach to communications (lessons 1–4)

2   The style and method of communications (lessons 5–13)

3   Rules to underpin all communications (lessons 14–18)

So what are the eighteen core communication lessons?

Lessons 1–4: Your planning and approach to communications

Communication lesson 1 – Plan your schedule of communications

Your approach to communications will ideally come across as confident, relaxed and natural, but this does not mean it should not be planned. Communications must be planned on a project like any other task. For a small project this can be very simple; on a large programme involving many people you may even have a dedicated communications planning team. In this context the word 'plan' means not only the formal plan you create, document and manage as a project manager, but also the mental rules and guidelines you develop, think about and structure your day-to-day interactions around.

Your communications may include a variety of people but should centre on your three key audiences:

- **The project team**. Plan regular meetings to assess progress, discuss issues, risks and changes, and also agree what the team will focus on for the next time period (do not leave this to everyone's individual interpretation of the plan). Agree a schedule and format of regular reports and/or meetings.
- **Customer reporting**. There are two primary groups to consider at the very least: the sponsor for ongoing updates and support, and the end users in preparation for the results of the project. Agree meetings and reports as required.
- **Stakeholders** – as part of your ongoing stakeholder management.

(In Chapter 9 I discuss the limits of project manager communications and the situations in which you may need some support from professional specialists in communications.)

Commence your communications planning by thinking about the objectives of any interactions, and then think about the actual message and approach to communicating. And remember that communications is not only about providing information and messages; it is also about building relationships.

There is no generic communications plan; it will vary from some informal thoughts on the smallest and simplest of projects, through to a complex piece of work on a major change project. Generically, your communication plan should be made up from three main components:

■ **Tasks within the project plan**. There will be some major communications deliverables and events that should be built into your project plan. These are mainly presentations and actions based around key milestones in your project. The specific events depend on the scale and type of project. Typical examples for a larger project include a mobilisation event, customer presentations related to acceptance of deliverables, and stakeholder events to prepare for the impact of the project launch. For complex programmes there may be a separate communications work package made up of multiple tasks. (See lessons 2, 3 and 17 below.)

■ **Guidelines and rules for project team members**. For small projects all communications will be the responsibility of the project manager. As projects become larger this may become impractical. It is good practice then to outline what regular communications are to be made, by whom and in what format. So, for example, the project manager may hold responsibility for monthly sponsor updates, but other customer groups may be updated by other project members. For large programmes such guidelines will need to be formally documented as a part of the communications plan. (See lessons 2, 7, 10, 11 and 13 below.)

■ **Ongoing communication approaches for the project manager**. These are typically the dynamic and undocumented thoughts of the project manager. I include in this approaches such as deciding to hold regular casual conversations with project team members. The fact that there is a constantly changing informal combination of proactive strategies and reactive tactics does not mean they should not be thought through. Great project managers look at communications as a holistic set of activities to support achieving the goals of the project. (See lessons 4, 11, 13, 15 and 16 below.)

Communication lesson 2 – Accept regular reporting as part of the job

To start your communications plan it is easiest to begin by thinking about the cycle of regular reports you will make and meetings you will hold as a project manager. Such regular interactions form the basis for a factual understanding of status, which is essential to determining what management action is required on a project. There are many options and formats. In practice, my experience is that a weekly report is essential for the project sponsor, supported by less frequent reports and meetings for other customer groups.

Many project managers complain about reporting on weekly or monthly cycles. You must accept that reporting is a core component of your work, and if it is difficult, you are not on top of your project. Once a weekly report has been created, the updates required for the following week should be easy. Try to manage the reporting overhead with standard formats and devise a format that suits as many audiences as possible.

In terms of your main weekly status report, it should at least provide:

- A very clear statement of status – are you ahead, behind or on track? Ideally this is covered unambiguously in the first few lines of the report.
- A simple description of any major issues that are affecting progress, what is being done about them, and when they will be resolved.
- A simple description of any new risks, or changes to risk status, that the audience for this report needs to be aware of.
- Finally, to specify anything you need in return from the report's audience (for example decisions, resources, help with issue resolution, etc.).

Keep such reports very simple and short. If people need more detail then they can come and talk to you. Very complex weekly reports risk people not bothering to read them, and the really important information being lost in too much detail (it is worrying how often I have seen status updates, read them, received lots of little bits of information, but had no idea whether the project was OK or not). My ideal report is certainly no longer than one side of a sheet of paper. Remember that you want and need the project team to communicate with you. Their behaviour will be influenced by yours, and if you treat project communications as a painful overhead or trivial bureaucracy, so will they!

Communication lesson 3 – Use formal presentations appropriately

Next on your communication plan will be some formal presentations. Opinions vary as to whether presenting to people (probably using the ubiquitous MS PowerPoint slides) is actually an effective use of time. It is a part of modern business life, and whether it adds value or is just part of the cultural ritual of contemporary business, you will have to do it.

You cannot predict what presentations you will require on a project. Sometimes during a project's life stakeholders will realise something is impacting them and ask for a presentation; perhaps customers will require an analysis of why a project is going wrong; perhaps project team members may need to understand more about some part of the project they are having difficulty with. So, leave some time for unplanned presentations, but start by planning the presentations you know will be required. Think about key times when you will have important information to report to customers and stakeholders. The basis for such a formal presentation schedule is your project's activity plan (see Chapter 5), so base presentation times around major milestones and critical events in the project.

The attitude to presentations must be to see them as part of the job. You should see them as an opportunity to shine rather than being the shadowy, unknown manager of the project. Project managers who make comments like 'I am doing so many presentations that I can't get on with my job' are failing to understand the critical importance of communicating. It *is* possible that a project team has to make too many presentations, if so; talk to your sponsor to reduce them. But, generally, complaining about presentations is missing the point. Presentations can be helpful to you and the project. Importantly, in the short run, they can provide an opportunity to get things that you need from your audience. Use them to get support, decisions made, resources allocated, issues resolved, and risks accepted. Points to remember are:

- Communicate to suit your audience, not to suit your process, existing templates, etc.
- Use different media wisely – slide presentations can be powerful, but can also bore people senseless.
- Think about what you and the project want from every presentation and include it in the presentation.
- Decide whether the material you are developing is only to be presented or whether it will be read as a standalone document. Some great presentations are almost impossible to understand without the presenter talking them through; similarly, some documents that are great to read are impossible to present. If you need to achieve both, plan it carefully.
- If necessary, press communication on your customer. If he does not want it, it is a good sign that he trusts you, but it may also mean he is not interested enough in the outcome and you may not be able to get him to do things that you want or need.

Communication lesson 4 – Use informal communications spontaneously and continuously

Finalise your communications plan by thinking about your informal communications. I am not saying you should actually plan out every little chat, but you should be consciously thinking about the balance between formal and informal communications. Informal communications score highly on a number of objectives, including building relationships and trust, finding out critical information quickly, and getting a variety of viewpoints when consensus does not exist. The fact that such communications are unofficial and relaxed does not mean they should not be deliberate. It's wonderful if you are one of those people who naturally network, know everything and everyone; but not everyone is, and even if you are one of these people, a little thinking helps to ensure all bases are covered.

No matter how formal the environment or culture you work in, do not rely on formal presentations as your sole communications mechanism. Over-reliance on formal communications will result in a lack of real understanding and trust between a project manager and his audience. Informal communications – short chats, calls, coffee machine conversations and e-mails (though see lesson 11 on page 51) – are a critical part of your ongoing work. In addition, if you really dislike formal presentations you may reduce the need for them by doing more informal communications. The more often you call your key audience members, catch them by the coffee machine or ask them out for lunch or a drink, the lighter your load on formal presentations will be.

Informal communications work well with certain customer groups, but are particularly important with your project team. The project manager who relies only on formal structured input is not likely to understand all the issues, nor will he develop a good relationship with the project team. Simply walking around the project team once or twice a day, asking them how they are, will bring all sorts of critical information to the surface, help to bond the project manager and project team, and, in a non-challenging way, can ensure the information being presented to you on progress and status rings true with what project team members are actually experiencing. It will also let you observe non-verbal communications to pick up information such as emotional states, which are essential to understand if you are to manage people optimally.

> **❝ informal communications are not just about telling people things; they are primarily about listening ❞**

Informal communications are not just about telling people things; they are primarily about listening. The best way to find out what is actually going on in a project is simply to go around and listen to project team members. Their comments must always be put in context and balanced with multiple views, but they are worth finding out. Informal communications are most effective when they manifest themselves as a dialogue. Dialogue is important not only because two-way information flow is essential, but also because it is the basis of building relationships.

Lessons 5–13: The style and method of communications

Communication lesson 5 – Use your audience's specialist language where appropriate

Most projects have specialists of one type or another, who each have their own jargon and communication tools. Additionally many organisations have a specialised language set because of the industrial sector they are in, the way they are organised, or because it is part of the organisation's culture. The ability to pick up and use the language of the various people involved in a project is critical for project managers. If you work in one company in one industry, this is normally not a problem as your communications will naturally be studded with the local jargon. However, if you are a mobile, contract or consultant project manager jumping from company to company and from industry to industry, you must learn to pick up the language around you.

Do not consider local vocabulary as irritating jargon, any more than if working in a foreign country you would consider the local language as irritating jargon. Jargon will have grown up for many reasons, and it can be an efficient way to communicate. Think of jargon as part of the environment you are working in. Your job is to fit into it and not to expect it to fit with you.

Communication lesson 6 – Avoid too much project management jargon

Project managers, like other specialists, have their own jargon. Do not assume that other audiences understand it, or even need to understand it. This lesson is the opposite of needing to use the local jargon yourself. I have heard people questioning the difference between a project and a programme manager, or between an issue and a risk, too often. In my experience certain terms cause regular confusion, for example:

- Work breakdown structure and organisational breakdown structure (or even more obscure, WBS and OBS)

- PID, Requirements Spec., Technical Spec.
- Change request
- Planning and progress control terms, e.g. PERT, Gantt, critical path, critical chain, earned value analysis
- Project roles, e.g. project manager, programme manager, portfolio manager, project director, project sponsor, project office manager.

In any project there may be many more terms that are not universally understood. If you do find yourself thinking about using these terms, my advice is:

- Ask yourself if the concept the term encapsulates is even required in the conversation you are having. (For example, the number of conversations in which you need to use the words WBS, PID or PERT should be quite limited!)
- If you do need to use such a term, try to find common everyday language alternatives. (For example, a Gantt chart may be described to most audiences simply as a plan; the fact that there are other types and formats of plans is normally irrelevant.)
- When you cannot find an alternative, explain the term before using it. (A term like 'critical path' is useful but not intuitively obvious in its meaning. Explain it, and then use it. Even terms like 'issue' and 'risk' are not clear to all non-project managers.)

Communication lesson 7 – Clarify what you mean by risks

A key piece of information that often needs to be communicated on a project is the degree of risk. It can be difficult not only for you to pass on the basic concept of risk, but for the person you are communicating with to understand the implications. I have seen lots of presentations to executives where the project manager lamely runs quickly through a risk register. It can come across as 'well, here are the risks, but don't worry about them because I will manage them away and I have only presented them because I was asked to'. Either this is wrong and the risks really may derail the project, or, if true, they are minor risks and you probably need not have communicated them to the executives in the first place.

Communicate a full understanding of risks. Ensure that your customer understands that the work may actually fail, not that they think you are simply telling them that this is something you are managing. Start by checking that the term 'risk' is actually understood in the context of a project as opposed to its use in colloquial English.

Do expect them to ask what can be done about it (if they don't it may well be that they have assumed it is not a problem for them or that they did not appreciate the possible impact of the risk), and have an answer to this question.

In Chapter 10 I talk more about risk management and contingency plans.

Communication lesson 8 – Present complex information in a clear way

Many projects over time become complex, either because of their scale, or sometimes because of the nature of their content. A real skill is the ability to explain complex information and detail about a project in concise, easily understandable terms. This is especially important when talking to senior audiences.

Learn to differentiate between what is complex, what people need to understand, and what is no more than detail. Very few people you will talk to need to know the detail about everything on the project, so don't waste your time and theirs by relating it. Tell them what is relevant and, if you don't know, ask them what is relevant to them. Similarly, complexity does not have to be explained in a complex way. (Chaos is complex, being an expert in chaos theory I'm sure is very complicated too, but some of the theories and specific algorithms for chaotic events are intellectually straightforward. It is possible to explain the fundamental concept in a few sentences. For most people this simple explanation is sufficient.)

When talking with people, take the time and effort to explain difficult concepts and do not assume automatic understanding. Confirm their understanding, and prepare a further explanation if necessary. However, although you should be prepared to explain complex ideas, check first with your audience whether they understand them. If they do, don't continue with the explanation but just move on to the next part of your presentation. People are easily irritated by having concepts explained to them that they already understand.

Do not underestimate what people may consider as complex concepts. For example, when talking to an engineering audience you may well patronise them if you talk about the need for a requirements specification. When talking to an executive audience you may not only need to do this, but also have to explain what a requirements specification is. I have been in many situations where the necessity for a requirements specification had to be explained to senior board members. It is not that they were stupid; it was just outside their experience. The best thing to

❛❛ if you really do not know, then ask ❜❜ do is to ask whether people are comfortable with concepts and, if they are, move on; if not, explain. If you are concerned that your audience may feel you are patronising them, start with a statement like 'I often find teams do not understand this term'. Then at least they do not feel you are specifically assuming they are idiots!

Communication lesson 9 – Tailor communications to the audience

Different audiences require different styles of presentation; don't assume you can use the same set of slides for a project team meeting as you can for an executive meeting. Yes, you should reuse materials if you can, otherwise you may constantly be developing communications materials. Don't assume, however, that what works well for one group will automatically suit another.

There are hundreds of different possible audiences, but those to start thinking about are clearly:

- The project team and separate work package teams
- Third-party suppliers to the project
- The project sponsor
- The executive (sponsor's peers or bosses)
- Customers
- End users
- Resource owners
- Other stakeholders.

The points to think about when presenting to these audiences are:

- **Why are you presenting to this audience?** Without understanding this, it is difficult to develop relevant communications. Very frequently people find themselves making presentations to audiences for less than totally clear reasons. (If you really do not know, then ask whoever has set up the meeting what she would like covered. If you have set it up yourself, you should know!)

- **What is relevant to this audience?** Many features of the project will not be relevant and the audience has limited time and patience. Also consider whether any of the information is sensitive and must not be communicated for practical, relationship or legal reasons.

- **How is it best to tell the audience this information?** In doing this you should consider what vocabulary you are using. Do technical or specialist words and concepts need to be explained?

- **What is the best type of media?** Is it formal or informal? Is it a presentation, an e-mail, a newsletter, a poster or something else?

- **What can you get out of this?** Different audiences can have different impacts on the project. For example, senior audiences can allocate more resources, a project team well motivated can do more work, etc.

Communication lesson 10 – Effectively communicate with senior audiences

One of the challenges to face new project managers is presenting to a senior or executive audience for the first time. A good presentation to a senior audience can make your life easy; a poor one can cause significant problems for a project. For a senior audience specifically it is therefore worth putting some real effort into thinking about the following:

- **What is relevant to this audience?** Many features of the project will not be relevant, and your audience have limited time and patience. A good starting point is to really challenge yourself – why are you presenting to this specific audience and what do they want from it? List the questions that your audience will be able to answer *after* your presentation which they cannot answer beforehand. Typical examples of these questions are:
  - What will be the outcome from the project, and will this still happen?
  - What will be the impact of the project on their parts of the business?
  - What is the current status?
  - What are the risks and issues?
  - What else do you think we should know?
  - Is there anything we can change to make it better/easier?
  - Typically, they will *not* be interested in things like the details of how your change control process works, or which version of MS Project you are using.

- If you cannot identify what questions your presentation answers, it is likely to be a failure. It is worth holding in mind what senior audiences are particularly looking for when projects are normally presented to them: confidence that you are in control of your work, and confidence that you are telling them the whole truth.

- **What are they feeling and thinking?** You cannot be a mind reader – no-one is, but everyone has some innate ability to feel what others are feeling and this is especially important with senior audiences. Try to get at least some feel for the following:

  - What mood they are in. You do not always have the choice but try to save difficult messages for times when people are in good moods.

  - What they are thinking as you present. They may be thinking 'this is interesting' or 'this is adding value'; alternatively they may be thinking 'this is boring and why am I here?', or they may be irritated. Try to analyse what you are doing to create any negative sensation and adapt your style and content accordingly. I am not saying avoid tough messages, but if information you are presenting is optional and they are obviously bored, cut it short.

- **How is it best to tell them this information?** There is no golden rule here other than tailor it to suit. Some executives love detail, others are 'big picture' people. Some like presentations and others like text. This is partly a function of personal bias, but it is also related to how expert the specific executives are with the subject you are presenting. It is best not to try to present high-level overviews if the executive is an expert. You need to tailor your contents for this as well. It's easy when you know your audience well, but there will be many situations in which the audience is new or unfamiliar to you. If you do not know the audience and cannot get advice on their preferred style, my general advice is to plan for a formal presentation. Keep it at a reasonably high-level, but be able to drill into detail if required. A good way to do this is to make a high-level presentation with a set of appendices full of detail should you need to go into it. Executives are generally more interested in the implications of a project than in the details of the project itself.

- **Is this better done formally or informally? Is it better done as a group or on a one-to-one basis?** The reasons you may wish to talk to someone informally rather than formally come down to personal style, the content you are communicating and the degree of risk you bear in communicating to a group. For example, contentious, unproven data that is new is generally best presented informally on a one-to-one basis.

- **What can you get out of this?** Senior audiences are the ones that have the power to reassign more resources to your project, sign off changes, and accept risks. On top of this they are the ones who can help your career progress. (This is a perfectly reasonable way of thinking as long as it does not become obsessive or over-played.)

- **Is this contentious or run of the mill? Are there any major surprises?** When senior audiences are being asked to make key decisions or to support an approach, or, generally, when you need their support and it is not certain that you will get it, it may then be worth 'pre-selling' to them on an individual basis before presenting to them as a group. If you present a major contentious decision to a senior audience without warning, and without giving them the opportunity to think about it, they will often respond badly, feeling that you are 'rail-roading' them into a decision. I remember one specific project which was stopped because the project manager surprised a powerful executive with something he did not support. The problem was not that the executive did not agree with the approach being taken by the project manager, but that it caused him problems with his own boss (the CEO). If the executive had been pre-warned on a one-to-one basis he would have had time to gain support from his own boss, tailor the message to suit, and possibly change the project a little to suit his needs. Having been surprised, this executive then lost confidence in the project manager and removed his ongoing support. This effectively killed the project.

- **How does this group make decisions?** Some groups and cultures like decisions made in forum with much debate, others like them made beforehand with the group effectively rubber-stamping an answer they have each already agreed to. Finally, most groups are not equal; there may be one or a few dominant individuals whose support you need to ensure. Working out the dynamics and politics of decision making is a great skill for senior project managers. If, for example, there is one dominant decision maker, try to get his or her agreement before you get the final sign-off on a decision.

- **Plan your presentation.** Even if it is for an informal chat with a senior executive, it is worth structuring your key points in your mind, and given that time with senior people is often restricted, structure your thoughts so you can cover them quickly. I often have a set of five or six points on status, key issues and any help I need, prepared and continuously updated in my head. I can then run through these if I bump into any senior executives in my daily travels around the office.

As you present you will get feedback from the executives. Some of this will be comments, criticism and questions, but some will be messages and ideas. Try and capture their suggestions and, if necessary, take someone along to take notes for this purpose. Once you have completed the meeting you should analyse their ideas and either take them on board or formally reject them. You may well need to involve your sponsor if rejecting someone's ideas. But there is nothing that irritates a senior audience more than to feel that their comments have been completely ignored.

If you do not know how a senior audience works, what things will excite them and what will irritate them, do some research. Someone you know will have had to deal with the very same group before. Ask them what went well and what went wrong.

The last point I will stress is to avoid obsessively worrying about your most senior audiences. They can be perceptive and difficult, but they are often the most balanced and realistic in assessing risks and problems. Do not underestimate the danger of failure or receiving the raw end of their temper, but remember that what can often be a topic for heated argument for a middle manager is accepted with a nod from a senior executive if managed well.

Communication lesson 11 – Do not rely on e-mails

E-mail is a feature of modern business life and is a great support in managing projects. It provides an excellent productivity aid and has some good functionality. It is a superb way for communicating to large numbers of people simultaneously, for distributing documents, and for those occasions when asynchronous communications are needed, such as across time zones. Project managers' lives would be considerably more difficult without e-mails. However, at times we all find them irritating. Sometimes it is the sheer volume of e-mails and at other times it is their content.

> ❝ I have seen well-meant jokes misread as insults ❞

I have not commented in detail on any other specific communications medium. I have picked e-mail as it is now so pervasive, very powerful, and quite dangerous! Most communication research shows that success in communications comes down to three components: the message you are giving (i.e. the words), your body language, and the tone of your voice. With e-mail you can only control the first. Missing out the other two makes it very easy to mis-communicate. There are other written media which potentially suffer from the same problem, but in my experience people tend to read reports for the words in them alone. When they read e-mails they interpret or assume a body language and tone to match, and I have seen well-meant jokes misread as insults. I am sure you have had similar experiences.

My advice on e-mail etiquette really comes down to four points:

- For one-to-one conversations always pick up the phone as a preference (if you cannot have a face-to-face meeting). Using e-mail to talk to one person when you can call them is really an abuse of technology.

- If you must use it, think through your words carefully and avoid language that may be interpreted with an emotional tone you did not intend. Just because e-mail is easy to use, there is no excuse for sloppy communications. I will often spend more time crafting an important e-mail than I do a presentation, precisely because I do not have the opportunity to amend it, or apply tone to my voice, once it is sent.

- Limit the number of people you copy an e-mail to. A long list of people's names after the 'cc:' smacks of political games. If people need to read it, send it to them directly. If they do not – don't. Personally, I auto-delete all e-mails copied to me. This may sound Draconian, but it saves me a lot of time and eventually people learn and send me only what is really relevant.

- Do not use the blind copy facility that is available on most e-mail systems. I have even insisted on it being disabled in teams I have been responsible for. No-one knows when you have used it except the recipient of the blind copy, but once people know you use it they will not trust you fully.

Communication lesson 12 – Be specific

The simple but fundamental lesson here is to avoid confusion, ambiguity and the opportunity for divergent responses by being specific in your language, and by cross-examining people when they use non-specific language with you. Words such as 'enough', 'sufficient', 'plenty', 'a little' should be avoided, especially in formal situations such as during require-ments definition or when presenting status. You need to define and understand precisely how many, how much, how long.

Try always to be specific. It is better if you occasionally come across as a pedant than if you miss the point or mis-communicate vital information.

Communication lesson 13 – Present key factual information in whole messages at discrete time intervals

Informal communications are best carried out in the style of ongoing dia-logues. Any information passed can be partial or incomplete, and you can update and adapt it on a continuous basis as the dialogue evolves.

This is the normal way for people to 'chat' – and it is an effective way for people to work together, build relationships and manage ongoing dynamic communications.

Imagine for a moment, though, that you are not the project manager, but instead you are someone being updated on project status by the project manager. You don't want a chat; you want him to tell you the status. When he tells you the status you may have questions, but ideally once the update is over you have a full understanding of status. The information you have been told is complete and makes logical sense as a statement on status. You may then want to discuss it and its implications, or drive down to more detail, but preferably your understanding of status is comprehensive. Additionally, when he informs you of status you do not want him coming back in five minutes saying '... and another thing ...', and five minutes later, '... and I meant to add ...'. You expect it to be a whole message. Finally, you don't expect him to come back an hour later, or probably even a day later, to tell you that it has all changed. Unless he has pre-warned you of something significant happening in that time frame which will alter status, you probably only want an update a week or a month later. You want to be updated at regular time intervals.

There is a variety of key information for which informal dialogue is not a suitable mechanism for sharing in a project environment – specifically, factual information such as project status, risks and issues, and instructions on what work needs to be done next. These need to be presented as complete pieces of information at discrete time intervals.

Why is this important? As intimated above, no-one wants to know half a risk, part of status, or a bit of the next activity you need to do. In these situations partial information is often meaningless, or worse still, it can transmit completely the wrong message, and it gives the impression that you do not really know what is going on. If you did, surely you would communicate the whole message? Finally, if you keep changing what you have said at short intervals of time, it undermines trust in your competence. Your audience's thought process would be something like 'was what you said a little while ago true or not? If it was, why do you need to change it? Why should I believe what you say now?' Status does change, but not significantly at very short intervals of time, unless you are out of control. This seems obvious, but very often project information is presented in incomplete segments. How often have you been updated by someone and felt that he or she has not really told you anything meaningful, or has left you suspicious because he or she keeps changing the information?

Completeness is relative to the level of detail that is appropriate for the audience you are communicating with. At the highest level a project status update needs to reflect whether you are on track or not, and whether you currently think you will stay on track. A simple statement such as 'we are on track, and currently expect to remain on track' is a complete message. At a slightly lower level a project status update may require a statement such as 'we are on track within expected tolerances, and expect to remain on track. There are two risks we are managing, and think unlikely now to occur, but if they do we will be late by six weeks'. This may be a complete message, as long as there are not other facts relevant to this level of detail. The skill here is determining what is actually relevant to a specific level of detail. That judgement is based on knowing your project and the level of detail your audience needs.

Lessons 14–18: Rules to underpin all communications

Communication lesson 14 – Tell the truth

Tell the truth. Avoid lying. Acknowledge your mistakes and errors. There are situations in which telling the absolute truth is not productive, but these situations should be rare and avoided as far as possible. I am not saying that you should not tailor your message. If there is bad news, sweeten the pill, and choose your timing carefully. This is common sense and good people management. If you do find yourself being tempted to lie, ask yourself what risk is involved – is it personal or is it project? If you get found out, which or who will suffer more: the project or you personally? (See Chapter 10 for a fuller discussion.)

If we ignore morals for a moment, the problem with non-trivial lies is that they will often come back to haunt you. You risk killing your relationship and feeling of trust with your manager, customer or other team member if they realise you have lied to them, or have even withheld information. If you do feel tempted to lie, ask yourself what the chance is that they will find out anyway. Ask yourself what weaknesses you are trying to hide.

Another aspect of telling the truth is being open with the full truth. If we consider ourselves to be truthful and yet not open, I believe that we are paying lip service to being truthful. There is a right and a wrong time to impart a bad message, but it is best to assume that you will be doing it. Relevant information is not only that which is true, but also that which is complete and timely. This requires real openness with your customer.

Almost as important as telling the truth is looking like you are telling the truth. It is very common to hear statements like 'well, I did not believe him as his body language was all wrong', or 'he just looked shifty'. Generally, as a project manager you don't just want people to trust you, you *need* them to. Building a reputation for straight-talking honesty is a big bonus for the project manager and comes from both telling the truth and making it look as though you are telling it.

Communication lesson 15 – Maintain only one version of the truth

There is nothing more frustrating to the customer of a project team than repeatedly getting different and contradictory information on status and risks, but it is quite common. I have regularly been the sponsor of projects where on talking to different members of the project team I get radically different interpretations of project status. There are many causes of this. Some project members will have only partial information, some will have historical information that is now no longer true, others will interpret facts in a different light, and occasionally people will deliberately spread wrong information. This can cause significant loss of confidence in the project. In your life, if your car is in the garage and the receptionist tells you it will be ready at 5 o'clock, the engineer tells you there are major problems and it will probably be another two days, and the salesman tells you not to worry as it is already sorted, how do you feel? When this occurs it is frustrating and destroys your confidence in the garage. You have spoken to many people but you still do not know the truth with any degree of confidence, and tend to assume the worst.

To counter this you need to get the project team to communicate consistently 'one version of the truth':

- Regularly bring the project team together and discuss the project status so everyone has a common view. Agree with the team that anyone who really wants or needs a full status update should be directed to talk to the project manager.
- When critical activities are completed, or major issues occur or are resolved, communicate this to the whole team so that no-one is retelling past history to the outside world. A short e-mail is sufficient.
- Agree with sponsor and other customer groups who they should come to for status updates, and warn them that any other source will not have the full picture. When I am running projects I like to agree at the start of the project with my sponsor that he or she comes to me only for status information – not because I am blocking them from talking to anyone in the team, but to ensure that when they are forming judgements on the project's status they have the full picture.

Communication lesson 16 – Obsessively manage expectations

The phrase 'manage expectations' could be the perfect project management mantra, and anyone working in project management circles will hear it all the time. But what in reality does it mean?

One of the critical success factors for project managers is to manage their customer's expectations throughout the life of a project. Like a good politician the project manager needs to ensure that what is delivered at the end is what the customer expects. This is quite a different thing from saying that what is delivered at the end is what was agreed upon at the start. Things change, even with the best risk management unforeseen events occur, and customers change their minds, which has an impact on timelines and costs. All project managers know about managing expectations in theory. Yet, as a customer, I have regularly been surprised by things going wrong without warning on projects being run by apparently competent project managers on numerous occasions. If you surprise your customer you are not managing his expectations.

> ❝ if you surprise your customer you are not managing his expectations ❞

I have seen many projects deliver a fraction of what was originally requested and yet be seen as a major success because the customer's expectations were properly and iteratively managed downwards as the project went forward. On the other hand, I have seen projects actually over-deliver against the original baseline but be greeted as a complete failure because the customer's expectations expanded without check as work progressed.

The best approach to managing expectations is to use the following easy instructions. These thoughts should be close to your heart at all times:

■ Think through and be explicit with yourself about what sort of issues and risks you need to tell your customer about. This is about both understanding your customer (does a 0.5% cost overrun matter to him, or does it need to be 5% or even 25% before he is bothered?) and understanding your own appetite for personal risk (do you think you can easily recover the situation without sponsor involvement?). There is a balance in involving your sponsor, which I discuss more in Chapter 4. This balance must be considered when thinking about escalation (this is dealt with in detail later in the book, but escalation is calling upon more senior management for support, action or approval). In simple terms you should realise that if you escalate everything you are adding no value. Yet, on the other hand, if you escalate too late you will find an irritated sponsor, not only because it is irritating in its own right but because he in turn may need to manage upwards. He will have his own managers and will want the chance to manage the subsequent conversation with them. By surprising him you may have lost an opportunity for him to do something to help you.

- Try to gain an understanding of your sponsor's appetite for risk and information. Some sponsors like to have a micro-understanding; others want only higher-level information about issues and risks at regular scheduled meetings. My general rule is: if in doubt have an informal chat with the sponsor. At the start of the project ask the sponsor what her preferred style is – is she 'light touch', or does she want daily detailed updates? This simple question can avoid huge amounts of tension later on.

- Have a no-surprises mindset. No-one likes it when things go wrong, people like it less when no-one predicted things might go wrong, and they hate it when they learn very late that things have gone wrong. If there is a major risk of derailment make sure the customer knows about it. Do not put your head in the sand and pretend it is not happening or hide it because you are afraid of your customer's temper. The longer you leave it the worse it will be (and you are in danger of converting an unpleasant conversation about problems on the project into significant personal risk). If something occurs that will make an impact on the project, make sure the customer knows about it. Put yourself in your customer's shoes. It is far, far easier to deal with a known change in plans than suddenly have to deal with something unexpected. Consider your private life. Would you rather a builder phone you up the night before your house is going to be re-roofed when the scaffolding is all around to say he is going to be a month late, or would you prefer him to ring you a month in advance and tell you he will be a month late? Would you rather know your plane was going to leave two days late when you arrive at the airport or a week in advance? Most people prefer the latter.

- When you are realigning expectations make them proportionate to where you are in the project. For example, with a few possible exceptions, it is inexcusable in my mind to say to customers one day before final delivery, 'oh, by the way we will be a month late'. It may have been acceptable to warn them there was a risk of this happening a couple of months before the end, and perhaps to tell them it was going to happen a month in advance. Similarly with cost. You have failed to manage expectations if at the last progress meeting you told your customer you had spent 10% of the budget and were 10% of the way through, but now without warning you are going to say you have spent 50% of the budget but are only 12% of the way through. You should at least have warned him of the risk of this occurring. Anything else is poor risk management and very sloppy project management.

- When you need to reset expectations do it in the customers' own language, and in a way in which they will understand the implications. Tell them the impact in measures they use (money, time, more people, fault rates, etc.). For example, project managers will often say 'there is a risk of x happening'. Customers often interpret this as 'there is something that will cause the customer some pain, but I will deal with it'. If you want your customer to understand the risk, say more clearly that the impact of this risk is something like 'a 25% chance that you will need to spend an extra £100k; if you want to be certain the project will deliver you must hold a contingency budget'. Your customers will almost certainly not like this, but it is better to forewarn them than to simply start overspending the money. Make it clear that you will do your best, but that if the risk happens you may not be able to manage the impact away.

- Stick to the principle of 'one version of the truth' (communication lesson 15).

- Deliver on your promises. Every time you make a promise you are setting up an expectation with someone. The commonly held guideline to under-promise and then over-deliver is good guidance. Think of yourself as having a personal brand, and wanting this brand to generate belief and confidence in yourself. For this to be true you need to live up to your promises. Nothing produces more poor expectations for the future than a track record of failing to keep promises in the past. *If you are not sure, do not promise*, and when you are definitely unsure, definitely do not promise anything. (Avoid at all costs the tendency to promise to keep people happy. A promise should be built on a foundation of reality, not wishful thinking.)

- Be consistent. If you need to say 'no', stick to it. If you say 'yes', do it.

- Always try to offer your customers solutions, or at least routes to a solution, whenever you give them a problem. Even if you know the solution is unacceptable to them, it helps to present problems in the most positive light.

■ When there is bad news to communicate, communicate it early. Ensure that your customer never finds out bad news about your project from someone else or via the informal grapevine. This reduces trust and does not give confidence that you are in control.

Managing expectations is simply about understanding the status and risk in a project and matching this with timely and sufficient communications with your customer.

Communication lesson 17 – Communicate to deliver (don't deliver to communicate)

Throughout this chapter I have built up a picture of the communication skills that drive success in project management and tried to raise awareness of the critical importance of having and developing such skills. But don't fall into the trap of thinking that communication is a substitute for real delivery. Occasionally when we have not completed something we are all tempted to talk our way out of it with clever words – if we get away with it too often, talking rather than doing may become a habit.

Project management is about delivery, in the same way that football is about scoring goals. To make this happen you need to have good communication skills, as delivery is built upon people interaction and successful, productive interaction requires communication. It is the fundamental project management skill, but do not think that communication is a replacement for delivery, any more than a footballer's dribbling skill is an alternative to scoring goals.

Don't be tempted to ameliorate poor progress with clever progress reports. Don't replace real progress milestones with communication events. Don't use talking as a proxy for action. Don't build your plans around your communications; build your communications around your delivery plans. Don't confuse setting up and having meetings with making progress. Keep on talking and talk *as* you deliver.

If you do nothing but keep talking, you may get away with it for a while, but you are not really achieving what you can. Communication is an essential support for delivery, and some of your deliverables may include a communication element, but communication is not delivery.

Communication lesson 18 – Remember that you are the role model

However you lead, the project team will tend to follow. It's not important for you just to communicate; part of your role must be to see that the whole team communicates. Some people will naturally be more open than others, some will be better formal presenters than others, and some of your specialists will tend to stick to jargon that only they really understand. But you will not be able to manage the project unless the whole project team is constantly exchanging relevant and understandable information with you.

With your encouragement, coaching and a little instruction, most team members will open up and start to give you the information that is the life-blood of being a project manager. Most important of all is the visibly consistent performance of yourself as the project manager, showing how important and valuable you think communication is. Your behaviour as a communicator will act as the role model for the rest of the team. If you do this, your team will follow.

The eighteen core communication lessons are summarised in Table 2.3.

table 2.3 The eighteen communication lessons for project managers

No.	Communication lesson and capabilities for project managers
Your planning and approach to communications	
1	Plan your schedule of communications.
2	Accept regular reporting as part of the job.
3	Use formal presentations appropriately.
4	Use informal communications spontaneously and continuously.
The style and method of communications	
5	Use your audience's specialist language where appropriate.
6	Avoid too much project management jargon.
7	Clarify what you mean by risks.
8	Present complex information in a clear way.
9	Tailor communications to the audience.
10	Effectively communicate with senior audiences.
11	Do not rely on e-mails.
12	Be specific.
13	Present key factual information in whole messages at discrete time intervals.
Rules to underpin all communications	
14	Tell the truth.
15	Maintain only one version of the truth.
16	Obsessively manage expectations.
17	Communicate to deliver (don't deliver to communicate).
18	Remember that you are the role model.

chapter 3

What actually is your project?

This chapter defines a simple approach to building a full understanding of what your project needs to be designed to achieve. This understanding I call scope. In some situations project managers define the word 'scope' much more tightly than this, but to me the most useful way to consider scope is the collection of information you need before you can go on to develop a meaningful activity and resource plan for your project. It is the basis for your management of the project.

The importance of understanding scope

Key lesson

The foundation on which all good projects are built is a clear understanding of the scope. Without it a project manager will struggle to deliver successfully.

Once you have been chosen to work as project manager on a specific development, defining the scope is where the real project management work starts. Defining the scope well requires great judgement: it must consist of all the information you reasonably might need to plan a project, but defining the scope cannot be an exercise that takes for ever. The scope needs to be concise and easily understandable, yet comprehensive and complete.

The importance of a good understanding of scope cannot be overemphasised. The scope is the foundation stone upon which all further project management activities are built. The scope defines what is in and what is out of the project. Before you understand the scope, you must not start to develop your project in any detail. Do not rush into developing solutions until you understand the scope.

One way to think about defining scope is as a risk reduction exercise. By defining the scope you do not remove all uncertainty from the project, but by bounding the project you at least place limits to that uncertainty. Much of project management is about clarifying understandings and removing uncertainty, and this starts with an adequate definition of scope.

As described in Chapter 2, scope is different from requirements. Requirements are the detailed and unambiguous definitions of what the final deliverables of a project must conform to. The scope is the instructions that enable you to build a good project plan in the first place, a part of which may be to do with requirements capture. The scope needs to be complete, but it is at a much higher level of detail than requirements. In addition, scope contains an understanding of factors that are important to the process of delivery of the project, but which have no relevance once the project is complete (for example, how your customer wants you to work on the project). The relationship between objectives, scope and requirements is shown in Figure 3.1.

figure 3.1 The relationship between objectives, scope and requirements

> **" before you understand the scope, you must not start to develop your project in any detail "**

For a project manager a full understanding of what is within and, almost as important, what is outside the scope of a project is essential. An inability to understand and communicate the scope of a project is as close to a cardinal sin as it is possible to get in project management.

When you have talked with your customer and developed an understanding of a project's scope, the next thing to do is to write it down. The first reason for writing it down is obvious: it will not get forgotten and it can easily be shared. Also important is that the practice of writing down the scope in a coherent manner is a good test of whether you actually understand it or not. If you cannot write the scope down you probably do not fully understand it, and will almost certainly have difficulty communicating it to other team members.

The key scoping questions

Key lesson

The scope of a project can best be understood by going through a set of structured questions with your customer.

There are many ways to capture the scope of a project. Often project managers have a variety of template scoping documents which they complete. Others use their experience and intuition to collect the information that defines the scope. In either case, collecting scoping information is about communicating with your customer, not about creativity on behalf of the project manager. Irrespective of the specific mechanism a project manager uses, underlying it must be a series of questions that the customer is asked.

The following sub-sections run through eight key and twelve subsidiary questions that you can use to ensure that you have really scoped out the project. It is acceptable to determine that the question is irrelevant in the specific context in which you are working, or to determine that you cannot answer it yet, and that in the early stages of the project you will undertake action to get an answer. However, in this situation you must accept that when you get the answer it may have an impact on your plans and require you to change them. An inability to answer any of these questions adds to the project's risk.

In defining these questions I am not suggesting that in every situation you simply go through them one by one with your customer, though this is a valid approach that is viable on some occasions. However, you must determine the best way in which to ask them in the environment and context of your project. At the end you should be able to go through these questions and either answer them comprehensively, be clear they are irrelevant to your project, or understand you are working with a risk derived from incomplete information.

The scoping questions are presented in Figure 3.2, and also as a checklist in Table 3.1 at the end of the chapter.

Scoping question 1 – What is the overall objective of the project?

The aim of this question is to produce a simple statement, ideally one sentence, which encapsulates what the project sponsor wants to achieve. This statement provides both a framework in which you can operate and flesh out the remainder of the project, and also the base communication that everyone involved in the project can share and understand why the project exists. Everything else you are told about the project can be compared to this objective statement, if it is not consistent with it, or not relevant to it, it should not be considered as part of the project. Every requirement placed on a project should be related to achieving this objective, if it is not, it has no place being delivered by the project. It is, therefore, critically important to get this right.

Some simple examples of valid objectives might be:

- The objective of the project is successfully to design, develop and launch the new product for the SME market consistent with the business strategy and focus.
- The objective of the project is to tailor and implement the new financial accounting system within the finance department and the corporate office.
- The objective of the project is to design and complete the refit of the Northumberland offices so they can meet the growth requirements of the 2010 growth strategy.

These are simple statements which are clearly understood, but which also provide a basic scope for the project and from which anyone can easily determine whether activities they are performing fit within the project.

It is worth being aware of a couple of warning flags. If your objective can only be defined as a series of statements and can only be linked in one sentence by using 'and' several times, you should question whether this is logically a single project or a set of unrelated tasks. Secondly, in writing down your objective, check it really is the objective. It is very easy to assume an understanding, and easy for a lazy customer to accept your definition without really thinking about it. Make sure the objective is correct. This is one part of the project it is absolutely essential to get right, as *everything* else in the project is derived from it.

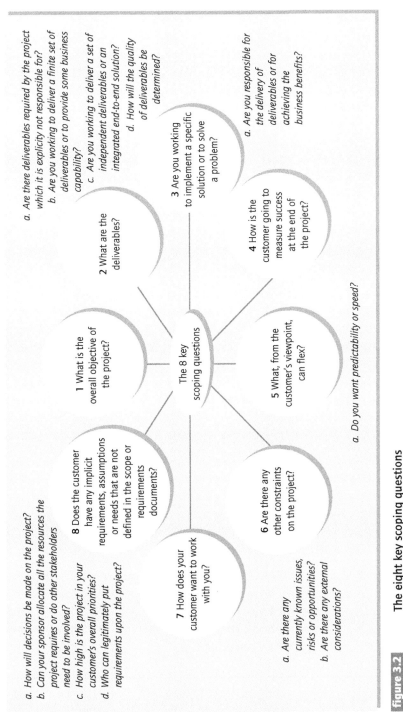

a. Are there deliverables required by the project
   which it is explicitly not responsible for?
b. Are you working to deliver a finite set of
   deliverables or to provide some business
   capability?
c. Are you working to deliver a set of
   independent deliverables or an
   integrated end-to-end solution?
d. How will the quality
   of deliverables be
   determined?

3 Are you working
to implement a specific
solution or to solve
a problem?

2 What are the
deliverables?

1 What is the
overall objective of
the project?

The 8 key
scoping questions

4 How is the
customer going to
measure success
at the end of
the project?

a. Are you responsible for
   the delivery of
   deliverables or for
   achieving the
   business benefits?

5 What, from the
customer's viewpoint,
can flex?

a. Do you want predictability or speed?

8 Does the customer
have any implicit
requirements, assumptions
or needs that are not
defined in the scope or
requirements
documents?

7 How does your
customer want to work
with you?

6 Are there any
other constraints
on the project?

a. How will decisions be made on the project?
b. Can your sponsor allocate all the resources the
   project requires or do other stakeholders
   need to be involved?
c. How high is the project in your
   customer's overall priorities?
d. Who can legitimately put
   requirements upon the project?

a. Are there any
   currently known issues,
   risks or opportunities?
b. Are there any external
   considerations?

figure 3.2　The eight key scoping questions

Scoping question 2 – What are the deliverables?

Every project produces some output, known as the deliverables. The production of these deliverables is the *raison d'être* of a project, and until they are produced the project will not be over. The deliverables are chosen to fulfil the objective, but there may be several different ways to fulfil any objective and it is the choice of deliverables that sets much of the shape and direction of a project. It seems obvious, therefore, to say that the starting point for planning a project must be to get a definition of what the deliverables are – obvious, but often not done clearly enough, or assumed rather than captured from conversations with the customer. I have seen numerous projects in which the project manager, when asked what the deliverables are, has been unable to reply with full confidence or clarity, or where the project manager has been surprised at a late stage by something the customer is expecting to receive that the project manager has not considered.

The first thing to understand with any customer, on any project, is what the expected output will be. What does the customer expect you to deliver? This is not about performing a detailed requirements capture or even necessarily a complete deliverables list, but getting an understanding of the customer's expectations of what the project needs to produce. Without this understanding it is not possible even to get as far as planning a project with any degree of certainty. The most important, and simplest, scoping question the project manager must ask therefore is 'what is the expected output from the project?'

The deliverables may include tangible objects such as a new building, intangible outputs like the development of some intellectual property or software, or some result such as a business change. Whatever it is and however it is defined, the project manager must hold this definition close to his heart for the life of a project. Only when this is understood is it worth asking the remaining scoping questions.

If it really is not possible to describe the deliverables or outputs from the project then you may not be ready to start the project. One solution is to run a short exploratory project or concept review to begin with. The deliverable from this concept review is a full definition of the objectives and deliverables from the main project.

Subsidiary question 2a – Are there deliverables required by the project which it is explicitly not responsible for?

Meeting the objective of a project will require the development of a range of deliverables, but there may already be other projects running that are producing some of these. There is no point in doing something twice, and in fact trying to do so can cause problems (think, for example, of the situation where two projects are both trying to deliver the company's new financial system).

In this situation you must identify what you are *not* responsible for delivering and, instead of developing a detailed plan with component activities, simply show an external dependency. This removes the delivery task but gives the project manager the very different task of managing an external dependency. (You should, however, be certain that what your project delivers, plus delivery of this external dependency, will achieve the objective.)

> you must identify what you are not responsible for delivering

Subsidiary question 2b – Are you working to deliver a finite set of deliverables or to provide some business capability?

This is a somewhat subtle point, but it is fundamentally important. I have seen many projects that were a success in the project manager's view but a failure in the customer's eyes because the project manager had delivered what he was asked to deliver, but the customer could not use it fully. A classic example of this is the case of an IT system. As the project manager for a project, are you delivering a piece of software, or are you delivering the business capability to use it? The first means your team would predominantly comprise software developers, the second that you would have to consider all sorts of other issues: staff training and possibly staff recruitment, business process change, staff access to the software and much more. An IT system is just a piece of software; a business capability is the full set of skills and ability needed to utilise the software and deliver the associated benefits.

When you have agreed your list of deliverables with the customer, look at them and think of any reasons why this alone may not enable the customer to fully utilise it. What does that set of deliverables do for the customer? What additional capabilities does it give him? Is that capability achieved completely with just these deliverables? Ask your customer if he needs the other things too. Check whether your customer can really achieve what he wants with those deliverables alone. If not, go back, re-scope and re-plan the project and include the missing items. It may take longer and cost more, but the project will fail without doing this.

For many business projects it is worth considering the process, systems and organisational impact of any project. If you are delivering a new IT system, do you need associated process and organisational changes as well? If you are delivering a process improvement, are there implications for the organisation design and the supporting IT systems? If you are delivering an organisational change, such as downsizing, are there implications for business processes or IT systems?

Subsidiary question 2c – Are you working to deliver a set of independent deliverables or an integrated end-to-end solution?

Most projects have a number of discrete deliverables. These may have a sensible and complete existence as discrete entities at the end of the project. On the other hand with many projects, especially technology projects, these deliverables need to be integrated together. The integration of separate items, such as separate IT systems or other pieces of technology, is not a trivial task. And yet I have seen dozens of projects that deliver these discrete items very effectively only to get to the point at which someone points out that they now need to be integrated together and there is no systems integration team and no time or tasks planned for integration. Sometimes the need for integration can be quite obvious, as when delivering several pieces of software, while on other occasions it can be more subtle. (Think of setting up a computer system, and then linking it over a data network to another system. People will generally test the systems, and someone will generally test the data link, but who is responsible for testing both together?) It is far better to work this out at the start of the project.

Subsidiary question 2d – How will the quality of deliverables be determined?

Depending on the nature of your project and the type of deliverables produced, you may have specific chunks of work to include within your plan which encompass quality checking and acceptance of the deliverables. In most cases, if you are familiar with the business context of your project you will already know this and may feel you do not need to ask this question. No competent IT project manager would design a plan without including a full testing regime. No experienced new product project manager would develop a work structure without thinking about customer trialling. However, it is worth asking your customer whether there are particular testing, trialling, assessment and auditing needs or whether there are specific defined standards for deliverable compliance (which may include legal and regulatory standards, etc.).

Quality is arguably the most important dimension of a project's deliverables and in the longer term is usually the only thing that matters. One or two years after a project completes, everyone will have forgotten that you were a month late or 15% over budget, but they will still remember you for delivering an excellent set of deliverables – and they will remember you even more if you deliver something sub-standard that creates problems for them every day. Good quality is not about the best possible deliverables, but about their being fit for the purpose they were intended for. It is critically important to be clear up front about the level of quality required.

Quality can be difficult to define and harder still to assess. Customers often struggle with defining quality standards more than any other sort of requirement. For this reason, although you need to set the basis for the level of quality required in the scope, it needs ongoing dialogue with customers throughout the project. Customers must understand what is being delivered, the level of quality, the quality implications of any time or cost compromises made on the project, and the impact on their business brought about by the quality of deliverables that will be handed over at the end of the project.

Scoping question 3 – Are you working to implement a specific solution or to solve a problem?

In other words, are you working in the solutions set or the problem set? This may sound a little esoteric, so let me put it another way. Is the project you are running set up to solve a specific problem to which the solution is not yet known, or are you working to implement a solution that has already been defined? This is best shown by an example. Let's consider the case of a company that is running a project to achieve some growth in sales. A possible way to deliver the growth in sales is to deliver a new product that can be sold to a new market segment the company does not currently address. Your project could be defined either as having to deliver the new product, which achieves the benefit of the sales growth, or as actually achieving the sales growth. Isn't this the same thing?

Well, no, not really. In the first case you will be successful if you implement the new product, whether or not it actually achieves the sales growth. That is the solution you were asked to deliver. In the second case, where you own the problem of sales growth, you may well decide to do something altogether different which delivers better sales growth, and if you do decide to deliver the new product and it does not achieve the required sales growth, you have not achieved success. If your project is framed around solving a problem, the first step will most likely be some analysis and selection of possible solutions prior to their implementation. If your project is framed around delivering an already selected solution then there will be no such step.

It is driving for an understanding as subtle as this, at the very early stages of project formation, that will change an ordinary delivery of requirements into a value-adding project management job. It may also completely change the direction and outcome of the project.

A specific example I was involved in was a project in which we were asked to increase the geographic area in which a television station could be picked up. We worked hard, but could not come up with an economic way of expanding the station's coverage. Actually we had missed the point, because the problem the customer had was not really how to expand their coverage – but how to convince their board that they were doing a good job. The board was convinced the management were failing because they thought that the coverage could be expanded. The solution the management asked us to come up with was expanded coverage, even though they themselves doubted it could be done. The alternative would have been to have asked us to help them convince the board that it could not be done. When we really understood their problem we developed a very structured and rigorous analysis of why coverage could not be expanded and presented it to the board. The board accepted our analysis, and from that time fully supported the management. The unfortunate thing was that developing this analysis, while complex in itself, was a fairly small piece of consultancy work. The original project to expand the network had been far more expensive!

Subsidiary question 3a – Are you responsible for the delivery of deliverables or for achieving the business benefits?

This is an important, but specific, variant on question 3. Let me phrase it another way: if you deliver the agreed deliverables and these do not achieve the benefits expected, who is accountable? Are you? If you are, then focus on the benefits, not simply the originally scoped deliverables – they may well not deliver the benefits required (or may over-deliver, implying the project could have been done more quickly or cheaply).

You will need to track benefit achievement through the life of the project, not simply assume that the benefits will be met by handing over the deliverables at the end of the project. Your work will not be over until the benefits have been achieved.

To give you an example, a colleague of mine was involved in a project to cut the cost of a company's order processing. The chosen solution was a new order processing system. He was employed to implement it, which he did successfully. The problem was that the sponsor did not achieve the benefits that had originally been expected (i.e. the cost was not sufficiently lowered), and he felt that this was the project manager's responsibility. My colleague had unfortunately never fully clarified his responsibility and felt it was simply to implement the computer system. There was much argument and difficulty as a result.

If you are new to project management, my advice is to take responsibility for the deliverables, not the benefits as that is the project sponsor's role. If you are a skilled project manager, you really want to earn your keep, and you have the option, then take accountability for the benefits too. People value someone much more highly who says things like 'I will achieve the cost savings' or 'I will see the profitability of the company delivered' rather than 'I will deliver the IT system' or 'I will launch the new product'. However, if the sponsor wishes you to take responsibility for benefits, you may in turn require more decision making and scoping powers than a project manager typically has. The key point is to be absolutely clear about what you are responsible for. (If you do take responsibility for the benefits, you may then want to ask the question whether you are still really a project manager or a more general business manager, but that is a detail!)

Scoping question 4 – How is the customer going to measure success at the end of the project?

At the end of every project the customer will assess whether success has been achieved. This may be done formally through some structured process, or it may be an informal assessment done on 'gut feel'. Although you may be more comfortable with the gut-feel approach as it can seem to give you some leeway, my advice is always to get success criteria formally documented at the start. As a project manager you need to know how the customer will assess the success (and this may be much broader than simply listing the deliverables). If you do not have this guideline to measure against on a daily basis, you cannot be sure that you are moving to deliver everything that is required. In addition, the customer's views of what is a success will often change as the project progresses, and without formally documented success criteria you do not have any baseline to control these changes against.

Scoping question 5 – What, from the customer's viewpoint, can flex?

Every project manager knows that at some point on almost all projects things do not go according to plan. In fact, if they always go to plan, in most cases either the project is something so simple that a project manager was not required, or you have so over-engineered the plan as to cover all eventualities and have therefore absorbed much more resource than was absolutely necessary. I believe that if things never went wrong you would never need a project manager!

So when things go wrong, what can we do? It is at this point that project managers should start thinking and talking about time–cost–quality trade-offs, the argument being that you cannot keep fixed on all three of these. If you absolutely must stick to the cost and quality of the deliverables, you may need to flex the time it takes. If you absolutely must stick to the time and cost, you may need to flex the quality. Project managers regularly mention this time–cost–quality model.

I completely agree with this fundamental project manager model – although I think it is a four- rather than a three-dimensional trade-off – time, cost, quality and scope, or functional richness. I separate quality (how well the end deliverable matches the needs) from functionality (how many of the original requirements have been met), as they can be flexed separately. As an example, I can change the functionality of an IT system (i.e. make it do more or less) without impacting the quality; alternatively I can alter the quality (i.e. make it more or less reliable) without impacting the functionality. The importance of these four factors is that they can all be flexed and often there is a trade-off between changing one dimension and changing the others.

> ❝ if things never went wrong you would never need a project manager ❞

So far most experienced project managers will be thinking 'so what, this is old news'. Perhaps true, but what project managers who understand this well often forget to do is:

■ Ensure the customer understands this at the start of the project. Tell the customer that at some point he or she is likely to be returning to make decisions based on trading off the length of time a project takes, its cost, its scope and the level of quality. This is an easy, if somewhat abstract, conversation to have at the start of the project. It can be very tricky if left until later, when these trade-offs are required. It is worth formally presenting the implications to the project sponsor in one of your earliest meetings with him or her.

■ On top of this, project managers regularly assume they understand what the trade-off balance is. Project managers are notorious for making trade-off decisions without clearly understanding the customer's own priorities. I worked in one company in which the project teams strove hard to make sure the projects did not come in over budget again and again. The company was generally short of cash so they concluded this was the right thing to do. They regularly hit the cost targets for the projects and hence thought they were doing a great job, yet the particular department they were working for was not so restricted on budget, it had more money to spend than was currently allocated to projects, but what it could not afford was any time delays. Ironically, in the effort to minimise spend on resources and hence save money, the projects regularly overran on time. In another organisation I saw a team valiantly working all hours to bring a project in on time and budget, and to achieve this, the quality was jeopardised. As the final result was a consumer product for sale in a competitive market, bringing it in late would have resulted in a financial loss for the company. However, lowering the quality was a total disaster as the product simply did not sell.

Let me challenge you, if you are working on a project right now: can you say with absolute confidence whether delivery time, total cost, quality of deliverables or the scope of the deliverables is more important to your customer? Can you say with confidence by what amount you can flex these factors? If the answer is 'no', or a statement like 'we cannot move any of them', then you need to go back, check and deepen your understanding.

Do not be surprised if your customers find a conversation about trade-offs difficult. They may initially at least give contradictory answers, or state that they need everything. This is not helpful, but from a customer perspective it is actually quite a sensible state of mind. The customer may reasonably question, if you have already agreed to deliver a project to time, cost, quality and full scope, why you are now asking to change it. To counter this, you need to ensure that the customer understands that you will try to deliver everything on time and cost, and to the full quality and functionality, and this is not an excuse or get-out for you but a way of ensuring delivery *if* problems or changes arise. To refine clarity, ask questions like 'if *x* occurred would you rather *y* or *z* happened?', where *y* and *z* are shifts respectively in time, cost, quality or functionality.

Start by asking generically, for example, 'would you rather the time increased or the price?', then move to specifics: 'would you rather the time increased by one week, or the price by £20k?'. In this way you can start by getting a general prioritisation that you can use on regular decisions (for example, if I have an issue to resolve, is it better if the resolution impacts time or cost?). By driving to specific values you can start to understand absolute tolerances – time cannot shift by more than a few days, quality needs to stay high, functionality can be de-scoped a lot, and cost cannot increase by more than 20%. These tolerances will vary from project to project, but give you the basis for great management control once you understand them.

In doing this, find out whether there are any absolute constraints on any of the four dimensions of project management:

- Is there a time when, if the project goes beyond it, it becomes pointless? (Is there a critical event that must be hit, or does the business case start to break down after a point in time?)
- Is there a cost which the project cannot go beyond? (Is there an absolute budget, which irrespective of business case is all that is available? Is there a cost which once hit means the business case starts to break down?)
- Is there a minimum scope below which the project will not deliver anything of value?
- Is there a minimum quality standard which in practice or for external reasons cannot be undercut?

Once you understand what the customer considers to be his or her possible points and levels of flexibility, do test them for *reasonableness*. Customers may make bold statements without thinking through the full implications. Your job is not to ignore their needs but to ensure they understand the implications of what they are asking for. I was responsible for running a programme once where the sponsor was very clear that the thing that mattered more than anything else was the delivery date. He reasonably told us we could increase the cost if necessary, and we could reduce the scope to a limited degree. From a project management perspective he seemed an ideal customer, he knew what he wanted and understood he may have to make trade-offs to get it. He was also not concerned about quality, or at least he did not really understand the issue when asked. To hit the time we had to make compromises on quality, because we could not do the full testing we ideally wanted. We kept asking for delays to build in quality by better testing. His driver was only time. When we completed the project it was a major success for his company and the share price duly went up and up. It was only after a few months when his end-customers kept complaining about the fault rates in the product they had bought, and started to turn away from the company, that the true cost of hitting the date at the expense of lower quality was revealed and that he fully understood the requirement he had imposed upon us. This was a painful lesson for me; if we had done a test for reasonableness at the start we could have foreseen the outcome.

Subsidiary question 5a – Do you want predictability or speed?

There is a specific trade-off question that is worth asking if your customer rates speed of delivery as of paramount importance. Speed can be critically important and late delivery can often adversely impact a business case far more than people realise. However, sometimes when people ask for speed what they really want is to be able to predict delivery times. This is particularly common where your project is a part of a large set of activities that must all be brought together at one point in time. Predictability is quite different from speed; when stated bluntly, this is obvious as the words have different meanings. It is, however, quite common subconsciously to confuse the two, or to have a mental model of the word in which they are closely related. In reality they are quite different things, and are often contradictory.

Scoping question 6 – Are there any other constraints on the project?

When a project is initiated there are often some constraints on how it can progress. Common examples include solutions that are unacceptable in the particular environment, people who must not be used or involved, maximum budgets that are available, or maximum time that can be taken to deliver. Before you develop your plan you must know these constraints.

Subsidiary question 6a – Are there any currently known issues, risks or opportunities?

Assessing issues, risks and opportunities for improvement is a core part of project work. However, it does no harm to ask the question at this stage to identify anything the customer is aware of that may take you some time to find out.

Subsidiary question 6b – Are there any external considerations?

Many organisations are subject to a raft of external considerations that must be understood and considered by the project manager. Typical examples of these are legal issues, regulatory concerns, specific social guidelines because of the nature of the organisation, and health and safety rules. In some cases these can fundamentally alter the approach that must be taken to a project, with significant implications for the resources used and the timescales taken.

Scoping question 7 – How does your customer want to work with you?

Successfully working with people is not just a matter of doing what people want; it is also a function of working in a way that people like, or at least are comfortable with. So, for example, does your customer like daily verbal updates, weekly reports by e-mail, or monthly presentations? Different people like different approaches and you should not assume you know best. Meeting your customer's preferred working style may be a small detail, but at the other extreme it may create a significant overhead and, as it is a critical success factor, it is well worth determining now. In addition, if his or her demands are unreasonable, now is the time to start managing their expectations. A short discussion on how they like to be briefed on issues, risks, progress and spend, and how they like to be involved in development and decision making, and so on, at this stage will enhance your relationship and avoid misunderstanding as well as aid plan development.

Subsidiary question 7a – How will decisions be made on the project?

During the life of a project you will need to make a continuous sequence of decisions. A project will never simply follow a series of pre-arranged steps. Resources need to be shifted around, options to solve problems chosen, different changes must be accepted or rejected. You can save a significant amount of pain and wasted time by broadly agreeing now with your sponsor what type and level of decisions you can make within the project, which ones you need to go to the sponsor to agree, and finally which decisions need to be made by other customer groups or stakeholders.

An example of this is whether you, as the project manager, can raise and authorise unplanned purchase requisitions, and to what value. Essentially the question is what is within your decision-making authority, and who you should involve for other decisions.

Subsidiary question 7b – Can your sponsor allocate all the resources the project requires or do other stakeholders need to be involved?

The task of resource allocation and resource management is described in Chapter 5. Needless to say it is important to understand who you must work with to get resources allocated to the project. Ideally your sponsor should be able to allocate all the resources you require. In practice this is rarely true, and although legitimacy for the project comes from the sponsor's involvement you will frequently have to deal with a range of resource-owning managers. This adds to the complexity not only at the start of the project, but also through its life, as these people may remove resources at any stage unless the relationship with them is well managed.

Subsidiary question 7c – How high is the project in your customer's overall priorities?

You do not actually need to know the answer to this question to scope out a project, but you really do need to know it to plan the project once you have the scope. All projects require resources, whether of money, specialist equipment or people. Your access to these will be a function of what resources the customer has and what else they are being used for. The determining factor will be how high the project sits in a customer's list of priorities. If the priority is set as high as possible then you can assume the customer will give you access to the resources he has available. If it is low, you need to plan accordingly and the timescales or scope need to be adjusted to reflect this. What really matters is not absolute priority to the customer, but priority relative to other things your customer is doing. For example, even if yours is the second most important activity a customer wants completed out of hundreds, it does not help if the highest priority project uses the resources you require.

> **“ what really matters is not absolute priority to the customer, but priority relative to other things your customer is doing ”**

The prioritisation may also impact the type of resources you require. For example, a low priority project will typically not have access to key staff members who will be allocated to higher priority work. Therefore lower priority projects may rely on contract staff or consultants. As such resources are usually more expensive, this ironically increases the budget required for lower priority projects.

I discuss prioritisation in detail in Chapter 10. All I will say here is that at first your customer may be reluctant or find it hard to give you a prioritisation. Although everyone has an implicit list of priorities, few people have an explicitly documented list. If you think of your own life it is quite hard to prioritise all the activities you do relative to one another. It is hard because it requires making decisions about options and this is difficult, but your customer must do this. (Customers also sometimes employ assertive project managers specifically to get projects delivered in the face of low prioritisation.)

You do not need an absolute priority ranking but you do need to get a view on whether you will be within your rights to get people allocated from other work, or if there is work at a higher priority you should not impact if it can be avoided. I firmly believe that you need to understand this point. Your job as a project manager is to get the work done, but it is not to go against your customer's wishes. I have frequently seen project managers working on low priority projects forcing through success on a project by their personal drive and, especially, nagging people to do the work required. The project succeeds, but if it does so at the cost of delaying other work with a higher priority in the customer's mind then you have not actually helped your customer.

Subsidiary question 7d – Who can legitimately put requirements upon the project?

A list should be drawn up and agreed of the people whose input must be actively sought to define detailed requirements once the project is running. This may affect the complexity of a project depending on the size of the list of names given, and the nature of the people on the list. Additionally, since many people may have an opinion about a project and want to influence its direction, you need to know whether you should listen to them or not. A project with a single person acting as the source of requirements may be unusual, but in such cases it is simple to collect the requirements. Larger lists not only offer problems of the logistics in collecting requirements, but also mean you may have to get involved in resolving conflicts between different stakeholders' views of requirements.

If the list of names becomes very extensive, challenge and discuss the implications of this in terms of time and resource usage with the sponsor. Also, be clear what sorts of requirements different people can contribute towards. Some may have a remit only to comment on and add to requirements in one specific part of the project.

Scoping question 8 – Does the customer have any implicit requirements, assumptions or needs that are not defined in the scope or requirements documents?

This is effectively a re-stressing of the point made in Chapter 2 about not making assumptions, and regularly checking understanding. Needless to say, keep checking with the customer throughout the development of both the detailed requirements specification and the project's scope definition that they cover everything the customer has on his or her mind.

All the scoping questions are presented as a checklist in Table 3.1. Use this to determine whether you can or cannot answer each scoping question. If you cannot, is that because it is not applicable, or because it is a risk to the project? If it is a risk, what will you do about it?

table 3.1   Scoping questions checklist

Scoping questions	Can you answer?		
	Yes	No	
		N/a	Risk
1. What is the overall objective of the project?	☐	☐	☐
2. What are the deliverables?	☐	☐	☐
a. Are there deliverables required by the project which it is explicitly not responsible for?	☐	☐	☐
b. Are you working to deliver a finite set of deliverables or to provide some business capability?	☐	☐	☐
c. Are you working to deliver a set of independent deliverables or an integrated end-to-end solution?	☐	☐	☐
d. How will the quality of deliverables be determined?	☐	☐	☐
3. Are you working to implement a specific solution or to solve a problem?	☐	☐	☐
a. Are you responsible for the delivery of deliverables or for achieving the business benefits?	☐	☐	☐
4. How is the customer going to measure success at the end of the project?	☐	☐	☐
5. What, from the customer's viewpoint, can flex?	☐	☐	☐
a. Do you want predictability or speed?	☐	☐	☐
6. Are there any other constraints on the project?	☐	☐	☐
a. Are there any currently known issues, risks or opportunities?	☐	☐	☐
b. Are there any external considerations?	☐	☐	☐

Scoping questions	Can you answer?		
	Yes	No	
		N/a	Risk
7. How does your customer want to work with you?	☐	☐	☐
a. How will decisions be made on the project?	☐	☐	☐
b. Can your sponsor allocate all the resources the project requires or do other stakeholders need to be involved?	☐	☐	☐
c. How high is the project in your customer's overall priorities?	☐	☐	☐
d. Who can legitimately put requirements upon the project?	☐	☐	☐
8. Does the customer have any implicit requirements, assumptions or needs that are not defined in the scope or requirements documents?	☐	☐	☐

Some key traits

This chapter defines the key personality traits required by project managers.

Imagine I need a project manager to manage a piece of work for me. I have a number of choices, and so I am going through a selection process. If you have ever had to employ project managers I am sure you will be familiar with the procedure. I have someone in front of me with a good CV. So far this person sounds good, they know how to communicate and they seem to understand all the things a project manager should know. What else am I going to look for? Beyond basic fitness for the role I am going to try to find out three things about this person:

- Do they have a sense of ownership for what they do – and are they involved in it?
- Do they have good judgement?
- Can they be creative?

Beyond communication skills these are the other things that really differentiate the excellent from the average project manager. They are shown in Figure 4.1 as three of the pillars of project success.

figure 4.1 The building blocks of project success

The sense of ownership and involvement

To be the most successful project manager, you must feel and externally display a sense of complete ownership for the project and its outcome.

A sense of ownership is a pattern of thinking that drives people to care passionately about how well and how hard they work. It is an emotional state that derives pleasure from success, and displeasure from failure. It is the mentality that makes someone act as if they are fully accountable for something, even if they are not. It is the force that makes people get involved in an activity and avoid being remote from it.

when a project manager has delivered without this sense of ownership, it is usually because the project has not been that difficult or complex

If you are a project manager you cannot control everything within the project, but you still need to feel accountable for it all. We can have a debate about the difference between accountability and responsibility, but in terms of the sense of ownership required these two need to blur. You are the one and only person who has overall responsibility, and in addition you need to feel as if you have full accountability. Don't evade it. Take ownership even when a project is a mess. The true sign of someone worth having around is the person who puts up their hand and takes ownership for things when they are going wrong. Act like this and people will thank you, reward you, and seek you out to work with them again!

A project can be delivered by a project manager who does not have a real sense of ownership for its content or outcome. I have been involved with lots of projects that have achieved their goals when they were managed by someone without a full sense of ownership. But when things go wrong, get tricky or are otherwise demanding, the sense of ownership drives success. When it is midnight and a little more is needed to complete the work, passion will drive you. When a project manager has delivered without this sense of ownership, it is usually because the project has not been that difficult or complex.

How can I tell when a project manager has this sense of ownership? You can only tell when the going gets tough. The project is going to be late, maybe for justifiable reasons – perhaps an issue has arisen which changes things. Do you feel, 'oh well, I have managed the process and this is the result. I have done my job and can do no more', or do you ask yourself, 'OK, this has occurred, what can I do to bring it on track and keep it on track?' If the former applies to you, you are going through the motions; if the latter, then you have that sense of ownership for the project.

If I am recruiting a project manager, what do I look for? Essentially, I will question and probe them to tell me about situations when things have gone wrong and ask them to describe what they did and how it felt. I will ask them about situations in which they have failed to deliver. What did they do and how did it feel? What I am looking for is a picture of someone who is tenacious in overcoming obstacles, who derives pleasure from overcoming them, and who feels he or she has failed if they cannot.

How can you know if you have this sense of ownership? My trite answer to that question is like the old answer to the 'how will I know if I am in love' question – the wise simply respond that you just do. You know when you are committed to something. If you are unsure, ask yourself this question: how will you feel if the project does not achieve its end goals for reasons outside your control? If you are simply going to shrug your shoulders and think, 'well, it was not my fault', then you do not have the sense of ownership; if, on the other hand, you are going to feel disappointed and unsatisfied then you probably do have it.

Great project managers feel passionate about meeting project success goals; they do not treat project management as an algorithm that either comes up with the right answer or does not. Great project managers will go that extra mile to find solutions and ways around when things go wrong; they do not accept answers from their team about how long things take, or how much they cost, without rigorous and structured challenge. Great project managers escalate issues to get things done, not to dodge responsibility. When you have escalated to the most senior person available, you still know you are the one who has to bring the project in and you treat the escalation as simply another task you must manage, not a handing over of responsibility.

Great project managers not only use their sense of ownership to drive themselves to deliver, they shine this passion onto the teams they are managing, and onto the customers they are delivering for.

A good analogy is with sports. Everyone can participate in some sports. Most people can win in some situations or against some opponents. But being really successful is not about winning when you can choose your competition, or winning only now and again. It is about consistently winning. This cannot be achieved without the passion to win. All sports psychologists will tell you that while ability and fitness are necessary to excel at sport, your mental state and attitude is also critically important to success. Similarly, project managers need project management competence and abilities, but they also need passion and drive.

Such a sense of ownership is not about project managers achieving impossible things. It is about project managers having an emotional state of attachment and engagement with the work so that their personal feeling of success or failure is aligned with project success or failure. I am not saying that without this you cannot ever competently manage projects; you can. You can be competent, but you will never excel. You may keep busy, but people will not go that extra mile to seek you out to manage their projects.

Ownership is not a remote sense. Ownership needs to be experienced and displayed through total involvement in a project. As a project manager you are not an absentee landlord who occasionally returns to make sure that your tenants are behaving well. You must be an integral, active member of the team sitting at the centre of the action. Ask yourself a question: what is your mental image of yourself as you deliver your project? Do you see yourself as a knowledgeable observer of the project, trying to put some shape and structure onto a series of events you have only partial control over, half-impotently trying to change things, your main weapon being your ability to track what is going on and bring more senior management in when you need to escalate? Do you see yourself as a powerful but impassionate deity sitting above the project whose role it is to oversee, report, and occasionally give directions and move people and tasks around in a giant game of chess? Or do you see yourself as a core component of the project, responsible for its delivery, fighting alongside everyone else to get it done and fundamentally involved in the day-to-day workings of the project? If your image is anything like the first two, you are doing the wrong job. You must be a core component of the project.

If you want to be great you need to feel total ownership for the project and remain intimately involved in it throughout its life. A final factor that makes commitment important is that work is personally more enjoyable if you are committed.

Good judgement – project management style

> ### Key lesson
>
> Each and every project is different and a project manager needs to adapt to each one. Although tools and processes will help, the basis for this adaptation must be the project manager's judgement.

Project managers have a whole family of processes and tools and may also have checklists and systems to support them. However, project management is not an exact science that can be applied like a mathematical equation to provide a precise answer. It is in the definition of a project that it is a unique endeavour. If every project is different, then the approach to managing each project must, to some extent, be unique as well. Project managers require judgement to tailor their management approach to the demands of the project. (In the rest of the book I will repeatedly refer to the need for good judgement.)

❝ I cannot give you good judgement – you have it, you develop it, or you don't and never will ❞

Judgement, by its very definition, is more an art than a science. Occasionally people seem to be born with good judgement, but usually it comes with the scars of practice. It is learnt by experience rather than taught in the classroom or learnt by reading a book like this. It is not a theoretical subject, and I cannot give you good judgement – you have it, you develop it, or you don't and never will.

However, I can be of some help. Good judgement is critical to the project manager, and if I cannot bestow good judgement, I can at least point out some areas in which your judgement needs to be applied. The following list covers a sample of fifteen key areas where a project manager regularly needs to apply judgement. It is not an exhaustive list. These points are not like Euclidean geometry providing, with absolutely logical certainty, unquestionably right answers in every situation. They require you to make decisions based on balancing different issues. Being able to find this balance is what makes really successful project managers. I have chosen these specific examples as they represent everyday decisions project managers must make and give a feel for the spread of judgements required.

The fifteen areas for judgement I have selected are:

1　What is in scope?
2　What should be in the plan?
3　Which elements of the project management process to apply and which to ignore
4　When to escalate
5　When to get into the detail and when to skim
6　When to do and when to delegate
7　Who can you trust in your project team?
8　What is an acceptable level of risk?
9　What is an acceptable level of parallel activity?
10　What is an acceptable level of change?
11　When should you enforce the change management process?
12　When is it reasonable to progress based on an assumption?
13　How many levels of project management organisation do you need?
14　When to consider broader stakeholder groups
15　When is the project complete?

Judgement 1 – What is in scope?

In Chapters 2 and 3 I outlined the importance of understanding a project's scope and defined a series of questions you they can use to ensure you know it well enough. I also described an inability to understand or communicate the scope as the closest a project manager can come to a cardinal sin. It is one of the most important things a project manager discusses with his customer, and by using the questions I outlined you should get a good definition of scope. However, the reality is that unless you are working for a very structured customer (or perhaps an ex-project manager), the final definition of scope is subject, to some degree, to the project manager's judgement.

An assertive project manager can usually influence a customer in the definition of scope and support defining it more or less broadly. A less assertive project manager may simply be at his customer's mercy. Project managers usually understand the issues to do with scope better than their customers, so they can, to a limited degree, if unscrupulous, manipulate it to suit themselves. In each case there is a danger. Over-rigorous definition of the scope to a very constrained set of deliverables may help to ensure delivery, but it can risk effective project failure. If not everything that is actually needed is included you may, on paper, have achieved the result required but, taking a more customer-centric view, you have failed. It also risks producing unsatisfied customers. No matter how well it is documented and signed off by the customer, if the end result is less than their expectations then they will be unhappy. The counterbalance to this is that an over-broad definition of scope can lead to a situation in which a project never finishes. The skill, therefore, is to help your customer define a scope for the project that is achievable with the available resources and time, and which also meets their real needs.

Common actions that can result in an over-broad definition of scope come about from what is normally known as scope creep, and the customer's desire to use a project to deliver a host of unrelated needs. Scope creep is the tendency for apparently successful projects to be subject to a constant series of additions to scope (sometimes without change control, but even if change control is applied it does not work as each change is acceptable in terms of its incremental impact, but the cumulative impact of many changes pushes the project to failure). Customers may also add unrelated requirements to a project's scope, simply because a project team exists and they may feel it can be used to achieve all sorts of extras they may need. Scope creep is dangerous; it can lead to a point at which the project becomes too big to complete. Unrelated requirements added at a customer's whim have the same, if not greater, dangers potentially affecting a project team.

The judgement you must make as a project manager is to balance the following questions:

- Is the scope defined broadly enough to add value for the customer?
- Is it defined narrowly enough to be achievable with the resources and skills available and in the time required?

▧ Is it defined in a meaningful way that is consistent with the project's objectives and can be easily communicated?

▧ Will it meet the objective (and nothing else!)?

Judgement 2 – What should be in the plan?

Once a project's scope is defined, the next thing a project manager must do is to build the project plan. I discuss planning in Chapter 5, but it is worth taking an early look at the subject.

Project planning in itself is not a conceptually difficult activity and it is very powerful. The project plan will form the basis for deciding the resources required and the length of time the project will take, and will also throw up other issues and risks the project manager must resolve.

The judgement in project planning is essentially to do with the level of detail the plan includes, and how many activities that are not within the project's scope should be included in the plan (external dependencies). A common mistake for new project managers is to make a massively complicated plan, showing every activity down to a very low level of granularity. At the other extreme some project managers simply spend a few minutes putting together a very high-level summary.

Before deciding the correct approach it is worth making sure you understand what the plan is actually for, and how you will use it in practice. One way to look at the purpose of a plan is that it should help you achieve the following five management tasks:

1 The process of planning helps to explore the project and develop understanding. If done in an open fashion, planning promotes constructive dialogue between the project team members and the project customer. It can reduce uncertainty and hence reduce risk.

2 The plan enables you to understand how long the project will take and what resources are required through the various stages of the project to deliver it. In doing this it needs to have the capability of enabling your 'what if' analysis. (For example, if you add one more person to a team for a few weeks, what will be the impact on the plan, or what will be the impact on the plan if you remove some people for a period of time?)

3 The plan will enable you to allocate work to the various people or teams involved in the project and to ensure that the tasks they perform all come together to achieve the end result required.

4   The plan helps you measure progress. Without a plan it is not possible to decide in any one period of time whether you have done enough to get to the end point, or whether you should have done more.

5   The plan is a communications tool to explain to people in the project, customers and other stakeholders, what they want to know and what you need them to know.

The next thing to understand is how the plan will be used in practice. It is a tool and not an end in itself. It needs only to be good enough to achieve the five purposes outlined above, and nothing else. It will be subject to change and needs to be a living document throughout the life of the project. No matter how well you plan, on a project with any degree of complexity, tasks will have to be added and timings will change, and the plan will help you manage this. Make it too complex and the task of updating it will become unmanageable.

Too high a level of planning and you will not be able to achieve the results defined above. For example, if a major programme is defined in single tasks, each a month long, you cannot work out the resources required. Too low a level of planning and the plan becomes an end in itself and as the project manager you will spend too much time creating and updating it. Also, it then becomes easy to get bogged down in low-level detail and stop seeing the wood for the trees.

If your plan is sufficient to achieve the five purposes described above, it is sufficiently detailed. Include any more detail and you are just making work for yourself. The primary aim is to show the work that falls within the scope of your project; external dependencies should be shown, but only at a very high level. Do not try to plan out all the external dependencies in detail in your plan. (However, see Chapter 10 for issues in managing external dependencies.)

Judgement 3 – Which elements of the project management process to apply and which to ignore

If you try to apply every project manager discipline in every situation, you will spend your whole life applying process and nothing will actually be delivered. There are some things (like planning and managing issues) which probably need to be done on every project, but there are others which can be excluded. I regularly see project managers producing all sorts of documents and following processes which are not relevant to the project they are managing, simply because they are mandatory in the organisation they work in. There does need to be a minimum mandatory set of common activities for project managers, but this should be a small set with the implementation of other processes being dependent on the judgement of the project manager. For example, if levels of risk are low and the impact of late delivery is minor, don't bother with contingency plans.

You should remember that the project management process is there to help you, not to hinder you. So use it carefully when it helps, but on the occasions it gets in the way or does not add value then ignore it. There is an overhead in using good process, but this overhead will be repaid in greater efficiency, effectiveness, or lower risk in the longer run. However, where it is not achieving these returns, work without it. As a project manager your management approach should have priority over the process. If you are a junior or inexperienced project manager, use the process. One of the key things to learn as you become more experienced is when to break away from it. As project manager it is *your* tool, not your straightjacket.

Judgement 4 – When to escalate

The judgement required here is not only to keep to the 'no surprises' rule (see Chapter 2, communication lesson 16 on expectation management), but also to avoid overloading the sponsor and adding no value. Put simply, if you escalate everything then you are adding very little value. Your job is to resolve issues and manage risks, not simply to act as a channel to more senior managers. When you hit a roadblock your job is to remove it. On the other hand, you need to give sponsors and customers adequate warning of issues and risks that you will not be able to resolve. If you escalate too late you increase the risk of failure. Being able to judge between when it is inappropriate to escalate and when it is essential is a key capability.

> **when you hit a roadblock your job is to remove it**

It is also important to remember that when you escalate you do not cease to be accountable for resolution of the underlying issue. You are still the project manager and you are still responsible for delivery; it is just that one of the tasks is being done by someone more senior.

Judgement 5 – When to get into the detail and when to skim

To some extent this depends on the size of the project. But assuming I am talking about big projects or programmes, this becomes a critical decision. Skim too high and you are likely to miss important details; go too low and you will stop doing the project manager's job and become overloaded. The secret is to identify the members of the team who are fully reliable and those who are not. Go into more detail with those who are not, rather than in the area you happen to be most comfortable or knowledgeable with. The second thing is to make sure you have a robust progress tracking mechanism; this will soon show up where you need to focus your attention.

Judgement 6 – When to do and when to delegate

This is a general management challenge that all new managers struggle with but must learn. Asking and trusting other people to perform key tasks rather than doing all of them yourself comes naturally to people who are experienced in their jobs. It is often difficult the first time you manage people. All managers must delegate; if you cannot then you should not be a manager. It is easy if the task to be delegated is not in your area of competence; then it is obvious that you must rely on your experts. However, you must also use delegation regularly even for tasks you feel you can do well. It's not just that you don't have the time, but your team members will never learn if you do not let them try. Of course, if someone is inexperienced they may need more help, but at least let them try to do it.

If you are managing the project properly you will not have time to do anything other than managing it. Doing other work means you will be disregarding your primary responsibility. But always remember a good rule from the military: don't ask your team to do anything you would not be willing to do yourself.

Judgement 7 – Who can you trust in your project team?

The project manager will have to look across a wide range of areas, managing progress and helping to remove any roadblocks. The main control mechanism the project manager has in this situation will be progress assessments against the plan. Where issues or problems occur the project manager will need to get into more detail. In big programmes it is frequently true that the project manager cannot cover all the areas in sufficient detail to be absolutely sure of progress and resolution of issues all the time. A good way to cover this is to be able to determine which members of your team you can trust to be good at following the agreed project plan and who will escalate to you when they need help. Then you can focus more of your time on those members of the team who need more detailed tracking.

There are two dimensions here that the project manager needs to be aware of. Trust on a personal basis means that when someone says they will do something you believe them. There is also trust based on whether someone has the skills and competencies to do the work required, so that when they say they will do something, you know they are capable of doing it thoroughly.

Judgement 8 – What is an acceptable level of risk?

There are three separate risks you have to be aware of when managing a project: risk to a business (i.e. if this project goes wrong what is the impact on the business?), risk to the project (i.e. what can derail it and how likely is this?) and personal risk (i.e. what is the risk to yourself in terms of things like reputation should this go wrong?).

Business risk should not really be the project manager's concern. That is for the project sponsor to worry about (although it obviously helps to provide good advice to the sponsor). I cannot talk about personal risk, as by its very definition it is an individual issue. It is something you should be conscious of and have a good self-awareness of. The degree of project risk that is acceptable varies from project to project, and from organisation to organisation. Assuming you have a robust risk management process and do actually understand the degree of risk you are undertaking, the things to think about when assessing whether the level of risk is acceptable are:

- Do you fully understand the risks you have identified or are they just the tip of an iceberg?
- Are the risks independent issues or are they interrelated and cumulative?
- Have you got a way around risk – can it be reduced, can you mitigate it happening, or do you have a contingency plan should it happen? (Is the plan viable and are there resources to implement it?)
- How risk-averse or risk-favouring is the organisation you are working in?
- How critical is it that the project is delivered? If the risk derails the project, will that have a significant impact on your customer or will they cope easily?
- How good is your project team? A strong team is usually better able to handle and resolve risks.

Judgement 9 – What is an acceptable level of parallel activity?

To many people the ideal way of doing anything is to perform one task at a time, in other words to do things sequentially. Some activities have to be done sequentially. As a trivial example you cannot physically test a new car until it has been built. However, if you conduct all activities on a project sequentially then it can become impossibly long. Hence, most projects have a degree of parallel activity – in fact, you could argue this is why you need a project manager to manage across the various parallel work streams (in the case of a project) or parallel projects (in the case of a programme). Usually, the issue becomes a problem only when in the desire to speed up activity, or the desire to catch up following a delay, tasks that were originally planned as sequential become parallel. This can increase risk and you should feel instinctively uncomfortable when too many tasks are brought together in this way. The questions you need to ask yourself are:

- Do you have sufficient resources to do the work in parallel? It may speed up progress but it will also eat resources up more quickly.

- Are any of the tasks now in parallel logically only possible sequentially? However much you may want to complete some tasks in parallel, perhaps they should or may only be done sequentially.

- What is the impact on testing, training and handover? I pick these out, as testing, training and handover are normally the last tasks on a project. It is often therefore testing, training and handover that are squeezed into shorter and shorter blocks of more and more parallel work. Acceptable testing shortcuts involve developing test and training plans before deliverables are ready for test, and testing individual components before all components are ready. The risk becomes higher when integration tests, user acceptance tests and operational readiness tests are performed in parallel. Cut testing at your peril. Reducing the focus on handover will only come back and bite you when you try to release project resources.

- Can you, as the project manager, actually manage this and can your team do it? A project with half a dozen parallel tasks is much easier to manage than one with twenty. Managing twenty tasks in parallel increases the management overhead and also the skill required. Effectively making task pathways more parallel removes the margin for error and makes delivery to date critical. In most projects, if a deliverable date shifts by a small percentage it can be recovered. When all activities are performed in parallel this may not be possible. Parallel working increases the need for a skilled and experienced team.

You should also differentiate between parallel activity of the project and parallel activity for individual project team members. Plenty of evidence shows that no matter how much we value people who can multi-task, multi-tasking is inherently inefficient; sometimes as much as 40% of effort can be wasted swapping between tasks. Of course we often have to multi-task, but if you do not it is much more efficient to work on tasks sequentially. Hence, try to avoid a plan, even one with many parallel work streams, in which individuals are regularly swapping between tasks. Have them work on one task at a time as far as possible.

Another reason to avoid parallel working is that it can slow down delivery of benefits. If you work sequentially individual tasks are completed quicker, and if these lead to business benefits then some benefits will be delivered earlier. This is usually more of an issue on programmes than on projects, but it is worth considering. Figure 4.2 shows this.

One final point about too many parallel activities, it is not only the planned tasks that you have to avoid becoming too parallel. If too many issues and risks are arising which need resolution, you can get to the point where work on these also becomes too much to manage, and a simple roadblock becomes gridlock. Although it is not a good point to reach, the pragmatic project manager does have to accept that sometimes not all issues can be resolved at the same time and, potentially, additional time has to be added to the project plan to resolve some issues sequentially.

Judgement 10 – What is an acceptable level of change?

The project manager's dream project is often one on which nothing changes. When nothing changes it is easier by far to deliver reliably. In fact, some project managers use the change control process more as a mechanism to stop change rather than to control it. And yet, change will occur; it is a reality. In some situations it may be a positive benefit. Many professional companies selling project-based products and services to a customer often make most of their money on changes as opposed to delivering the base requirement. However, as a project manager you do have to be able to manage the degree of change to some extent. Constant change makes a project almost impossible to complete. If the degree of change is too great, you must talk with your sponsor to reduce it (which may be achieved, for example, by slowing the project down until requirements are better understood, or by agreeing that you will deliver against the existing requirements and deal with the changes as a separate, subsequent project).

The judgement you need to make is to determine at what point the level of change becomes too great to successfully deliver. In many ways assessing whether the degree of change is too great is like deciding whether the level of risk is too great: different projects can absorb different amounts and there is no absolute rule. The key things to do are:

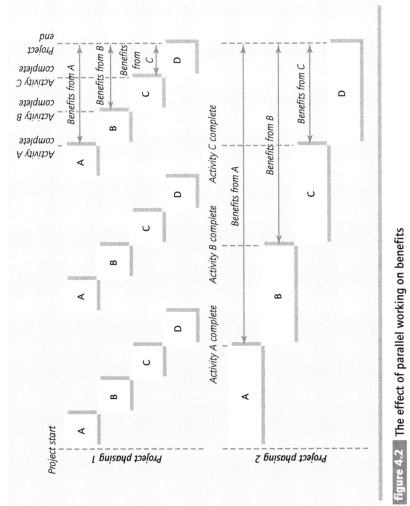

figure 4.2 The effect of parallel working on benefits

▓ Make sure the project has a robust change control process in place. People often focus on the forms to log and raise a change. This is important, but there is more to a change control process than this. Critically, there must be a clear process for accepting change, which needs clarity over who has the final say in accepting changes. It is also important to make sure that the project team do not agree to changes without using the change control process.

▓ Develop an ability to explain the impact of change unemotionally. Do not get caught in the trap of disliking changes because you personally find them irritating. This will show in your communications with the customer. It is your customer's project and if they want to make the change they can, but they need to understand the impact fully. When customers really understand the impact of a change on timescales or costs of projects, they will often not go forward with it. Unless you take time to explain this, then from a customer's perspective making changes seems essentially to be 'free', and they will tend to ask for changes willy-nilly.

▓ Determine how important the change is. Is it nice-to-have or is it really essential? It is worth challenging hard. It is interesting to see how many so-called 'critical' changes, when really analysed, are not desperately important when people fully understand their impacts, especially if they are asked for more money or delays to the project to implement them.

▓ Determine the impact of the change on the project. How does the change affect the customer's time–cost–quality–scope trade-off? If a customer really has a time priority for delivery then change generally needs to be minimised. On the other hand, if the scope and quality of the end result are of paramount importance then the amount of change that can be incorporated is greater.

▓ Assess how the project team are handling it. Too much change can eventually be demotivating for a project team, especially if hard work is wasted as a result.

Judgement 11 – When should you enforce the change management process?

The judgement here is to ensure the change management process achieves what it set out to achieve: to manage the process of changes occurring to the project, to manage the risk associated with change, and to ensure that the change is fully assessed and its impact understood before it is implemented. So, in general terms, the change management

❝ project management approaches are often fairly accused of too much bureaucracy ❞ process should be activated whenever it is applicable. On the other hand, project managers and project management approaches are often fairly accused of too much bureaucracy, and with the best will in the world change management processes will always have some degree of administrative overhead.

Two factors for a project manager to consider when thinking about changes are:

- The impact of a change upon a project depends not only on the change, but also on when it is asked for. It may be fairly easy to make what are fairly fundamental changes to a project early in its lifecycle without affecting the overall cost or schedule. On the other hand, at the end of a project even minor changes may require significantly more work. (A simple example: if you have a project to build a car from a kit, and you decide at the beginning you want to change it from a two-litre to a three-litre engine, it may be easy, but at the end of the build when the car is complete, changing the engine size will be complicated and will delay completion of the project.)

- Many people may want or request changes, but some (such as the sponsor) have a more legitimate right to expect their changes to be implemented than other stakeholders.

When it comes to changes, there are small things that are asked for early in the project's lifecycle that can be done with a very minor impact on the project and which do not need to go through the full change management process. If a change is not going to alter the time, cost, resources or plan for a project, it is reasonable for the project manager to accept it without fuller assessment, though even here it should be an occasional and exceptional change rather than become a behavioural pattern.

This is a useful judgement to be able to make. However, if you are in doubt do stick to enforcing the change management process on all changes. I would also never tell the project team that it is permissible to avoid the change management process lest uncontrolled change becomes the norm.

Judgement 12 – When is it reasonable to progress based on an assumption?

People make assumptions all the time, and projects are not immune. Sometimes it is done as an explicit action; on other occasions it is implicit in activities and thought processes. In projects people make assumptions when they do not have full information. For example, in a project to deliver an IT system you may need to know the number of users to scale the hardware required for the system to run on. It may be that you can make an assumption that the same number of people will use this system as another similar one. This is not a proven fact, but it may seem a reasonable decision to allow you to progress with hardware planning. A further example may involve the delivery of a new product and you do not know how many will be sold. You may assume a sales rate based on your experience of other product sales, and from this plan your manufacturing volumes.

The power of assumptions to a project manager is that making an educated assumption allows rapid progress to be made when there is not time, it is not possible, or it is not pertinent to actually prove something. The danger with assumptions is that they may be wrong, and this may have a detrimental impact on the project. Making assumptions is a perfectly valid thing to do. Never making assumptions will usually lead to a very slow development activity, and there are many things you can assume without too much risk to a project. If you try to make everything certain you may never progress, but making too many assumptions or taking on too much risk by making critical assumptions around key components of the project needs to be avoided.

The judgement required of a project manager is to find a balance between the answers to the following three questions:

1 What is the impact of not making an assumption? (Will your work be delayed, cost added, etc.?)

2 What is the risk of making an assumption? (How likely is it that it will be wrong, and what will be the impact if it is?)

3 How easy or difficult would it be to confirm the assumption you want to make?

Underlying this is a need to understand when assumptions are being made, and to make them explicit; and to have an assumption management process to manage them through, linked to your risk assessment. (In Chapter 10 I lay out the essence of an assumption management process, which I regard as a core project management skill.)

Judgement 13 – How many levels of project management organisation do you need?

In various projects I regularly see many layers of work-stream, work-package, project and programme managers. It is important to remember the end goal is to deliver, not to manage delivery. Once the project is complete all that matters is that the deliverables exist, not that there was a magnificent management structure. Only the very largest of projects should need several layers of management. The issue is as much one of presentation (too many layers look inefficient, like empire building, and like laziness on behalf of the person at the top – all of these factors look bad to customers, sponsors and project team members). One simple way of looking at it is how many people do you have *managing* work as opposed to *doing* work? If your number of managers is not a small percentage (less than 25%, perhaps as low as 10%) of the doers then you have too many layers of management. I have seen projects where 40–50% of the team seem to be managing rather than delivering. This is too high. Countering this, if you have significantly less than a 10% management overhead you probably have too few managers.

Judgement 14 – When to consider broader stakeholder groups

If the group of stakeholders includes anyone who has an impact upon or is impacted by the project, this could include virtually anyone in an organisation. This is obviously too big to manage. On the other hand, if you ignore stakeholders beyond the immediate customer, you may miss people who can disrupt progress or have another impact on the success of the project. To decide which stakeholders are important, start by using your intuition, but also do formal stakeholder analysis to identify those people or groups with potential major impact. This is a risk mitigation activity, the aim being to reduce the risk of external impact on the project. The types of people to consider are:

- Those who can have a major influence on the continuing allocation of resources.
- Those who can influence the acceptance of the project, its deliverables, the resultant change, or the achievement of business benefits.
- Those who may otherwise cause significant risk to the project.

In Chapter 10 I look at stakeholders again and discuss processes around this more.

Judgement 15 – When is the project complete?

It is theoretically very easy to understand when a project is complete. It is complete when it has met the agreed requirements. For some projects this is black and white, but for many others the situation is less clear. The reality is that a project is complete when both the customer and the project team agree it is complete, and there are many situations in which reaching this agreement can be contentious.

The lack of clarity normally involves handover periods and bedding-down situations. For example, a new piece of computer software will normally have bugs in it – does the project end when the formal development is complete, or once all the bugs have been found and corrected (noting it may take many months or even years for some obscure bugs to become apparent)? Alternatively, a project team may be required to support new users through a training and familiarisation period. Once the users get used to having support all the time they may be unwilling to let go. After what length of time are users capable of supporting themselves? A different example occurs when a new building is finished. It may have faults or snags. Normally a snagging list is agreed and the items on it must be fixed before a customer accepts that the building work is complete. But when is something legitimately a snag and when is it a change of requirements?

Achieving completion may also be contentious when, at the last minute, the customer suddenly understands that they cannot use the deliverables for some reason, or realises there is a gap in them. I have been in several project handover meetings when someone representing the user community or customer says 'but we need this as well, otherwise we can't use it' or 'otherwise we won't achieve the benefits'. There may be a gap in requirements and scope, though you may have delivered absolutely everything you were asked to. There is still a problem that you cannot just walk away from.

You should not leave your customer in the lurch with poorly functioning or sub-standard deliverables, or deliverables they cannot use. Even if the gap is the customer's fault it is not productive to state, even in the most politically correct language, 'that was not in scope, so it's completely your problem'. On the other hand, if a project team is never able to disband, it is at the very least an ineffective use of project resources. It may directly cost money, resulting in arguments about who should pay, and there is an opportunity cost arising from the alternative work the team members could productively be doing if they were not still tied up on the project.

In terms of finishing support for projects once they have gone live, the secret is to:

- Ensure, from the outset of the project, that the customer is aware of their responsibility, especially in thinking through their full needs. Although it may seem obvious, regularly remind the customer that the project will end, the team will leave, and one day they will have to use and maintain the deliverables by themselves.
- Ensure you manage a robust requirements capture process in the first place. This reduces the likelihood of customers turning round at the end and saying there are other things they need.

- Agree both a timescale and clear criteria for support to end once the deliverables have been handed over.
- Think through the implications of the project on the stakeholders. What do they need to be happy to let you finish your work? Build this into your project plan.
- Plan to release staff incrementally through the support period.
- Build upon good expectation management about the quality and impact of deliverables.

With regard to the timescale and criteria for support to end, agree this early on, not at the end of the project. Then you can build the support time into your plans and budgets. Add some contingency around it. For example, in a project to launch a new product, the project team may support live operations until end users are sufficiently familiar with any new supporting processes and to cover any problems that might arise with the product once it is in end customers' hands. A guideline may be agreed such that support will be provided for one month post-launch and until no major issues have occurred for two weeks. Although these criteria may not coincide (so, for example, you may have run out of planned time, but still have had more than one major issue in the last two weeks), they at least provide a basis to manage expectations around and provide a framework of understanding which you can use to extricate yourself from a project you consider complete. In my experience, post-launch support is never completed more quickly than anticipated, and the less pre-planned the longer it takes. For complex deliverables post-launch support may need to last several months.

Setting exit criteria should not be arbitrary, but normally cannot be done totally scientifically either. Deciding what is a major issue that stops launch versus a minor issue which can be lived with requires constructive dialogue with the customer. You need to balance your desire to close a project when there are more effective and efficient (or interesting!) uses of your time, with your customer's ongoing need for help.

You do not have to maintain all the staff on the project team through a post-launch support period. It is generally most efficient to let the team diminish gradually until you have only a skeleton crew in the final stages of support. Ideally you should set up an agreement with team members' line managers that any key team members you have released can be re-assigned back to you if major issues arise.

The other basis for successful completion is managing the customer's expectations about the quality of deliverables and the likely impact on their organisation. If the project's timelines and budgets have forced you to make compromises, tell your customer. A customer who understands that a deliverable will not be 100% perfect, and will cause some pain as well as benefits to his organisation, is more likely to be supportive of letting the project team go than one to whom this comes as a complete surprise.

The alternative scenario, when, at the last minute, the customer realises that the deliverables are not complete or are unusable even though the project has delivered its full scope, is more complex to resolve. There is no single approach to fixing this problem and its solution ideally rests on a strong relationship with your customer. Whenever a conversation starts debating whether a deliverable set is complete or not, there is always the danger of confrontation between project and customer, but if you get to a point of confrontation then disaster is looming. When you have a perceived gap between deliverables and customer needs, make sure you and your customer are communicating, both listening and talking. If you are just arguing, you will get nowhere. Try to keep the debate open and resolution focused rather than pointing fingers. If you must do it, the finger pointing can be done once the problem is solved.

If the customer really has forgotten something it is not unreasonable for you to point out, in sensitive language, that this really is their fault. But you should not simply wash your hands of it. Agree an extension to the project and do the work; if you are an external company then, yes, you should be paid for this, but you should also do it. You don't want your customers saying that what you delivered does not work, whatever the cause.

The greyest situation of all occurs when project requirements have been omitted by the customer, but when you were hired as a subject matter expert in this specific type of project. The customer may legitimately think that although they signed off the requirements you should have advised them on any omissions. I can remember several meetings with consultancies when they have claimed they did not do something because they were not asked to, only to have the response that they were employed as experts and advisers and should have noticed the gap. *This is a reasonable view for the customer to hold if you have sold yourself as a subject matter expert.* Cracking this problem will vary from situation to situation. My advice again is to focus on resolution and not on pointing fingers. Be willing to compromise on responsibility (and hence cost). Try to make reaching resolution a negotiation and not a dispute.

Finally, do not confuse the act of completing a project with meeting a date on a plan. Ideally the two coincide, but regularly they will not. Often organisations focus on time at the expense of all other issues, and it can be in a project team's own interest to complete on the due date. There can be an explicit, or more often unconscious, conspiracy to finish on time at all costs between project teams and certain stakeholders. You should avoid the temptation to put your or the project team's needs in front of your customer's when it comes to delivering on time. While late delivery is bad, it may often be a lesser evil than simply stopping when the scheduled time is up. Your thinking may be 'if I don't complete on time, I have missed the deadline for the project, surely this is failure?' Missing deadlines and project schedules on a regular basis is symptomatic of poor project management. But you must not let your need to be perceived as a heroic project manager who always delivers on time get in the way of supplying a high quality deliverable. Do

> **❝ missing deadlines and project schedules on a regular basis is symptomatic of poor project management ❞**

not make the mistake of confusing the importance of hitting time and the fact that very occasionally it is *the* critical factor, with the knowledge that in most situations a specific date to finish the project is an artificial constraint. Unless there is some critical event – such as completing building works for the start of the Olympic Games – which is not going to move, time is important but only one factor among several that are important. Cost is important, scope is important, quality is important, business benefits are important. Yes, if you do not deliver in time you have not achieved full success, but if the cost of hitting the timeline is a sub-standard deliverable, or worse still something that actually disrupts the organisation it is being implemented in, then you need to make a balanced decision about what is best for your customer. This may mean drifting beyond the end date, and if your personal reputation for delivering on time takes a little knock, so be it.

Let me give an example where speed of delivery was put ahead of 'real' completion of a project. I worked for an organisation which was implementing a major software package that could significantly enhance operations. As with such packages the work to implement it was highly complex and required much data collection, data cleansing, process design and process change, as well as organisational change. The package was implemented, and the result was operational chaos. Parts of the system did not fully function as expected, the data in it was not fully accurate, and the impact on existing operations was greater than expected. This was explained as normal teething problems, but those involved in operations knew it went far deeper than that. The organisation survived and eventually thrived, but not without great pain. At the end of the project, the project manager proudly announced that the software had been implemented in six months less than in any other organisation. No doubt this improved the project manager's reputation, but left many of us thinking it would have been better to have taken six months more to get it working properly. A poorly launched set of deliverables can end up costing far more than the business benefits it was meant to deliver.

Project management judgements – summary

This list of areas where judgement is required could be continued almost indefinitely, as there are many judgements a project manager has to make day in, day out. Some of these will be specific to the project he or she is running. All I have done here is to give you some key points to think about.

I'm afraid that beyond this I cannot tell you how to develop a sense of judgement. I would love to be able to. It would enable a lot of new project managers to short-circuit painful experiences. But I would be lying if I did not say that experience and scars have tremendous value. It is not that a brilliant inexperienced project manager cannot deliver a complex project; it is just that you will find it harder and often your fingers will get a little burnt on the way.

To begin with as a project manager you may struggle to find the balance point, especially as it varies from situation to situation. However, if you find, over time, that you cannot develop this judgement, it is really worth asking yourself whether project management is the right career for you. But assuming you get better over time, when things do go wrong, learn from them and be positive about it. Very few, if any, people are born with perfect judgement and therefore accept occasional mistakes as a learning opportunity. Good project management process requires you to review projects when they are complete and at periodic intervals during projects. When things have gone wrong ask yourself, 'if I had made a different judgement in that situation would it have gone better?' If the answer is 'yes', learn for next time.

When things have gone wrong I find it helps to reflect on Nietzsche's famous phrase – 'what does not kill me makes me stronger'!

A touch of creativity

Key lesson

Never be creative with your customer's requirements, but always look for creative ways to deliver those requirements.

Project managers are responsible for managing the delivery of particular sets of things – be they documents, processes, computer systems, buildings, new products or otherwise. They deliver them against a requirements specification, and generally according to a defined project management process. Typically the solution itself is defined not by the project manager but by some specialist person or team, such as a group of design engineers, whom the project manager manages. They are doing this work normally for someone else, a customer, who needs the end result. In this situation, surely the last thing needed is creativity, and surely what is really required is an ability to manage a process robustly and effectively?

There is some truth in this statement, and, in fact, there are many parts of a project that you do not want a project manager to be acting creatively in. A creative attitude towards your customer's requirements is generally unacceptable. Project managers who change the project requirements to ease the work or reduce risk (and I have seen it done) hazard almost certain failure to meet the customer's needs. Such changes must be driven by the customer.

So where is the place for creativity? The place for creativity comes when it is necessary to solve problems and remove roadblocks from a project. Things happen on projects that are unplanned and that get in the way of progress. Such roadblocks need to be removed or worked around for success to be possible. To do this, creativity helps. For example:

- **Customer challenge** – the project manager is there to deliver the customer's need and not to define it. This does not mean you should feel you are not in a position to challenge the customer's requirements if you see they will result in problems. The mindset to avoid is one in which you, as a project manager, are thinking, 'you do not really want that'. However, based on your experience and what you can see when you plan the project, it is very productive to help the customer understand if any specific requirements add significantly to risk, cost or timescales and help the customer to understand that they could get a shorter, simpler or easier project if they removed them. Alternatively, you may see that additional requirements may easily be met by the project. Again it is worth raising these with the customer. The mindset to adopt is of a professional adviser. The customer in the end must decide, but sometimes a little creative advice can be helpful. If the help is not wanted then stop giving it, but if you do this with sensitivity, you will find that in many situations this helps to build trust and a productive relationship.

- **General planning and approach** – your plan defines, to a great extent, the approach you will be taking to delivering a project. There is always more than one way to do anything. For example, there are multiple ways of defining a work breakdown structure for a project, and then to plan out the sequencing of work following this. This becomes especially useful when resources are scarce, or time to complete is short. When you have completed your plans, really challenge yourself – was there a better way to organise the work? Remember you can change the plan any way you like as long as it meets the needs of the scope.

- **Project organisation and structure** – how will you arrange the team on the project? Again there are normally multiple ways of doing this, which will have different strengths and weaknesses. If you are finding team interaction and team management problematic, try looking at the way you have organised them and come up with some alternatives.

- **Issue resolution** – finding the way around a problem or roadblock for a project is a great use of creativity. It is amazing how often seemingly intractable problems can be resolved with creative insight.

- **Risk reduction** – how often as a project manager have you seen a risk as a *fait accompli*? The risk is a fact and you feel there is nothing you can do other than accept it. Rarely, in fact, is there *nothing* you can do about it; you are probably simply not being creative enough.

- **Contingency planning** – developing good contingency plans and alternative options that do reduce risk and do not excessively increase the cost overhead for a project requires broad thinking and an ability to develop new ideas and options.

- **General challenge and insight** – challenging specialists without being a specialist and without taking everything they say at face value can be helped by looking at the problem they are trying to solve from different angles. The stereotypical specialist is notoriously conservative in his thinking in his own field, and challenge in new and novel ways can often result in better solutions. As the project manager you are not responsible for specialists' work, but it is part of your job to probe and challenge and ensure the solution they are proposing is fit for the purpose. Project managers need to become adept at recognising creativity or a lack of creative thinking in the project team.

In addition to this list I would argue that people management can be improved by creative thinking about the way you engage, motivate and drive the project team. This is not a request for constantly off-the-wall behaviour or bizarrely novel ways of interaction for the sake of it – more a desire to see project managers use their judgement about *when* an alternative approach is required, and to creatively seek it out and apply it.

Creativity has its roots in many places. In practice, the main sources of creativity are:

- **Yourself and the project team** – the most obvious and easily available source of creativity is yourself and other members of the project team. Do not fall into the trap of thinking you are not creative. Everyone has creative potential in the right situation. This may mean simply mulling things over overnight, or cutting yourself off from the project for a day or so – to give some breathing space for creative thinking, as there is nothing like work-overload to destroy creativity. Encourage a project culture where people need to deliver their tasks according to plan, whilst knowing that creative thinking, and innovation are valued. As long as progress is being made to plan, hold regular discussions. Bouncing ideas around should be praised. Encourage unusual suggestions even if you do not implement them. One of the keys to creativity is to develop an environment in which people are excited by the concept of coming up with new ideas.

  A significant factor to consider with yourself and the team is the phenomenon of 'group think'. Put simply, the team starts thinking the same way and enters a creative straightjacket. Oddly, this is a particular risk for close and high-performing teams we otherwise praise. They can convince themselves that there are no solutions other than those they currently see (equally, they can convince themselves that what is actually a major risk is minor). Real creativity sometimes entails a willingness to take a degree of risk. Obviously this needs to be managed and understood, but creative risk appropriate to the outcome is acceptable.

- **Other people** – people outside the project environment can often be a great source of creative insight if you are not finding solutions within the project or project team. You should remain open to other people's ideas. In a project situation getting external advice can help.

Ideally, choose someone you trust, and clearly and concisely structure the problem you have without giving too much contextual information (as this can inadvertently constrain thinking). Then go to this independent third party and see what their view is. Often a fresh pair of eyes really can add creative insight. If you can find someone who will listen, without breaking client confidentiality, then take advantage. I know many project managers who will talk through such issues with their life partners, finding they can give naive responses which are surprisingly helpful.

■ **Formal processes** – there are a number of formal approaches to creative thinking that are useful. These can be as simple as the well-known brainstorming technique, or can be more complex and involved. If you regularly find yourself needing to search for creative solutions then it is well worth seeking out some formal training in these methods for future projects.

Table 4.1 provides a short checklist to summarise this chapter. You can use it to think about your own personality traits, and areas you may wish to try to improve in. It is about identifying not simply those traits you have, but those that you exhibit and use when managing projects.

table 4.1 Review your own personality traits

Personality trait	Do you exhibit this on projects?		If no, what will you do to improve on it?
	Yes	No	
Ownership and involvement			
Judgement, e.g. answering:			
What is in scope?	☐	☐	
What should be in the plan?	☐	☐	
Which elements of the project management process to apply and which to ignore?	☐	☐	
When to escalate?	☐	☐	
When to get into the detail and when to skim?	☐	☐	
When to do and when to delegate?	☐	☐	

Who can you trust in your project team? ☐ ☐

What is an acceptable level of risk? ☐ ☐

What is an acceptable level of parallel activity? ☐ ☐

What is an acceptable level of change? ☐ ☐

When should you enforce the change management process? ☐ ☐

When is it reasonable to progress based on an assumption? ☐ ☐

How many levels of project management organisation do you need? ☐ ☐

When to consider broader stakeholder groups? ☐ ☐

When is the project complete? ☐ ☐

Creativity, e.g. using it for:

Customer challenge ☐ ☐

General planning and approach ☐ ☐

Project organisation and structure ☐ ☐

Issue resolution ☐ ☐

Risk reduction ☐ ☐

Contingency planning ☐ ☐

General challenge and insight ☐ ☐

Getting your project started

This chapter looks at the work required to take a project manager from the situation in which he has a definition of what he is meant to be delivering (the scope), to the position in which he knows how he will do this and has the resources ready to start delivering. Like getting a large boulder to start rolling – planning activity, estimating, resourcing the work and mobilising staff are often the hardest part of a project. Having the idea to get it rolling was not difficult, keeping it rolling is not always so tough, but overcoming initial inertia can be very difficult.

A lot of good planning and resourcing has less to do with the art of being a project manager, and more to do with a real understanding of project management mechanics and tools. I make no claim that this is a particularly exhaustive or complete study of these topics. This section overviews the principles and provides some context for the rest of the book. It includes many tips I find useful to remember. For the person who is not an expert in project mechanics this will add value. The real benefit of this chapter is to give you a framework to help you think and test whether the way you are approaching planning and resourcing is sound. In addition, it looks at the reality of doing this in a live environment and the difference between the theoretical situations in which you may learn project management, and the real-life experience of setting up a project.

In terms of what you have learnt so far, implementing the knowledge in this chapter in practice will depend on the clarity and completeness of the scope you have defined, your continuing ability to communicate, critically your good judgement, and to some extent your creativity. The other point to hold in mind is that every project is unique. Use your plans and resources from prior projects to help your thinking, but adapt them to the specific situation you are now managing.

The way you plan and resource your project will set the framework and constraints within which you will operate through the project. Take the time and make the effort to do it properly.

Planning

The first skill that new project managers learn, and the activity that non-project managers most closely associate with project management, is

planning. Planning is fundamental. Without a plan, thinking or saying that you are on time, late or early, on budget, over or under budget is meaningless. To scale its criticality I know of some very successful project managers who can spend up to 30% of their time scoping and planning a project.

" simply entering data into a project planning tool will never deliver a good plan "

I think it is important from the outset that you differentiate between planning and planning tools such as Microsoft Project. It is like the difference between writing and a word processor. The software is extremely useful and you would be foolish not to make use of its powerful facilities, but simply entering data into a project planning tool will never deliver a good plan. Good planning requires you to use your brain.

Before you start planning you must ask yourself what you are planning for. If you cannot answer this question it is likely that the plan you develop will not be particularly useful. There are typically three possible answers to this question:

1　You are developing a plan because you need to form a view of what tasks there are in a project and thus how long it will take, and from this be able to derive what resources will be required. This is the plan as the project manager's core work.

2　You are developing a plan to explain to senior managers and other stakeholders how a project will be delivered. This may be to get approval and support for your plan, or simply to explain status and issues to people who need to know. This is the plan as an external communications vehicle.

3 Finally, you may develop a plan to enable people involved in the project to be allocated to work and for them to understand how their work fits within the project. Understand that a project plan is as much about ensuring that people are allocated to the right tasks as it is about looking at timings. This is the plan as a work management and internal communications vehicle.

The reality is that at some stage in most projects you need a plan to be able to do all three of these things. These three tasks should be inter-related and the plan that is used in each case should be derived from the same base information. But do not assume it is the same representation of the plan in every case. As a project manager you must be able to alter the level and scope of detail and the style of presentation in each of these situations, and potentially in different variations of these situations. A senior management presentation will typically want to see a high-level milestone chart, an individual working on the project will want to see the activity breakdown relevant to them, and you as the project manager will need various views depending on the task you are undertaking. Every time you present a plan, therefore, you must be clear about:

- The level of detail required in this situation.
- The presentation format. (For example, a work breakdown structure, Gantt chart and network diagram communicate different things to different audiences. Network diagrams are a very powerful project management tool but are of limited value as a senior management communication vehicle. Milestone charts are great for those interested in the outcome of the project rather than the details of how it will be done.)
- The degree of 'specificity'. For example, is it generic about resources and resource type, or is it specific and names a particular individual?

The process of planning is in theory not desperately complex, though in practice it can be both intellectually and physically(!) demanding. Good planning starts with a full understanding of scope. Although you should start thinking about planning while developing the scope, 'planning in anger' cannot start until the scope is clear and understood. The basic process is:

- Build a work breakdown structure – there are many formal definitions of this term. In this context I mean simply to break the overall project into its component tasks, and then iteratively decompose these tasks into lower levels of detail until the plan is detailed enough to manage.

- Identify and build in the dependencies between the tasks.
- Add the lengths of time each task will take – this is where estimating skills come into play.
- Determine the resource types and quantities you need to meet this plan.
- Add in your actual resource availability – in some cases this will lengthen tasks, in some cases it may shorten them. Once you have done this you have a complete first-cut plan. You may need to iterate this step several times, refining the plan as a result of actual resource availability before you produce your baseline plan. This is shown in Figure 5.1.
- Add appropriate levels of contingency.

In implementing this process there is a complex set of more detailed and difficult considerations to layer on top. How much you need to go into these will really depend on the scale, scope and complexity of the project you are managing. In my perspective the most important considerations are listed below. Each one of these is the subject of many millions of words of documented debate and opinion. For some project managers it is essential to build up in-depth capabilities in these. In my general experience, on the average project, understanding the top-level basics and applying common sense to the situation you are in is quite sufficient.

- **Who helps you develop the plan?** In a project of any complexity you will not have the knowledge or skills to develop all the plans. You may not have the specialist skills to understand the work breakdown for some tasks, and you will not be able to estimate the task durations. You will need to call on others' expertise to input into the process. However, whoever is involved it is still your plan, you must integrate the components and you are fully accountable for the end result.
- **Milestones.** A plan is a list of tasks and you can, as project manager, track and report on every single one. More constructively it is helpful to break the project into a series of stages, the completion of each stage being marked by a milestone. These stages may overlap or may be purely sequential. The aim of a milestone is to have points on the plan that enable a *visible*, *measurable* and *communicable* show of progress. For example, in developing a new product, saying to someone that you have determined the colour is typically not useful

Identify tasks and develop work breakdown structure → Define dependencies between tasks → Make initial estimate of task length → Compare to actual resources → Refine estimates and plan → Define resource requirements → Assess risk and contingency required → Produce baseline plan

figure 5.1 Developing a project plan

in providing an idea of how much progress has been made; on the other hand, having a milestone to say all the requirements have been captured is. For milestones to be really worthwhile they should not simply be the measure of the completion of a set of tasks, but they should result in the development of a useful deliverable, usually but not always in a tangible form. Views on milestones have changed over the years; my belief is that good milestones should be relatively frequent on a project. For example, on a very large project lasting more than a year, I try to have a milestone every month or so. Without this it is difficult to keep up the pressure to drive progress on a project. It is human nature to strive to meet targets and milestones, as externally visible targets help the project manager in driving progress.

▓ **How many plans**? One of the mistakes new project managers often make when they start their first very large project is to try to put everything in one master plan. A better way is to have various components of the project broken down into their own plans. A summary of these is shown in the master plan only. Otherwise the master plan ends up having thousands of lines, which may look very impressive when put up on a wall, but in practice almost no-one can actually manage against this type of plan. This is easy with modern planning software which allows the rolling up of individual plans into an overall higher-level project or programme plan.

▓ **The level of detail in your plan**. I discussed this in Chapter 4 in the section on judgement. It is a very common issue for inexperienced project managers. The level of detail should enable you as the project manager to allocate work, and then measure progress against the tasks. This does not mean you need a minute-by-minute, hour-by-hour or even day-by-day plan (though there are exceptions). Typically, breaking tasks down to about a man-week level of decomposition is sufficient. If you have an experienced and trustworthy delivery team then it can be longer than this, although much longer than this and control of individuals can be lost. If you need or decide to go to a lower level of detail, do not be surprised if plan management and maintenance start to become unwieldy. It is also easy with very detailed plans to lose sight of the overall objective and timelines.

▓ **Differences in levels of detail in different stages of the plan**. Having decided what level of detail your plan requires, the next consideration is whether you can or should plan the whole project at the same level of detail. For simple or short projects the answer is almost always 'yes'. For complex programmes lasting many months the answer is often 'no'. You may not yet know enough about later stages to plan them in detail and doing so can be a waste of effort. In this situation you need a high-level plan for guidance for later stages, but really breaking it down into very detailed tasks and times is likely to be fruitless. You should explicitly differentiate between those parts of the plan you can define in detail and those you cannot. Reasons why you cannot plan in detail beyond a certain point include:

– Your customers have not decided what they want in sufficient detail beyond the immediate deliverables. If you do not know what you will be delivering beyond a certain point in the project, there is little reason to plan in detail beyond that point.

– Your business's strategic horizon is shorter than the length of the project. In a modern business this is often true. There is no point planning in detail beyond six months' time, if you don't know what the business strategy and direction will be.

■ **Task size.** Task size needs to be set not simply to reflect the length of time a task takes, but also to give you a management framework. To manage you need small, discrete pieces of work that you can measure progress against on a regular basis (weekly is a good guideline). If you find each of your tasks is several months long, decompose it into smaller activities you can track the completion of.

■ **The types of dependencies.** The way dependencies are built into a plan, and hence activities are scheduled, has a fundamental impact on project length. The first type of dependency everyone knows is where one task cannot start until another has finished. Such 'start-to-finish' dependencies are the most common, are the easiest to manage and communicate, and will result in a clear sequential plan, which often is very long. You can make tasks dependent in many other ways, the most useful of which are:

– Finish-to-finish – one task cannot finish before another one does.

– Start-to-start – one task cannot start until another one does.

– Offset – a task starts or ends a defined number of days after another.

Working through the dependencies in a plan and ensuring they are correct is one of the more intellectually demanding tasks for a project manager. If you are unsure stick with start to finish. Figure 5.2 shows different dependencies in a Gantt chart format.

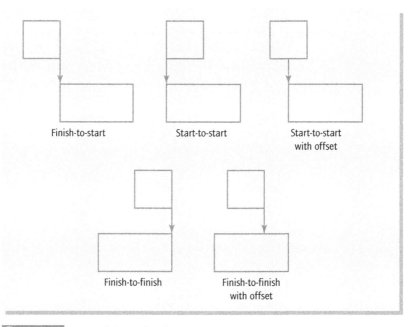

Finish-to-start Start-to-start Start-to-start
with offset

Finish-to-finish Finish-to-finish
with offset

figure 5.2 Types of dependencies

▨ **How much parallel activity will you allow?** Once you pull your
plan together you may end up with it all sequential, which generally
results in unacceptable lengths of time to complete. Alternatively, an
aggressively managed plan can result in it all being parallel. Highly
parallel plans are inherently more risky and require more focused and
able project management. (See judgement 9 in Chapter 4 for a longer
discussion of this issue and the problems of parallel activity.)

▨ **What consideration will you give to risk?** There is a strong linkage
between risk management and planning. Gaps and mistakes in
planning are a source of a significant amount of risk. On the other
hand, you can use your plan to build in actions to counter risk, if you
think about it up front. Before you finish your plan think through –
*what can go wrong and should I include something in this plan to overcome
this? Are there events that if they occur will kill the project, and if so, is it
worth putting in place activities to make the event survivable or not?* You
need to take a balanced approach to risk. If you decide it needs to be
reduced or minimised, this is far easier to achieve by building tasks
and resources in the plan to overcome it.

Whatever way you develop your plan, do it with the expectation that it will need to change. No one can absolutely accurately forecast or foresee all eventualities (and I for one am inherently suspicious of projects that actually run exactly according to a plan). The success of a good project manager is not *never* changing a plan. It is meeting end goals in the face of a changing plan. For this reason it is worth finding the balance: you need to take enough time to make your plan robust and representative of what is required, but do not spend for ever on it – it will never be perfect.

❝ you must always remember that the plan is a tool, not an end in itself ❞

I have presented planning here as fairly manually mechanistic, and there are lots of wonderful tools you can apply to make planning easier and more robust. Not using planning software nowadays is foolhardy at least. Remember, though, that however well they present your thoughts and facilitate planning activities they do not create the plan. You do.

Like most other project management tasks, judgement is critical (see Chapter 4). In addition, you must always remember that the plan is a tool, not an end in itself. This is sometimes forgotten by the more over-zealous lovers of control and beautiful documentation. It needs to serve a purpose; as long as it does this, it is good enough.

> **Key lesson**
>
> Be prepared to change your plan – the measure of success is not an unchanging plan, but meeting the end goals within the reality of continuous change.

Estimating

Often the activity of determining the tasks within a plan is comparatively straightforward. It is never easy, and developing a robust work breakdown structure that has no gaps and is a good way to structure the work is a good achievement. However, the hard work of planning is often in estimating the task length and resources required.

Occasionally, when you look at a plan there are a series of tasks you are very familiar with and you can easily and quickly identify the time it will take to deliver them. However, most projects have some tasks you will not be familiar with, requiring you to answer the question *how long will a task take that I have not done before?* Unfortunately, there is no magic answer. Sophisticated project management techniques enable you to handle variations in risk levels of tasks, but fundamentally understanding how long a task takes is about understanding what is involved.

The classic project management answer is decomposition. Break the task into smaller components and then estimate their duration. This can help, but only so much. If you do not understand a task it is quite possible you do not know how it decomposes. Even if you do, guessing the length of half a dozen short unknown tasks versus one unknown task is inherently no more accurate. So, what can you do? The following list provides some tips.

- **Estimate task length for tasks you understand.**
- **Make sure the requirements are clear.** Good estimates are based on clear requirements. If your requirements are ambiguous or constantly changing, then your estimates will as well.
- **Look for someone with experience to help you.** Someone in the organisation has probably done something similar at some time.
- **Break a task down into smaller known tasks if possible and if this helps.** It does not always work, but often it will help.
- **Look for similar activities to model on.** Some tasks are similar to others and can be estimated against each other.
- **In the worst case – make an assumption.** But build risk contingency into plan. The more guesses, the more uncertainty, and so the more contingency you need in your plan. If you find yourself having to make assumptions, try at least to put some bounds on uncertainty: *'I don't know how long this task is – but I do know it is not less than a week, and not more than two.'*

Finally, take care presenting your estimates back to sponsors and customers. Even if you caveat them they may be taken as committed facts, not assumption-based assessments. If your plan is uncertain make sure you make this clear, and do not present figures to very specific numbers. Saying *'it will take about a year'* implies a broad estimate. Saying *'it will take 237 working days'* sounds like an accurate statement, and will be understood by some of your stakeholders as a commitment no matter how much you caveat it. Either of these statements could be generated from exactly the same plan, with exactly the same level of certainty, but the way they are presented will result in radically different expectations in the listener.

When presenting time, cost or resource estimates, correlate the detail and precision of your estimate with the level of certainty associated with it.

Resourcing

Simple logic determines that having completed your plan you should go on to look at the resources to deliver it. In practice, the activity of resourcing must be integrated tightly with planning and estimating. A good project manager iterates rapidly between planning, estimating and resourcing. If the theory behind good planning can be complex, that underlying resource management can be truly intellectually demanding.

In this book I am not going to go to those extremes. Again this is because I am more focused on the art of project management than on the mechanics, but also because only in the most demanding situations is it really necessary to understand the fine points of resource allocation, resource levelling and other resource scheduling activities.

As with planning, the starting point for resourcing must be to ask why you are resourcing. The obvious answer is to determine what resources you need for your project and how you can get them allocated. It should not be considered as simply an exercise in accumulating talent and skills, but as process to help you achieve your project goals. It will also help to build the bridge between your project and the organisation you are working in, and this should be an important consideration in both the people you ask for, and the way you organise your team.

The problem with resourcing is that it is the point at which your project stops operating in a vacuum. Until you need to start getting resources, as a project manager can happily develop scope documents and plans by yourself with a little input from stakeholders and supporting experts. Now your project clashes with the basic reality of everyday business life. The resources you need could well be allocated to another task, and there are always more tasks than there are resources to do them. Whatever resource planning you do within the confines of your own project, it must fit within the broader resource planning and allocation of the organisation you are working in.

Assuming you can determine resource needs from your plan, resourcing is not then simply a matter of getting the resources for the tasks you require. There are three additional questions you need to be able to answer for yourself at least, as a project manager:

1　Where are you going to get resources from? Do they have to come from the organisation you are delivering for, or can you make use of additional external resources such as contractors and consultants? Does your sponsor have the authority to allocate the resources you need?

2　How are the people allocated to the project going to interact with the organisation in which they work? So, for example, are they going to be allocated to a project 100% of their time, be located in a special project space and managed purely by the project manager for the life of the project, or remain in their line functions, with the project manager managing them in a matrix function in coordination with their line managers?

3　How are you going to organise the project team members within the project?

The basic points to resource allocation are:

- To determine from the plan what skills you require, and how many people with those skills you need for how long. How long in this context does not mean the elapsed time people can be involved in the project for – it means the actual number of hours they are available to work on this project (not on holiday, sick or working on other things).

- To work with resource owners (generally line managers), to get the necessary people allocated to the project.

- To reflect on the degree of risk and contingency required on the project. Is the project fully understood so resources can be cut to the bone, or are there risks and commitments, meaning that there has to be contingency in resourcing levels?

- To aggregate resource usage across the plan to understand your points of overload and underload. Focus on the resources that are continuously overloaded as this is the key risk area. These are used to replan and reschedule. (You can use the facilities of any software planning tool to do this, though take care with the resource levelling function. It may help to think about rescheduling, but if you are constantly overloaded it cannot really help as it cannot create resource. Also you should try to understand what it is doing. The various planning tools use different algorithms and approaches for this and will not all come up with the same answer. You should assume that however good the tool, it will need manual intervention.)

- To avoid falling into the trap of thinking that the solution to every problem is to add more resources. Adding resources does reduce the workload for others on the project and may make tasks possible that otherwise are not, but each additional resource increases management complexity and the project manager's coordination and communications overload. Hence with every project there comes a point at which adding more resources reduces rather than increases efficiency and effectiveness.

■ To reiterate the plan taking account of the actual resources available, which may be different from those you originally requested. You may reiterate between planning and resourcing several times. (In fact, to some extent this is a continuous interplay for the life of the project.) It is the combination of resourcing and planning that provides you with the actual framework in which you will deliver and manage delivery. I often see plans without consideration of resources. These can provide help and guidance but offer no degree of accuracy or certainty.

One thing that people often forget is that resourcing is not only an input to your plan, the tasks of resourcing should be included in the plan. The sorts of things you must consider are the order you need resources in, and the lead time to get them. If, for example, your plan requires six contractors on 1st March, there needs to be an activity some weeks before to start to find contractors, to interview them, to select the ones you want, and to put the necessary contracts in place. For some resources the lead times are relatively quick and they can be available in a few days, but for some specialist resources it may take several weeks. (For permanent team members it may take months to find and recruit the right person.) This lead time will affect your whole project schedule.

Once you have some idea of the people you need, you will have to define how they will be organised for the project. There is no right or wrong answer, but the factors you need to consider are:

■ **Size of project** – the larger the project the more you will need a formal and structured organisation with very clear roles and management levels.

■ **Stage of a project** – the organisation may adapt as the project progresses. A project in a feasibility stage, during implementation, or during post-implementation support may have very different needs.

■ **Complexity of the work** – is everyone doing very similar tasks or is there a large variation?

■ **Type of staffing** – are they dedicated or part time? Are they junior technicians or senior specialists like lawyers? Each need to be managed in different ways.

■ **Relationship to end users** – are you working with end users during the project, or are you separate from them and will hand over once complete?

Like other aspects of planning, resourcing is an estimate. Do not go into infinite detail (like the hour-by-hour resource scheduling I once saw). Reality will always bring in many factors to move your plans and resources around. Your resource plan provides the baseline to manage against.

Allocating resources to tasks must be done in such a way that accountability for delivery of each component of the plan is clear and lies with either a single individual or, on bigger projects, a single team. This is more to do with management of delivery than resourcing, but it impacts the resources and the task breakdown. You do not want to be in the situation of having to resolve the question 'if an individual item needs to be allocated to several people – who is accountable when it is late?' To avoid this problem, ensure you allocate tasks to single points of accountability; if you cannot, decompose the task further until you can.

When planning around the people on your project, do not assume full-time availability. If you are running a big, well-funded project that is accepted widely by the business as being critical then you may have a complete full-time project team. In practice, much of a project manager's time is normally spent coaxing and cajoling work out of part-time resources who have twenty other tasks to do. This is highly inefficient, but it is what happens, and unless you are in an organisation which has projects as its core business, it is unlikely to change. When combining your plan and resources, you must understand not only who is available to you but for what proportion of time. For part-time resources it is then essential to confirm that their assumed availability actually matches their real availability (businesses constantly overload key resources). (See judgement 10 in Chapter 4 for the perils of multi-tasking.)

The final point to make about resourcing is that we generally focus on people. Actually we need a whole load of other resources which need to be managed and allocated in the same way. This can be money (a budget – see below) and specialist equipment required. A typical resource problem on a new project is access to desks, PCs, and even building passes if you are using contractors or consultants. If you cannot provide these resources at the time the contractors or consultants start working, then you will be wasting at least some of your money as they will not be fully effective until they have such things. Build these into your plan!

Budgeting

I could use the word budgeting with regard to any resource, but in this context I mean planning the amount of money you need for your project. Budgeting and tracking of spending are often the weakest part of project management and some organisations ignore it almost altogether. One reason for this is that it is often easier to get away with overspending, as it can be hidden in many ways, but it is hard to get away with being late. To be a fully qualified project manager you must understand how to budget and manage cost and manage trade-offs between cost, time, quality and functionality.

There are many costs that must be budgeted for, but the main components are:

- Items the project must buy as components of deliverables (for example, raw materials used, or computer software that is purchased).
- Items the project must pay for as they are required to do the work in the project (for example, do you need to rent office space, or pay for PCs for the life of the project, etc.?).
- External resource costs – contractors and consultants. (May be on a day rate or at a fixed cost. Do not forget expenses, which for top-end consultants may add 20% to the cost.)
- Internal resource costs – staff from your own organisation. Even if you do not actually cost for them, you should at the very least track time they spend on the project. It is best practice to cost internal time. At the very least there is an opportunity cost for having resources tied up on your project. If internal resources are not charged for, they tend to be treated as if they are free, which creates inefficient allocation and usage.

At the simplest level your budget is a total cost from all of these items. There are, however, a number of other factors to consider. The key ones are:

- The finance system and approach of the organisation you are working in. For example, is there a cross-charge for the use of internal resources, or are these effectively 'free' to the project? Are some activities capitalised and some not, and do you need to be able to track this? What are the reporting and tracking requirements?
- What is the attitude in the organisation to overspend? Is it better to forecast an accurate budget and hence risk overspend, or is it better to forecast a full budget and hence risk having money left over at the end?

- How is budget allocated, and how is spend approved? Do not fall into the trap of assuming that just because you have a budget you can spend it. Authorisation may still be required for actual spend even if you have a fully approved budget.

- How will you track spend against budget, and, for example, do you need to link into the company's finance systems or not? If so, be aware that the finance systems may be structured in a very different way from how you think of your project finances.

- What cost was assumed within the business case for the project? Most organisations require business cases for any significant project, i.e. assessing the cost against the benefit. The business case cost is often a broad estimate, and reality in detailed planning may come up with a different answer. Often the business case cost will act as a maximum budget you must operate within.

- What are you expected to pay for from the project budget? Sometimes you may be required to pay for activities which are not strictly part of the project, for example training staff to be able to

6 6 **often the business case cost will act as a maximum budget you must operate within** 5 5

perform certain project activities. Often it is in your interest to do this to deliver the project successfully. However, it does require you to be clear about this up front. Getting the money at the start of the project is usually easier than half-way through.

I have left this section until after planning and resourcing as it is dependent on them. However, having layered your budget and your financial constraints on top of your resourcing and plan, you will almost certainly need to reiterate your thinking on the resourcing and plan.

Thinking about contingency and risk

Key lesson

Having contingency built into a plan is essential and is not a sign of poor project management. The critical factor is how much contingency, and how you allocate and manage this. This should be related to the degree of risk of your specific project.

To this point I have discussed the various aspects of planning as though we can plan and estimate accurately. This is never perfectly true and before you finalise everything you must consider the degree of risk on your project. The ability to understand and manage risk is an absolutely fundamental project management skill, and it starts now, at the planning stage.

The response to risk at the planning stage is contingency. Contingency is used in two related ways in this book:

- Contingency – as a buffer in your plans to enable you to respond to change and risk occurring. This should exist in every project plan.
- Contingency plans (see Chapter 10) – which are specific alternative activities carried out, usually in parallel, to your base plan. They are implemented only when the degree of risk and business importance of a project is sufficiently high to warrant development of an alternative solution (or partial solution), should the main plan fail to deliver. This is not discussed further in this section.

Having contingency built into a plan is essential. It is absolutely not a sign of poor planning or weak project management. What is important is the degree of contingency you build in, and how you allocate it. I am always inherently suspicious of project managers who always claim to bring projects in on time and budget and never show any risks. If it was so easy we really would not need project managers in the first place!

It is worth starting by thinking about the key reasons for uncertainty in our plans. They are:

- You simply cannot predict everything; risk at one level or another is inherent in everything we do.
- Things change. We can argue that change should be managed through a change control process. True, but the change may be due to something like a poorly understood or misunderstood scope or requirements. From a customer perspective nothing has changed. Alternatively, a team member being ill is not really a change in the change management sense, but it is a change in terms of the validity of your plan.
- Your estimates may be wrong. An estimate is simply that, an estimate. Estimation is a notoriously inexact science.
- Your sponsor or customer may expect you to be able to absorb a minor degree of change without recourse to formal change control and impact on the project.
- There is inherent risk specific to the project you are planning. This comes from four sources – technical risk (can it be done, has it been

done before?), management risk (how complex is this to manage?), requirements risk (is what is wanted really understood?), and environmental risk (something changes outside the project that has an impact upon the project).

The first step in building some contingency into the plan is to consider how you estimate task length. This depends on the type of task you are planning. To be able to estimate with any degree of accuracy, you need to have experience and expertise in the specific task whose length you are estimating. What typically happens is that people overestimate how long tasks take. *In extremis* they plan a task to give themselves virtually 100% certainty of completing it, even though this means that tasks are all longer than they will actually take on average, and the overall plan duration is then also far too long. I think people do this through a combination of wanting an easy life and not wanting to be seen to fail. A better way is to get people to estimate the tasks down to the length they think it will take on average, and not allow them to build in any contingency time. You, as the project manager, then need to build in blocks of contingency time which you can allocate when the inevitable happens and some tasks take longer than planned. The advantage with this is that you will almost always find many tasks are delivered on time, and overall project length is shortened. (The disadvantage is that it may make contingency explicit to other managers, with a poorer understanding of the reality of risk and uncertainty, who ask for it to be removed.) There are a number of cultural issues to resolve in holding contingency centrally. Essentially, you need to build a project culture in which people do not think they are being punished when they overrun and need to dig into the contingency pot, but balancing this they need to treat it seriously and try their utmost to avoid using it.

Put into a simple summary:

- Avoid building contingency into every activity.
- Hold your contingency pot centrally.
- Manage people to hit the plan – but release contingency when required.
- Manage and monitor your contingency pot. If it is disappearing faster than progress on the project, you have a problem looming.

Contingency is not just about time – it should also be considered with regard to the resource budget you have available. Finally, remember it is there to give you a tool to manage risk, not an excuse for poor performance or poor management!

Mobilising

You have a plan, you have a team of people to deliver the plan, and you have an approved budget to spend. There is no great difficulty in mobilising a project team when you are in this position, but mobilisation must take place. It needs to be a specific activity, which it is the core responsibility of the project manager to undertake. Mobilisation can be equated to the situation where a brigade of soldiers is ready for a battle, they have their weapons ready and they understand what they must do, but they still need someone to actually give the order to commence work.

The basic task of mobilisation is a communication task. You can use all the skills defined within Chapter 2. The style and approach you take to mobilising staff can have a significant impact on your relationship with them, and hence how successful you will be in managing them during the project's life. The objectives of mobilisation are:

- To energise and align the project team. If it is a large project team this may take some considerable effort (see Chapter 8).
- To ensure the broader stakeholder community is supportive of the project and ready for it (or you have activities planned to overcome resistance where necessary).
- To ensure project team members understand the objectives of their involvement, the specific work tasks that have been allocated to them, and how they fit within the overall plan.

Once this is done, project delivery can commence.

There is a final point to make clear to everyone during mobilisation. The plan provides the framework the team will work to and be measured against, but the team members are each individually responsible for their tasks. Having a defined plan does not remove the individual need to think. The plan is an aid for them and you, but it is not an abrogation of responsibility.

Projects in the real world – common practical issues to overcome

Key lesson

Project management theory often defines the ideal environment to set up and run a project in. In practice, not all ideal environmental conditions will be achieved, and as a project manager you must learn to deliver in sub-optimal situations, managing a variety of constraints and compromises.

> **❝ you are allocated people, but they don't actually have any time to give to the project ❞**

Like many writers on project management, I have avoided the constraints that occur in practice on projects. However much you plan and develop the right structures to manage, when you are working on a project you will be subject to a host of real-world issues. The list of these is endless, but in this section I will pick a few common issues to be resolved at project start-up and discuss what you can do about them.

Eleven real-world issues that I commonly experience are as follows:

1 Unclear requirements and objectives. It's quite difficult to deliver if the requirements and objectives of the project are unclear. Even if you go through the scoping process described in Chapter 3, if the customer fundamentally does not know the answers then you cannot just make them up.

2 The wrong team. You may be allocated insufficient people, or a team with sub-optimal skills or competencies.

3 You are allocated people, but they don't actually have any time to give to the project. This is surprisingly common. A manager allocates people to too many tasks at once. Alternatively, you are allocated lots of people but only on a part-time basis, which makes your logistics complicated and extends the project timelines.

4 Location and set-up of team. You are allocated a team, but they are physically located all over the place and getting them working together will add significant overhead to the project that you have not planned for.

5 Not being allowed contingency time or budget. The project has risk and you have planned it efficiently, but to cover the risk you have built yourself a pot of contingency time or budget. Your customer sees this and asks you to remove it.

6 There are too many stakeholders or requirements' owners. The effort to collect all their views and to input, assess and collate them and resolve any conflicts will prevent the timescales from being met.

7 Your sponsor does not actually have sufficient positional power to support the project. He wants it and has employed you to do it, but he cannot actually allocate the necessary people or budget to deliver it.

8 The project is more complex than any you have ever managed before and you are concerned that it is beyond your abilities.

9 The budget, timeline or resources are fixed before you plan, but they do not match your needs when planning has been done. This is the classic project management dilemma. The most common examples are having to keep to a budget that was set during an earlier budgeting cycle, or the advent of a 'critical event' – an event that must be met and cannot be moved in time.

10 There is no known solution for the problem the project is trying to resolve.

11 You do not have enough information to plan with any degree of accuracy.

These are all constraints on the project you are trying to run. Hopefully they became clear when you were defining the scope of the project. Sometimes they become clear later on in the project's lifecycle, and may, for example, become exposed through your assumption management process (see Chapter 10). There are many others that can exist but, generally, faced with a constraint of this type, what can you do about it?

- See the constraint as a constructive challenge – quite often you will find that a challenge does generate creative thinking about alternative ways of resolving problems.

- Plan your project without the constraint at first. If you start with the constraints there is a risk you will become more focused on these and not on meeting the requirements of the project. (If the constraint means you do not have all the information, make explicit assumptions and plan using them.)

- Assess the impact of the constraint. Do not immediately panic and get yourself into a negative mindset about it. If this constraint is real, what does it actually mean for your project? Statements like 'it's not possible' are not constructive; they need to be quantified. Specifically, what is not possible?

- Then review your approach to your project – are there things you can alter that would make this possible? What would the impact be upon the scope, quality, cost or time of the project? For example, if it is time that is capped much shorter than your plan shows, can you increase resource and cost to deliver on time, or can you reduce scope or quality to deliver on time? If you have a specific resource bottleneck, such as limited access to desk space or a specific system, can you work shifts instead of trying to use the limited resource in parallel?

- Look at the project lifecycle you are implementing and see if additional stages need to be added. For example, if there is no known solution to the problem the project is trying to resolve, perhaps you need some form of solution selection phase before you start your project. Alternatively, if you do not have enough information to plan with any degree of accuracy, put a formal feasibility stage in the project to provide this information.

- Are there mitigating actions you can take? For example, if your sponsor says you cannot have an explicit contingency pot of money or time, can you call it something else, or build it into the plan in another way? To take another example, if you have lots of people on the project but they are only part-time, can this be mitigated by at least arranging for them to have the same times available each week to work on the project?

- Talk to your customer and explore options. Start by making sure he understood your baseline plan and why it gives the answer it does. Then determine if this is an absolute constraint that cannot be changed, or whether it is something he has decided upon for some other reason. Sometimes managers put such constraints in place simply because it makes their life easier, or because they believe that setting a challenge is a good management approach. Make sure they understand and accept the implications of the constraint.

- In doing this, present them with options, not a *fait accompli*. For example, if your customer wants everything done in less time than you have planned, give them the option of giving you the extra time or an alternative such as extra budget or reduced scope to hit the timelines. Best of all is a range of options.

- Make an explicit decision on how you will manage this constraint – do not just fudge it.

- Having decided which path you are taking, re-plan the project accordingly and communicate the changes. Do not ignore the constraint and assume it will have no impact.

- Realise there is always a choice. Even the most critical of critical events are only worth achieving at a certain cost!

These steps are summarised in Figure 5.3.

A different issue occurs when you inherit a project that has been running for some time, possibly informally without proper project management, or for one reason or another where the original project manager is no longer available for the project. This is very common, and it is a time to

figure 5.3 Dealing with real-world issues

take care. If you do inherit a project, try to take it over on the basis that you can review it, and set your customer's expectation that you may need to change the time, scope or cost of the project. No-one likes hearing this, but if you don't say it you may find yourself in trouble later on. Of course, you may be lucky and have taken over that perfect project, but the chances are that if the project manager has been changed it is for a reason. Before committing to the project, go back and review, confirm and if necessary change the scope. Then review, confirm, and if necessary change the plan. This is more complex than in a project start-up, as you need to account not only for what needs to be done, but for what has been done and whether it has been done to a sufficient level of quality. Most project managers will frequently find themselves having to take projects over in-flight. This is the time to be assertive, and to promise you will do your best to turn it around, but not to commit to anything until you've had a chance to review the scope, plan and status. Once you have done that, reset expectations to what is really going to happen!

Finally, remember that project management is all about balanced judgement and creativity. There are often alternative ways to do things which can meet objectives within defined constraints, so look for them. But you must have room for manoeuvre, and you are not a miracle worker. No matter how senior and powerful or opinionated a boss you are working for, he or she will not make the impossible possible (see Chapter 11).

Table 5.1 provides a planning and mobilisation checklist, based on the contents of this chapter. Use it to review how you go about starting projects and where you may be able to improve.

table 5.1 Project planning checklist

Aspect of planning and mobilisation	Yes	No
Do you understand the different uses of plans and think about them whilst developing your plan?	☐	☐
Do you understand the different formats for plans and use the most appropriate one to present in any situation?	☐	☐
Use a logical process for planning? (See Figure 5.1)	☐	☐
Develop your plan to the most appropriate level of detail, both for the plan as a whole and for different stages of the plan?	☐	☐
If your project or programme is complex, do you split your plan into manageable sub-plans?	☐	☐
Do you involve the right people in plan development, to get a range of expertise, ideas and constructive challenge?	☐	☐
Do you show an appropriate set of milestones in your plan?	☐	☐
Is it clear who is responsible for the delivery of each and every task in the plan?	☐	☐
Do you identify all the dependencies, using the right sort of dependency according to the nature of the relationship between tasks?	☐	☐
Do you think through the best level of parallel planning, considering issues such as project timing, span of management control, levels of multi-tasking and benefits delivery?	☐	☐
Do you develop the best estimates you can, and link your level of estimation certainty to risk management and contingency?	☐	☐
Do you consider risk in developing your plan by applying the right risk avoidance or mitigation in your plan, and by including an appropriate level of contingency related to the uncertainty in your plan?	☐	☐
Are you clear about the assumptions you make in planning and do you link these to risks?	☐	☐
Do you review your plan to take account of actual as opposed to theoretical resourcing (including actual availability)?	☐	☐
Do you gain commitment to resources before assuming you have access to them?	☐	☐
Do you include lead times or ramp-up times for resources in your plan?	☐	☐
Do you load resources sensibly – neither overloading nor underloading individuals?	☐	☐
Do you put in place an appropriate project organisational structure, considering the characteristics of the project?	☐	☐
Do you ensure you have sufficient budget, considering all aspects of the plan and your organisation's approach to budgeting?	☐	☐
Do you put mechanisms in place to track budget and resource usage (including internal resources)?	☐	☐
Do you include appropriate mobilisation activities in your plan?	☐	☐
Do you consider the real challenges you are likely to face in practice and build your plan around them?	☐	☐

6

Personal styles

Key lesson

There is no right interpersonal style for a project manager; successful project managers have a variety of styles. But there are certain approaches to avoid, and some key attributes of style to develop.

This chapter looks at personal styles: firstly, those which I advise any project manager to avoid, and secondly those attributes of personal styles to be encouraged in project managers. If you do find you are drawn towards the first set of traits, it can limit your success and so you need to learn to moderate them. You may not naturally have all of the second set, but they can be learnt to some extent, or you can bring people into your team who have these skills.

Styles to avoid

Key lesson

Certain interpersonal styles will limit your success as a project manager.

There are many styles of project management, and there is no one type of interpersonal skill and style that ensures success. I have seen many thoughtful and introspective project managers, some who are extroverts and compulsive and continuous communicators, some who deliver by understanding the technology and using logical analysis to drive people to the right conclusion, and others who build a team and a consensus towards delivery without getting into the details. There are endless approaches and options. There is no single right personality style to be a good project manager, but what I do believe passionately is that there are some methods of interaction to avoid. Core among these are four styles you may recognise. These are stereotypes – but stereotypes based in reality, and you may be familiar with them already.

Stereotype 1 – Bully boys

You will probably be familiar with this type of person. The bully boy is known by everyone (I should say *bully person*, but it does not sound right and in my experience it is a more common trait in men than women). These are the people who manage by fear and when things go wrong start shouting. The general approach is to make sure that everyone knows they are the boss. They talk a lot about respect, which they confuse with power. They misunderstand leadership and instead like to 'put people in their place'. They thrive on people giving in to them, and they tend to be obsessed with titles and position in organisational hierarchies. This person is the grown-up version of the playground bully. In bullying they lack an understanding that delivery does not require bullying and is often impaired by it.

Use this style sparingly and at your peril! It is not so much that bullying never gets results. I would be lying if I said it never worked or that it is not occasionally useful to be able to direct staff robustly. Sometimes this is essential. It is recognising the difference between the occasional demanding request, and the grinding bullying of people into submission and delivery. In reality, apart from being an obnoxious style, bullying is a very poor way to deliver anything reliably and consistently. It has several core weaknesses:

- It does not develop trust (which is a two-way thing). If people think you do not trust them, they in turn will not trust you. Successful project teams which do not have trusting team members are hard to find. Generally, the most productive team is the one that works harmoniously and not the one that works in an atmosphere of fear.
- It creates problems from the very outset of the project. If people think they will be put under unreasonable pressure in an unpleasant manner when they are late, they will tend to overestimate the lengths of tasks to ensure they can be completed within the schedule.

■ People who fear you will avoid or delay telling you the truth, especially if it is bad news. People will seek to cover up or put things in a defensive way. Really good project management requires the project manager to know the risks early, and to know when things are going wrong immediately. I have seen situations, on several occasions, in which the project manager was the last to know that the project was going wrong because people were too frightened to tell him. I even remember one specific programme with a budget of several hundred million pounds, which almost everyone on the team knew was a disaster except for the programme manager. Needless to say it was a failure, and he was fired.

■ Sometimes team members you have to manage or get deliverables from or tasks done by are actually more senior than the project manager. Acting the bully boy in these situations usually will not work.

■ Team members working for a bully may work hard from fear, but are unlikely to be enthusiastic or passionate. Passionate, enthusiastic people will produce more, and what they produce is more creative. People who are bullied rarely deliver high-quality results. They produce just enough to stop the bullying and will often go behind your back whenever they can to undermine you.

■ Finally, people, and often the best people, will avoid you, and try hard not to be on your projects in future. Consistent delivery depends on other people too. The project manager is a participant, not the whole team.

If you are of this type, next time you feel yourself going red and being tempted to bang the table and shout at everyone, take a deep breath and calm down. Try to manage in a more humane way. The toughest, most demanding, effective and efficient managers rarely let themselves get to this state. Really ruthless people never do.

> **❝ passionate, enthusiastic people will produce more, and what they produce is more creative ❞**

Well-respected people get things done well because people want to deliver for them rather than because they are frightened of them.

Stereotype 2 – Process nuts, compulsive planners and detail obsessives

Another style of poor project management that is not uncommon is the person who is more obsessed about some detail or other of the project than its overall progress.

It is important to note that I am not criticising people who like detail more than high-level views. There is nothing wrong with being interested in the details, and being focused on too high a level can be dangerously risky. However, the project manager is there to manage the overall project and, except on the smallest project, usually does not have time to be aware of every detail of everything.

There are three typical forms this takes. Firstly, there are those who obsess about the process of project management more than the project itself. They focus on making sure they have carried out every possible project management activity and ticked every box on all their tick lists. Satisfaction comes only when they know they have done all the process tasks, and when the project goes wrong they tend to see this as inevitable rather than as a result of too much management process and too little managing. The correct use of process is to apply balanced decision making. Too little process can result in chaos, too much can be sterile. Good process is powerful, but it can never cope with every situation, and the skill is to use it rigorously when appropriate, but to be able rapidly to assess when it is necessary to go outside the process boundaries. The bureaucratic process obsessive will often think *'I will not do that, it is not part of my job'*. Some things are not the project manager's job, but if progress is to be achieved you are the person who needs to sort it out, and process constraints must not stop this.

Secondly, there are those who continuously focus on the plan, updating it at every opportunity in a vain attempt to keep it perfectly correct. On a daily basis there is a vast collection of status data, tasks are realigned and the critical path reassessed. I have known project managers spending literally hours every day keeping the plan up to date. The point they miss is that the plan is merely a tool; it is not a result in itself. Planning is essential, the plans are powerful – but they are a means and not an end in themselves.

Finally, and somewhat differently, there are those who become obsessed by the very low-level details of the content of the project. Often these people have a technology focus. They try to understand and have an opinion on every aspect of the project, and may even become stressed when they do not understand all the details. At best this type of project manager gets overloaded; at worst the project fails because the broader picture is being ignored.

There are two basic reasons for people focusing on these types of details. Firstly, they may be more interested in them than in the delivery of the project. If this is true and you do actually want to work on projects, you may be better off working in a project office than as a project manager. Project offices offer more scope for very detailed management of plans and focus on project management processes. The second reason is that they have not built up the skills and knowledge to do otherwise. Inexperience tends to result in poor judgement on what is important as a manager. When people do not know what to do they typically cling to a lifebuoy, and in this case the lifebuoy is feeling good because you are busy with the details. If this is true and you are unsure what else is important for you then seek out some help from a more experienced project manager.

Success for a project manager is measured only in terms of delivery of a project. Once it is complete the beauty of your plans, the completeness of your paperwork, and the depth of your understanding of every aspect of the work are irrelevant. Think in terms of other professions. A decorator wants good paintbrushes and will clean them well after work, but knows that all that matters to his customers is the quality of his painting. An accountant will worry about his compliance with agreed accounting approaches and processes, but what counts at the end of the day is the accuracy and completeness of the accounts he puts together. An engineer will try to use the agreed algorithms and theories in designing a new machine, but again, in the end all that matters is that the machine works to the performance parameters it was designed for. So it should be with a project manager. Use the tools and understand the details, but only so far as is necessary to achieve the desired results.

Stereotype 3 – The Teflon man

There are some people who can seem to get away with everything; when things go wrong they come up smelling of roses – it was always somebody else's idea. These 'Teflon men' (and women) never let anything stick to them. You will have come across them in any large organisation. They carry the scent of politics, but never show it directly. Somehow they are never incorrect, never in the wrong place at the wrong time, and always have a valid reason for error or failure.

This style of being able to dodge all bullets and claims to fault can be successful in the short term. The problem is that the profession of project management is essentially about taking responsibility. In every situation sometimes something will go wrong, and if you are taking responsibility you must shoulder some of the blame. If things never stick it means you are not fully taking responsibility. You are ducking the necessary sense of ownership.

The problem with this style is much more subtle than the problems with the previous two styles as some people have built apparently successful careers around it, and have even reached senior levels in management hierarchies. The main issue is as much to do with the project team as anything else. People resent others who work like this and can wriggle out of every situation, and therefore the project team is less likely to be aligned with the goals of the project manager who is like this. If nothing sticks, it may well be sticking to someone else who will have honest grounds for resenting you strongly. When your boss takes some painful flak to support you it generates goodwill and trust; when it constantly slides off your boss onto those around him or her it generates bad feeling. The same is true for project managers. I think we all know the answer to the question: would you rather have a team working for you which resents you or one which respects and admires you?

You may not fail with this style, you may feel you actually do quite well with it – but you will not excel, nor will you do as well as you can. Do not think *'oh well, it works for me'*; think *'how much further would I have got if I did not work like this?'* You may be getting away with it, but do not think it is invisible to your managers or your team.

Stereotype 4 – The panicking manager

Some people stay calm in all situations; they remain as cool as a cucumber whatever life throws at them. Many of us aspire to be like this, but these people are few and far between and can occasionally seem inhuman. Occasional doubt and feelings of lack of control are normal; however, do not confuse this with the tendency to panic. There are some managers whose first reaction when the pressure steps up or something goes wrong is to panic.

In the old BBC TV series *Dad's Army*, there was a character, Corporal Jones, who whenever something was starting to go wrong, which was often in this comedy, would start to rush around and shout 'don't panic, don't panic'. And, of course, he was rushing around aimlessly and panicking. This is precisely the problem with panicking. Someone panicking tends to spend more time managing their panic and trying to get their brain to work again than actually doing constructive work.

When you do feel the pressure, avoid panic. It is never constructive. If you do find the tendrils of fear grabbing you and pulling you towards panic, resist. It is quite normal to be concerned, even to feel a little stress, but once panic sets in you cease to be productive. Worse still, panic tends to be contagious – once one person panics it can spread rapidly. The worst person to panic on a project is the project manager. This sends a clear message to the team, and they will be thinking 'if he is panicking it must be really bad'. Over time, if you panic regularly people will lose trust and faith in you.

When things are tough it is the time for good leadership, and good leaders may be afraid and may even have doubts, but they do not display this to their teams.

Styles to encourage

Key lesson

Choose the personal style that best develops your personal brand. Build the attributes of good style to help you succeed.

This section defines the building blocks of personal style that project managers should consider.

There is simply no one best style for project managers. Different styles suit different people, different organisations, different industries, different project teams and different types of project. At heart I would always advise a project manager to try to be true to yourself, and to avoid going with a style that is completely unnatural to you. Adopting a completely unnatural style is often transparent and as a consquence can lead to problems. However, this is not to say that the project manager should not, over time, learn to have different styles for different occasions, or should not try to learn new styles. The style you adopt, display to people and use is to a large extent a personal choice: be conscious it is a choice and has an impact on performance.

Elsewhere in this book I talk about how you have a personal brand as a project manager. We all are attracted to branded products. A brand is something that gives people a feeling of confidence. We select things with brands because the brand is a promise of a certain minimum level of quality and to a specific experience. A brand is initially about presentation, but as any good marketing manager will tell you, unless the reality matches the hype a brand will not survive. If you are influenced to buy a certain type of car because of its brand, and it does not live up to your expectations, then the brand will be devalued in your eyes. A brand can be both powerful and fragile: every time you buy a brand of food or drink the experience can encourage you to buy anything with that brand again, or it can make you avoid it for ever. This principle can also be applied to people. We build up a brand over time, usually accidentally, but by choosing the optimal style to adopt you can manage and improve on your personal brand. If you want to be a successful project manager who is asked to run the most interesting projects, you must think what your personal reputation and brand is – and how you build and maintain it. Although a large proportion of people's judgement of us is related to our success in delivering projects, much of this is also due to the personal style we assume. I am sure you know people who are excellent at their jobs but do not excel in their careers because of their personal style.

> ❛❛ you must think what your personal reputation and brand is – and how you build and maintain it ❜❜

When thinking about your personal brand, you must therefore think through which attributes of personal style have the largest impact on people's perception of you. There are eleven factors I find are usually most important. They are really a combination of personality traits and competencies:

1 Empathy with your customer
2 Management and leadership skills
3 Ability to handle stress
4 Respect for people
5 Dynamism and positivism
6 Networking skills
7 Political sensitivity
8 Having sufficient presence
9 A sense of humour
10 Being sensitive to your environment
11 Adapting your style to the situation.

The following section is therefore less about whole styles and more about attributes of style. If you do not have these attributes try to develop them, or think about how you can bring others into the project team who have them.

Attribute 1 – Having empathy with your customer

A project manager is not the customer and needs, at times, to be able to distance himself from the customer. Constant affinity with the customer may start you thinking exactly like the customer and through this limit creativity and breadth of vision. And yet at the same time as a project manager you need to be able to think things through from the customer's viewpoint when it is relevant. For decades now the fundamental mantra of business has been 'the customer is king' and this is also true from a project perspective. Treating the customer as king requires an ability to see things from her viewpoint, and communicate in a way that is helpful to her. This is what I mean by empathy with the customer.

The times when it is really important to be able to adopt the customer's viewpoint are:

- When you are collecting the initial requirements and developing an understanding of what the customer wants.
- When decisions or changes need to be made to a project – if you were the customer is this trivial or is it a core issue that needs serious debate and consideration?
- When communications are being made or planned – what does the customer understand, what is important to them, and how do they like it being communicated?

Every time you are in one of these situations try to put yourself in your customer's position. Ask yourself:

- Why are they acting this way?
- What do they need?
- What help can I be to them?
- How is it best to approach them and provide this help?
- What are their sensitivities and how can I avoid these or approach them carefully?
- If I cannot help them, is there anything else I can advise them to do?

People who work to understand their customers best and respond in the most productive way are the most appreciated. This is not saying you should do whatever your customer wants. If you think it is wrong you need to say so; if you cannot do it you must tell them. But this should be done in the most constructive manner.

Attribute 2 – Displaying both management and leadership skills

There are huge amounts of paper dedicated to defining and explaining good management and good leadership. I will not try to encapsulate it in the few words here, but I will point out that while there is some relationship they are different activities. Project management by its very definition is a management task and it goes without saying that project managers need good management skills. Project managers, at times, also need to be leaders.

Without writing down all the things in a project management approach, the management task of a project manager relates to assessing the work that needs to be done, assessing the people available to do the work, and then providing the project team with clear roles and defined goals. The sum of the goals delivered by the specified roles will deliver the end project. The ongoing management task is then to monitor progress and remove issues as they arise. Although the approach is specific to project management, the basic task is the same as any manager has to do: prioritise and chop up the work that needs to be done, allocate it to the team you are managing, help them develop their skills and learn from the work they are doing, and manage them to complete their tasks.

Although much is spoken and written about leadership, and we all intuitively have a view about it, leadership is a more nebulous concept. At one extreme, leadership is about providing the motivating speeches and a good example to the team; these are important but are not the core task on a day-to-day basis. To me, leadership is about the framework which is developed for people to operate within – how do you present and communicate the objectives of the project? What is the culture of the project team? How much space do you give people to do their tasks in? How do you get and maintain approval and support from the project team? What examples do you praise and what behaviour do you clamp down on? What behaviour do you exhibit on a day-to-day basis to act as the role model for others? The need for leadership on projects, especially those which require large teams of people, is evident. The management role is solely the project manager's, whereas the leadership responsibility belongs to a wider group of people including the project sponsor. However, leadership is needed on a project and the project manager cannot assume this will be provided by the sponsor or anyone else. The project manager's leadership role is to assess what leadership is required, determine what is being provided and fill the gap with what is needed. There is no one leadership role for a project manager to take – it will vary from situation to situation, depending on both the leadership required by the project team and the leadership that is being delivered from other sources. A hands-on and inspirational project sponsor may provide all the necessary leadership, but a backroom decision maker who is invisible to the project team may provide none. A key task for the project manager is therefore to make an assessment of the leadership requirement and work out what she can do to fulfil this.

A core skill for project managers is to drive things to happen when you do not always have legitimate line authority over all the people on the project. We can all talk and dream about fully dedicated teams, but a lot of project management is about getting slices of people's time, time that is a scarce resource for them. So why should they give it to you? Well, this may be partly because you are perceived to have authority to do so, but it must also be that your management skills combined with the leadership you project encourages them to do so.

Project managers who understand and can implement their management role, and can determine the type of leadership required in each situation, will thrive. Being successful will require you not just to manage well, and when required to lead well, but also to be seen to be a good manager and leader.

Some important leadership and management skills for project managers to consider are listed in Table 6.1. This could be an endless list, and there is always debate as to exactly what leadership skills are. So, this is intended to give a flavour rather than be completely exhaustive.

Attribute 3 – The ability to handle stress

Projects can be tough environments to work in. The work can be intense, the work can be difficult, and the available time, budget and other resources can be limited. Project managers need to be personally committed to the end point or goal. The end result of this is that project managers are liable to great stress.

An example of a typical stress driver for a project manager is the rate of change. You need the ability to handle the fact that everything will change – timescales, requirements, resources, budgets. They flex, and yet you are expected to have the ability to manage through and deliver to expectations! Depending on your personality type, this can be stressful. Plan proactively, but be willing to react when you need to. People instinctively do not like change and a frequent response to such constant change is a feeling of stress.

table 6.1 Management and leadership skills for project managers

Management skills	Leadership skills
▦ Define team/individual roles and responsibility, and put an appropriate project organisational structure in place	▦ Set the vision for the project and the project strategy. Create a shared vision with the team. Position the project in a wider context
▦ Mobilise the project team	▦ Define and role-model the style of behaviour wanted from the project team (e.g. levels of energy, styles of interaction, etc.)
▦ Induct team members into the team	
▦ Assess skills needs for tasks	▦ Motivate the project team
▦ Assign appropriate tasks to team members, and set individual goals. Provide necessary levels of individual support (based on tasks allocated versus individual competencies and motivation)	▦ Adapt behaviour for the situation
	▦ Create an environment which brings the best out in project team members and in which they can safely and productively deliver
▦ Set priorities	▦ Influence the wider stakeholder community to facilitate delivery of the project
▦ Provide learning opportunities for team members	▦ Stretch and encourage team members to develop, without putting them in situations of excessive risk of failure. Provide space for team members to learn
▦ Define the management process for a project team (e.g. controls, delegated levels of authority, reporting and information collection, escalation, decision making, meetings, etc.)	
	▦ Listen, counsel and mentor project team members
▦ Motivate the project team	▦ Adapt the style to the situation – from the directive autocrat to the consensus-driven facilitator
▦ Resolve team and project conflict and issues	
▦ Provide performance feedback and guidance	
▦ Appropriately appraise, manage the performance of, and reward project managers and other project staff.	
▦ Ensure quality of deliverables	
▦ Provide project management expertise and put appropriate project controls and management processes in place.	

There are many mechanisms to handle stress, including being naturally laid back, doing a hard workout, having a drink or talking things through with people. Whichever it is, if you are liable to stress you need to find a mechanism to handle it or else a career as a project manager may end up being more trouble than it is worth to you. I have counselled several people liable to stress to reconsider their choice of being a project manager.

❝ I have counselled several people liable to stress to reconsider their choice of being a project manager ❞ The other point about stress is not only to manage it in yourself, but also to avoid displaying it overtly to your team. People are less likely to trust some-one who is regularly showing stress, and when things are hard people will often look to the proj-ect manager. They will sometimes be looking for help, but on other occasions they may be looking simply for confidence. A stressed-out manager does not exude confidence.

Finally, do not get stressed because things are going wrong from time to time. It is worth remembering that normally the world will not end if your project is late or over-budget. This is not to shrug off your sense of commitment to the end point, but to put it in context. Also, remember that if it all went smoothly there would be no need for a project man-ager. Recovering from difficult situations is the sign of great project management and something people value highly. It is true that if all goes perfectly well you may end up being invisible – and it is right to con-clude that that is a sign of success, not failure, but in reality people best remember those who have recovered projects from difficult situations.

Attribute 4 – Respect for people

Project management is largely about managing people. It is a job that is all about interacting with people on a daily basis. You need to respect the people working on the team for two reasons. The first is simply that people are more likely to respect you if you respect them; the second is that people work better when they feel they are respected and valued. You are dependent on your project team doing a good job and anything you can do to improve on this will increase your chance of success.

If you do not respect your project team because you legitimately think they are not up to the job, try to change the team. You may shake your head when this is suggested as it will be very hard, but unless you do, you will jeopardise the project and it is your job to enable its delivery. If you cannot change the team, try at least to hide your contempt.

Having respect for people does not mean being weak or wet. When you respect someone you tell them the good news as well as the bad; you give them constructive criticism as well as the praise they deserve; you ask them to do the tasks that need doing, not just the things they want to do.

Attribute 5 – Dynamism and positivism

There are two attributes that every manager seeks from every member of their team – a positive attitude to their work, and a dynamic style of performing work. This can be flipped on its head – good project managers should lead by example, display a positive outlook and attack work in a dynamic style.

The ability to come across as energetic will inspire energy in other people. Non-dynamic teams are less fun and people are less motivated. A dynamic project manager will help. Well-managed and funnelled energy will deliver a result many times that of an unenergetic project team.

A positive project manager develops a feeling of confidence in the team, and confidence helps people overcome everyday obstacles with ease. This is not a cry to underestimate or ignore problems, but to face them with the attitude that they can be overcome. I do not know how the human mind works, but when it comes to solving problems, people who face them in a positive frame of mind regularly solve the problem more quickly and more constructively.

I have often been in the situation of having to choose between well-qualified, cynical experts and a dynamic person with bags of energy. You need a good balance on your project team, and there are times when I have to choose the expert, but these are, in practice, in the minority, and when I can I will always choose energy and enthusiasm over experience.

Attribute 6 – Networking skills

Project managers need to get people onto their project teams, to be able to get help and other input during the project's life, and to engender an environment that is supportive to the outcome of the project. A great help in these situations comes from your personal networking skills.

One way to look at a network is to see it as a framework of personal relationships that you can call on when you need help or advice. You should build a network and use it for finding people and resources that you need, and for informal communications which underpin our daily lives (both to transmit and to receive information). Such a network is about having ongoing dialogues around the business so you know what is going on, you know who can help you, and you understand which people are good to have on projects. It is about having subtle negotiation skills that convince people to free resources to you, encourage team members to come onto the project, and induce people to support your work. A good network provides information and promotes action.

Some people are natural networkers. We can all think of someone we know who knows everyone in the office, hears all the gossip and news first, and can always lay their hands on whatever they need. But networking skills are possible not only to the gregariously extrovert. A personal network can be built deliberately by identifying those people whom it is useful to know and by engineering situations in which to talk to them. It is quite acceptable to be completely open about what you are doing. Most senior managers understand the need for personal networks and will respond well if you simply ask for a short slot in their diary (try 30 minutes, or even less), simply to introduce yourself. Having done this it is much, much easier to ask them for advice or support at a later date.

Ironically, one of the best groups I find for this is smokers. There are very few reasons to be jealous of smokers, but one is their informal networks. In modern environments smokers have to go outside to smoke and the people who go there often share information well. I would not suggest you take up smoking to get your project delivered, but do learn the example of regular informal communications and a personal network.

Attribute 7 – Political sensitivity

Project managers should avoid playing politics, but you do need to be aware of them. Projects often fall foul to political games going on in many organisations. You should try to avoid getting involved in them, but you do also need to develop the ability to feel when strings are being pulled behind the scenes and when you need to approach your sponsor for help.

Usually people play these games because they have some vested interest which is endangered or negatively impacted by the outcome of a project. Some good stakeholder assessment will often provide a good basis for understanding the political landscape (see Chapter 10).

Not everyone likes being in a political environment. If you really cannot stand the pressures of personal manoeuvring and vested interests then there are certain projects you should avoid. Projects related to topics such as business change, organisational transformation and post-merger integration work tend to be highly politicised. If you do not like politics, avoid these types of projects. Also, in some organisations there is a very political culture (for example, I find government bodies and academic institutions places where political games are played regularly), and projects in these are more likely to have a political undercurrent than in other organisations.

However hard you try, unless you stay on small or very focused projects it is unlikely that you can avoid politics altogether. Be sensitive to such issues, and seek help if they are interfering with your project.

Attribute 8 – Having sufficient presence

Not all project managers have natural presence, and it is not a critical problem. It can, for example, be balanced with the strengths of your key sponsor. I know some introverted and very successful project managers.

However, there will be times when you need to be able to hold an audience and generate respect. This is especially true for large programmes and for situations when things are not going well – then a project team will look to the project manager for guidance and confidence. There will also be opportunities to interact with senior managers and executives who respond well to presence. It is worth trying to develop; seek out feedback on whether or not you do have presence and what you need to do to encourage it.

Attribute 9 – A sense of humour

The ability to generate and enjoy humour is an extremely positive trait with a project manager. People enjoy working with someone who can raise a laugh. Project management can be stressful and the ability to laugh about it will help you manage your stress.

If you are not a natural wit do not worry. A good substitute is simply to smile a lot. People like people who smile. It sounds trite, but do not underestimate the value it generates. A well-placed smile can completely change the dynamics of a conversation and can lift an individual from a negative to a positive frame of mind.

Attribute 10 – Being sensitive to your environment

As stated many times in this section, project management is primarily about people management, and people and groups of people vary tremendously in how they behave and how they expect others to behave. A style of interaction that is perfect in one environment is completely unsuitable in another. As a project manager you must learn to be sensitive to your environment.

There are many triggers to different environments and different behaviours. There are four factors I always try to consider:

1 The country I am working in
2 The type of organisation the project is for

3 The type of function the project is working with

4 Anything specific to the organisation I am operating in.

At the highest level on this list is the culture of the country you are operating in. An example of cultural differences is the casual use of first-name terms versus surnames and even titles – in some countries first names feel obligatory, in others anything less than Mr Newton is just rude. Next is the culture of the organisation you are working in. In most media companies, if you are dealing with creative departments, wearing a suit will place you at odds with most people, but wearing jeans and T-shirt in a legal firm is also likely to be poorly regarded. Thirdly, I consider the function I am working in. Engineering departments have a very different ethos and language from marketing departments. Engineers tend to be focused and pedantic about detail; marketers are often very hard to pin down to specific requirements and will often talk in terms of ideas and concepts. Finance and legal departments often work alongside each other and are seen as 'corporate' functions policing people as much as helping, but their styles and approaches to work vary tremendously. Finance departments often start work early in the morning; I find legal departments usually do not, but they think nothing of still being in the office at 10 pm. Finally, there is the organisation itself. Some companies strive to develop a specific culture or attitude, whether this is open and honest, or driven and focused. Some companies have a caring culture where you help people succeed; others have a ruthless focus on delivery and any hesitation is seen as failure.

If you are not sensitive to the culture of the organisation you are working in, you will find that, over time, you do not develop support, people will try to avoid working with you, and confidence and trust in your abilities will not develop easily.

Once you have got used to a specific organisational culture you will find yourself naturally following its patterns of behaviour. This is good, but when the project is over do not take those behaviours to another organisation unless they are directly appropriate.

Attribute 11 – Adapting your style to the situation

The final thing to say about personal style is that not only is there no single correct style for all project managers, but any one style is not right for all situations. To take an extreme example, laughing and telling jokes is expected at a wedding but is out of place at a funeral. Most of us will automatically adapt our style when we move into a different situation, and we would not even need to think about the appropriate behaviour to adopt in my example of a wedding and a funeral. Projects are no different; on a day-to-day basis they will put us into many different situations, and just because a certain way of interacting works for you some or even most of the time, do not maintain it in every situation. Adapt your style as appropriate.

In many situations it is inappropriate to blow your own trumpet. Boasting and continually stressing what wonderful things you have achieved is normally frowned upon. Yet sometimes – for example when you are being interviewed for a job, or if you are trying to develop trust in your ability to lead a large programme – it may be essential. There are endless examples of situations in which it is appropriate to tailor the way you interact.

❝ any one style is not right for all situations ❞

However, do not automatically adjust your style without thinking about it, but *consciously* manage the style you adopt as this will avoid you inadvertently taking on a poor style. For example, if you feel yourself becoming defensive it is not always good to actually adopt a defensive style of interaction. Think about what will be most productive in any one situation. Failure to adapt your style can leave you looking wooden and unimaginative, and people will start to develop false assumptions about what you are feeling and thinking.

Table 6.2 summarises the styles from this chapter into three categories – individual styles, styles relating to interacting with others, and styles relating to the wider work environment.

table 6.2   Personal styles for project managers

Individual styles	Styles relating to interaction with others	Styles relating to the environment
Styles to avoid		
▦ Process nuts, compulsive planners and detail obsessives	▦ Bully boys	
	▦ The Teflon man	
▦ The panicking manager		
Styles to encourage		
▦ Ability to handle stress	▦ Empathy with your customer	▦ Being sensitive to your environment
▦ Dynamism and positivism	▦ Management and leadership skills	▦ Adapting your style to the situation
	▦ Respect for people	
	▦ Networking skills	
	▦ Political sensitivity	
	▦ Having sufficient presence	
	▦ A sense of humour	

Managing your project

To manage projects a project manager must understand what she should be managing, have a mechanism to provide information to understand when management action is required, and finally implement action when the information tells her it is necessary.

This chapter looks at the core daily work required of a project manager on a live project, actually managing the project. It may be surprising to some readers therefore that this is one of the shorter chapters in the book.

To be an effective project manager it is important to have a good grasp of project management processes, methodologies and tools. These mechanics are not the primary focus of this book and therefore this is not an extensive study of these topics. What this section will do is overview the principles and provide some context for the rest of the book. For the person who is not an expert in mechanics this will add some value. The benefit of this chapter is to give you a framework to help you test whether the way you are approaching managing projects is sound. More fundamentally this section is short because if you have set up your project correctly as described in Chapters 3 and 5, if you use the communications tools described in Chapter 2, and if you have the attributes of personality described in Chapters 4 and 6 – the truth is that day-to-day management of projects is not the hugely difficult and demanding task that it is often presented as. (This is reflected by the fact that it has taken me until Chapter 7 to even start discussing this topic.) On the other hand, if you have not worked hard to scope your project well or put the correct plan and resources in place and if you do not attempt to use good communications skills, then managing your project may soon become a complete nightmare.

To be able to control a project you need to be able to keep in mind what you should and can manage, understand what is going to trigger you to take management action and, following on from this, actually how you manage.

> ### Key lesson
>
> The degree of difficulty in managing a project is closely related to how well you have set the foundations (in terms of expectations, scope, plan and resources) in place.

What should you manage?

When you start out on your career as a project manager it is often easy to get bewildered by the number of things you have to do on a day-to-day basis. The plan is complicated. There are lots of people doing activities more or less under control, and more or less relevant to your project. There are various external stakeholders trying to influence the project. And finally there are huge numbers of things that are completely outside your control that you feel you must worry about. So what should you be managing?

" there are only five things that you are really responsible for managing "

In your role as a project manager there are only five things that you are really responsible for managing. These are difficult enough at times, but keep focused on these and your life will be much easier. Anything else you are involving yourself in should be because it has an impact on these five. They are:

1 **The time the project is taking to deliver** – this is typically measured as progress against your plan.

2 **The resources you are using to deliver** – again this is typically measured as resource expenditure (man/hours, money, etc.) against your original plans. This is generally harder than measuring progress and relies on a number of estimates. In addition, you must work to

ensure you continue to have access to the resources you need. This cannot be taken for granted. Often people focus totally on time and ignore or underemphasise resource usage – this can be because it is quite hard to monitor, and also because a less than fully scrupulous project manager can more easily get away with using more resource than with failing to deliver on time. Inefficient delivery is as much failure as late delivery.

3   **The quality of the work done and deliverables produced** – where the quality of a task is determined by assessing whether it is good enough to allow following tasks to be done adequately, and therefore allow the overall project's goals to be met. Quality of deliverables is an assessment of whether they are fit for the purpose intended. Additionally, you should look at quality in terms of the project process you are applying. This can be the hardest part of managing a project, though it is one often thought about least.

4   **The scope and outcome** – are you continuing to meet the scope of the project, and is this scope still relevant and linked to the desired outcome?

5   **Your customer** – are you still meeting their expectations?

One way to consider the activity of managing your project is to think about the goal of project management. The goal of project management is to convert a need, specified in terms of objectives and success criteria, into an achieved outcome. How this is done is by clarifying the objectives, translating the objectives into a scope, translating the scope into deliverable definitions, and then translating from the deliverable definitions into a project plan. These four steps are about preparing and planning a project. Having planned the project, the project plan is used to determine project team actions. The project team actions result in the production of deliverables. The deliverables fulfil the scope, and by fulfilling the scope the outcome is achieved. These next four steps are the delivery of the project. This overall process of going from needs through planning and preparation, into delivery and from that achieving the desired outcome is shown in Figure 7.1.

The project management process in Figure 7.1 goes through eight steps, which are numbered in the diagram. The project manager's management task is:

■   To translate fluently between steps 1 to 4 to result in a plan that will achieve the desired outcome.

■   On a day-to-day basis to manage the plan and ensure that the project team actions (in step 5) are those that are defined in the plan (created in step 4) and are done within time and cost constraints.

▨ However, the project manager also has to ensure that the activities performed will really lead through to produce the deliverables, fulfil the scope and achieve the desired outcome. Although the primary work is focused on ensuring there is a close linkage between the plan and the project team actions (i.e. between steps 4 and 5 shown in the figure), there also needs to be alignment between the planned deliverables and those developed (steps 3 and 6), between the defined scope and the fulfilled scope (steps 2 and 7), and between the objectives/success criteria and the outcome (steps 1 and 8)

One way of thinking about the project manager is to compare him or her to *both* the ship's navigator and its helmsman. Acting as the helmsman the project manager must steer the ship on a day-to-day basis where the plan says. But acting as the navigator the project manager also has to ensure that the daily movements of the ship are periodically confirmed to be taking the ship towards the expected destination. To get to the right destination you must make continuous comparisons between plan and activity, but don't forget also to periodically check alignment between where you want to get to and your current location and direction.

How do you know when to take management action?

A very large part of project management theory, processes and tools is given over to providing the project manager with mechanisms to deliver information to know when management action is required. These are described in more detail in Chapters 2 and 10, but in summary the key tools a project manager has are as follows.

▨ Formal progress reporting and progress monitoring:
  – Progress reports and other formal inputs from the project team. (One good tool that is frequently not used to its full advantage is timesheets for team members.) Do not forget that progress needs to measure what has been produced relative to time spent, not simply how much time has been spent.
  – Ongoing planning and monitoring – and there are a variety of tools available to help this, including mapping progress against plan and using tools like earned value analysis. Remember that such monitoring is not simply a measure of how much time has been used, how many tasks done, and how much resource used. It is a measure of how much has been used relative to where you expected to be.

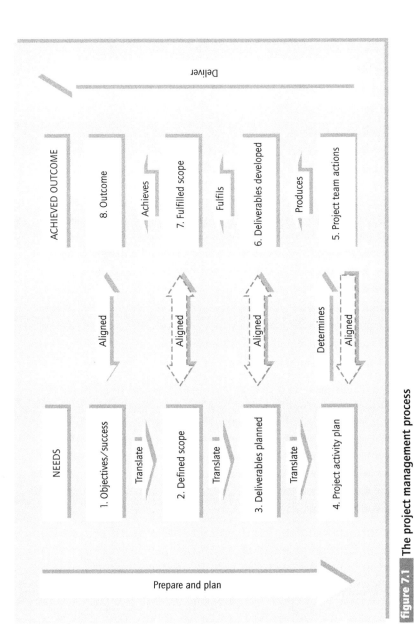

figure 7.1 The project management process

© Richard Newton, 2009.

- Budget and spend tracking – both from the project itself and from any financial systems supporting you.
- Project team meetings – the team's own assessment of progress.
- Use and assessment of outputs from project management tools, e.g.:
  - Risk management
  - Issue management
  - Assumption management
  - Change control.
- Quality control and quality audits of deliverables – both formal and informal. (This is normally not regarded as a project management tool as it is specific to the content of the project. My view is that as a project manager you need to know how quality of deliverables is going to be assessed, otherwise how can you know if the project is delivering what it is meant to be? For some types of deliverable such as software there are well-described processes and approaches for testing them. For many other deliverables there is no defined standard methodology.)
- Informal day-to-day conversations and communications. No matter how good formal information flows are, do not forget how powerful it can be to keep your ear to the ground.
- Direct feedback from the customer.

All of these tools provide different sets of information to a project manager, and as a project manager you must be aware of the range of tools in your armoury and use them appropriately. The combination of tools you use to manage the project is known as the *control system*. A good control system will measure activity progress (have I completed the tasks I expected to in the planned time and budget?), creation of deliverables (are the tasks delivering the output I expected?), and outcome or benefits (will the expected benefits arise?).

With all of these tools the depth and quality to which you use them should be a function of the situation you are in. They are simply tools and not the end result. When you need to hammer a nail into a piece of wood you will use a cheap hammer; when you need to break up several tons of concrete you need at least a pneumatic drill and possibly something bigger. So it is with project management tools. Their effectiveness should be measured in only one way – do they have the optimal balance of being as simple as possible, yet giving you the best information with which to make management decisions in the context in which you are working? When you are setting up your project you must determine which tools you will need and to what degree.

The decision to take action then comes down to your ability to structure the output from these tools to give you worthwhile information, your analysis of the information and your judgement of what action is required. Look for two things: firstly specific individual problems or issues and secondly trends. For example, a one-day slip from one team member in one team in a large programme is probably not relevant to the project manager, but a one-week or one-month slip is. On the other hand, a continuous trend of one-day slippages does need to be managed.

How should you manage?

If you know what to manage, the next question you need to determine is how should you manage? This is somewhat more difficult, but again if you have the fundamentals in place it is where all your hard work comes together, and this is where the successful project manager makes life look easy and the less able project manager struggles. This is also when a balance of analytical skills and a touch of creativity really come together. To use an old cliché, this is where the rubber hits the road.

Again, this is not intellectually complex if we think in terms of the actions a project manager can actually take. No matter how senior, how experienced and how clever a project manager you are, there is a very limited set of actions you can take in response to a need to manage something. The management levers you have are:

- **Change the way the team are working** – this may be as simple as encouraging them to work a little harder, asking them to work more time on your project, reprioritising or refocusing effort, or looking at the way they are actually working.
- **Change resources on a project** – if a project is running late, or occasionally if it is ahead of schedule, you can attempt to change the resource level – or release resources from the project. The basic parameters are to get either more resource or different resources. A more subtle but equally important thing to do when you need resources is to have the priority of the project changed to make accessing resources easier.
- **Change the scope of a project** – a project that is suffering can be made more likely to deliver by reducing the scope and focusing on a smaller

set of critical deliverables or requirements. (Alternatively, a successful project may have more deliverables or requirements added.)

- **Add tasks to the project** – not quite as broad as fundamentally changing scope, but, for example, in response to issues or risks you may add resolving tasks to the workload of project members.

- **Change the plan or approach** – a plan is only a plan; it becomes a statement of fact only on the day a project completes. If it is wrong it can be changed. This may be fundamental rewriting, or it may be to try to move some dependencies around to see if things can be improved. Projects often get fixated on one approach. There are normally many ways to solve a problem. If an approach is not working then it is worth taking a creative look to see if there is an alternative approach.

- **Change the quality** – changing the quality of deliverables of projects can make a huge difference to the time a project takes and the resources it absorbs. This should not be undertaken lightly and must be explicit. I have seen numerous examples on technical projects where engineers have striven for a level of quality that far exceeds what is necessary on the project and hence have used more time and budget to deliver. More often people cut corners to get their deliverables complete. In the intense focus on time and money that many projects operate under, changes to quality happen without really being noticed until a sub-optimal end result is achieved.

- **Make decisions and escalate** – one thing a project manager must do on a regular basis, either by herself or in conjunction with different customer and stakeholder groups, is to make decisions on actions (see the end of this chapter). All the changes noted above need some form of decision making, with external agreement, if significant enough but there will be other decisions required on a day-to-day basis by the project team. If you escalate, you are still responsible for seeing that some action is taken or a decision is made, even if it is done by someone more senior.

- **Terminate the project** – a valid option that is always available is actually to stop a project. Of course, this should not be done without serious consideration, but in my experience it should be done more often than it is. Any project which will under-achieve its original business case should be considered for termination, if the under-achievement is material to the decision to start the project in the first place. Of course, if you get to this place it is best to get there sooner rather than later, and don't fall into the sunk cost trap. What you have spent you have spent; what you need to focus on is how much time and effort it will require to complete the project from where you are now.

The important point about these levers is that this is really where individual judgement comes in. Most project management tools and texts are about getting you to a position in which you can make a decision on one of these activities; they will not actually help you that much in making the decision.

Taking action is the heart of managing a project. If you do not or cannot do this then you should not be a project manager. If what you love is understanding and analysing projects then consider a role in a project office. If you want to be a project manager it is about driving delivery through action. It is not just that you do this, but how well you do it.

When issues or problems occur that need management action, the action must be driven by getting a better result, not simply about understanding why it occurred. In fact, understanding how an issue or problem has arisen is less urgent than understanding how you are going to resolve it. A lot of time can be wasted determining who did what and who is to blame. This is generally unproductive and even if necessary can be done later when the more urgent task of solving the problem is over. When the problem is understood and some action is being taken to resolve it, it is sensible for you to give this some more focused management attention, but do not confuse that with smothering everyone with a need for constant and continuous updates. Updates are required – sometimes daily, sometimes even more frequently – but if people spend the whole time updating you they will not actually be resolving the issue. This is the time for good leadership and balancing your need for information for control and managing customers, and giving people the space to deliver.

> ❝ taking action is the heart of managing a project ❞

Once you have determined and agreed upon a course of action it needs to be communicated. You must therefore have a structure of meetings and communication channels in place to ensure this is done and the team should be prepared for it. The team should understand that the plan they are working to is a framework, and not necessarily the final answer. They must expect regular updates to agree what actually needs to be done given the current status of the project.

The success of a project manager depends on an understanding of what can be managed and the sources of information to trigger management action. The measure of success depends only on the taking of the action and its result.

Change control and management

Change control provides a mechanism for a project manager to respond to changes in a project's scope and requirements in a controlled fashion. It is essential to successful project management to have a robust change control process supported by ongoing expectation setting.

So far, in terms of both setting up the project (as overviewed in Chapter 5) and subsequently managing the project (as defined in this chapter), I have described the baseline for the work as the scope (described in Chapter 2). In practice, neither the scope of a project nor the detailed requirements stay static. The whole of the management process that is based on these being consistent is therefore in jeopardy. The response to this is not to reject change, but to control and manage changes. This is where change control and change management come into place.

The primary source of change should be the customers of the project – they want additional requirements included, or they desire to expand the scope. Alternatively, but much less commonly, the customer may want to decrease the scope or requirements – this is also a change and they may expect the project to be done more quickly or more cheaply as a result. There will be some changes that are driven by the project team rather than the customer (for example, if it is found that a chosen approach does not work and the plan needs to be modified). This is not to say that the project team cannot drive changes, but the volume of changes led by the project team should be limited. As a project progresses and the project team's understanding of what is required improves, it may be necessary to change plans and approaches to such an extent that it needs formal change control. Finally, changes may be driven by the environment in which a project operates. This may be something as fundamental as a legal or regulatory change that must be conformed to, through to more simply a change in an external dependency. Again, this should ideally be driven by the project customer. The drivers for change are summarised in Figure 7.2.

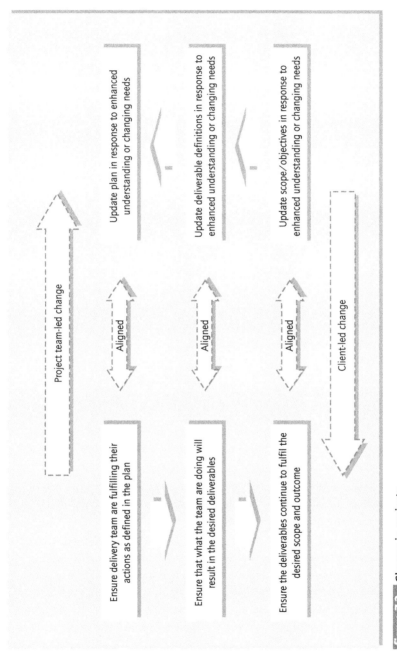

figure 7.2 Change in projects

© Richard Newton, 2009.

Figure 7.2 shows that no matter where or how a change occurs, it must ripple through to other aspects of the project. A customer may require the scope or objectives to be modified – for example because a performance target has increased. They may want changes to deliverables – for example the identification of missed requirements. Or they may want an update to the plan – for example because a deadline has been brought forward. Any of these must be aligned to the plan and activities of the project team. Alternatively, this can happen in reverse with the project team requesting changes for one reason or another to improve the project. It is this dynamic balance that change control seeks to manage.

There are some changes which are not optional, when something happens that must be responded to. But in most cases it is worth remembering that accepting or rejecting a change is an optional choice. A key part of change management is therefore about delivering the information to make the best choice.

While you may have built some 'fat' or contingency into a project plan to respond to minor changes, and as discussed in Chapter 4 you may occasionally accept small changes without explicitly using a change control process, change control is not an option for the project manager. It is central to project success. Poor change management is a very common reason for project failure.

The basic process for any change control system is fairly straightforward:

- Identify and log any changes that are proposed – what it is, why it is wanted.
- Understand and assess the change. Specifically determine the impact of the change upon the project. There are two views of the impact of a change:
  - *A project management view*: will it increase or decrease time, will it increase or decrease resources, will it change the cost, and will it impact the quality of the project?
  - *A customer view*: if this change is implemented, will it still result in a project delivering what the customer wants and will it still result in the necessary benefits or business case being delivered? The impact of change upon benefits realisation is often ignored and yet it is critical, as without it you may alter something that prevents the project from delivering what it was set up to deliver in the first place.
- Determine viable options for responding to the change and determine the resulting impact upon the project. For example, if the change is

an increase in scope, you may be able to respond by lengthening the project or by keeping the time the same and increasing resources.

- Discuss with the sponsor and agree whether to accept the change, and if so which approach to take towards it.
- Adapt your plans accordingly.

Figure 7.3 shows the change control process.

A key factor in successful change control is supporting it with good expectation management. Successful change control is not just about saying yes or no to changes – it is also about how the changes are implemented. Set the customer's expectations early on that if changes occur they will have an impact on the project, and when changes do occur communicate and reinforce the impact to make sure it is understood and accepted. An essential part of this expectation management should revolve around educating the customer. If your customer wants a project with an absolutely committed plan and minimal contingency in time, cost or resource, it is unlikely that you will be able to change anything significant without altering the cost, time or resource levels. Alternatively, if change is likely your customer should hold a contingency budget to be prepared to handle this.

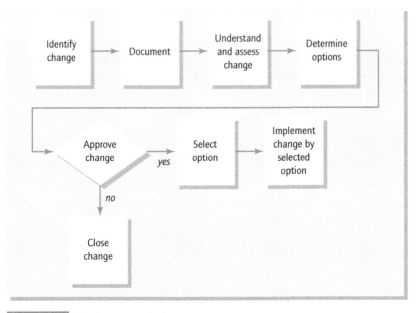

figure 7.3 The change control process

Decision making

Throughout this chapter I have mentioned the need for the project manager to make decisions. No matter how good and accurate your planning and preparation, things will occur that require decisions to be made to resolve them. Whenever there is an option you must make a decision. Therefore, while it is rarely explicitly mentioned, analysis and decision making are a core project management skill.

To make a decision you may either guess at the right answer (generally not a good idea) or, more constructively, rely on your intuition and experience of similar situations to make a 'gut' decision (which is fine for most decisions we make on a day-to-day basis) or finally, in the most structured way, decide what information you need to make a decision, gather it, identify options, analyse the information relative to the options available and then make the best decision. Good decision making is not 'free'; it requires effort to gather the information you need, and it takes time to perform the analysis. A trade-off that all managers must make on an ongoing basis is between making decisions sufficiently quickly to maintain progress and taking the time to gather the information required and to form a valid assessment.

> " good decision making is not 'free' "

Projects in this respect are like any other management challenge – all the tools and processes in the world will not provide you with all the information you need to be sure of a perfect decision in all situations. But you must make and implement decisions regularly, otherwise the project will stall.

The key points about decision making are that it is a constant trade-off between the following issues:

- How critical is the decision and what is the impact if it is wrong?
- How critical is the decision and what is the impact if you take too much time to make it? (Many decisions must be made within a certain period of time. The most difficult to make are those that must be made quickly but that also need lots of information and have a big impact if wrong.)
- Understanding who can and who should make the decision. Can you do it? Do you need an expert specialist? Does it need any level of formal authority to make? Is it something for your sponsor to decide?

■ What is the culture of your organisation? Some companies value considered decision making, others value speed and pace over accuracy.

Don't be afraid of decisions. In most situations it is important to make a decision rather than be absolutely certain it is right. Analysis and decision-making paralysis is usually far worse than making a few sub-optimal decisions. The key is to identify the small number of critical decisions and make sure that they are right.

8

The team

Getting the best from the project team

One of the main tasks for a project manager is to manage and motivate the project team to deliver all that is required for the project. Pure project management process and methodologies will not achieve this. A project manager above all else is a people manager.

During the life of a project the project manager will personally create a range of tangible deliverables that are critical to delivery. This includes things like plans, issue and risk registers, project charters and the like. The funny point is that at the end of the work when the project is complete these items are largely worthless. They have little or no value outside the life of the project. The real deliverables, the things desired in the first place, are produced by everyone else on the project. Whether that is a computer system or a new building, the people the project manager manages on the project produce the deliverables the customer wants.

This is important to remember, because project management is at its heart largely about people management. Project management is delivery through a team. Even though as a project manager you will usually have no permanent staff of your own, and may even have become a project manager to avoid line management, you will have to accept managing people as being core to your role. Without the project team the project manager's role is worthless. The main task for the project manager is to ensure that the project team is capable of delivering, that it does deliver, and that blockages in the team's way are removed.

So what are the key things that a project manager can do to get the best from the project team? To give a flavour of this I have identified seventeen people management tasks, split into four groups. Many of these you will do naturally, so try to identify which of these seventeen you are weaker at and need to improve on. The seventeen are:

1   Getting the basics right – right people, right skills, right tasks (tasks 1–5)

2   Motivating and building the team (tasks 6–10)

3   Project team management challenges (tasks 11–15)

4   The broader context (tasks 16–17).

Tasks 1–5: Getting the basics right – right people, right skills, right tasks

Management task 1 – Getting the right capabilities and skills

The first thing a project manager must consider when setting up a project team is what capabilities and skills are required to do the project. This should be treated firstly as a paper exercise, not a review of who you have. Once you have an understanding of what is required then review what people are available and assign them to relevant roles on the project.

Often there will be a gap between the capabilities and skills of the team you have, and that which you ideally need. Try to fill it as best you can, but it is naive to expect a perfect match between the skills you need and the people you get. This gap needs to be managed as a risk like any other risk. (A key reason for starting your thinking with what you need rather than what you have is to be able to understand this gap explicitly and therefore to be able to assess the risk this creates.) Lack of skills to complete the project should appear on your risk register. Do not just ignore this point and accept what resources you are given. Yes, in the real world you do not get a perfect team, but as the project manager it is your responsibility to manage the resultant issues. If the impact of the gap is small you can manage around it, but do not assume that the gap will be constantly small at all stages of the project.

Get a balanced set of capabilities and skills, and do not fall into the trap of choosing people who are all like you. In fact, look for people you can work with, but make sure at least some of them are *not* like you. They may see issues and risks you would not have thought of or may come up with creative solutions you may not see. Managing varied people assists in ensuring constructive challenge and helps to avoid the danger of group think. Group think is when a team of people think alike and become blind to issues. This is a risk especially on a small well-motivated and focused project team working in a closed environment.

> ❝ group think is when a team of people think alike and become blind to issues ❞

Find a balance between internal and external resources. Unless it breaches company policy or budgets are very tight, you should consider people external to your organisation. There are many good contractors and consultants who can help out. Some unusual skills which your organisation uses only occasionally are often best sourced externally. On the other hand, fully staffing projects with contractors and consultants is expensive and can lead to solutions that are inappropriate for your specific context. In addition, in-house staff often resent the use of a high percentage of external staff.

Management task 2 – Go for quality rather than quantity

If you remember no other point from this section, remember this one. When people plan and scope out projects and look at the number of people required, there is a tendency to treat people in purely numerical terms. Do you need five, ten or twenty people – as if there is no difference in the quantity and quality of the outputs from some people? When in doubt always go for fewer, better people. They will be easier to manage and will produce more. I can quote numerous examples where a smaller group of people have delivered far more than a big team. I have seen situations where a single senior executive goes away on a Friday and comes back on Monday morning with a fully scoped strategy that the strategy project team of ten consultants has struggled over for weeks. I have seen small teams of motivated fitters do more work in one weekend when a building is required than a team of builders twice as big achieved in the week before. I have experienced a group of four superb software developers creating better, more functionally rich and robust software in a matter of a few weeks than a team of twenty or thirty from a major software house would develop in six months. Life is full of examples where a small group of motivated people have delivered far more than a much larger group of less able people. In terms of people, quality always wins over quantity. Get the best people you can afford even if the resulting cost means you end up with fewer.

Do not simply accept the resources you are offered without question. If there are better capable, better qualified or better motivated people elsewhere in the organisation, try to get them rather than the people you have been offered. You may need to act as the salesman to these individuals to get them interested in coming onto the project, and work as a negotiator with their line managers to get them released. This effort will be rewarded as the project progresses.

Management task 3 – Assign clear roles and defined objectives

The starting point for management of anyone in any team is for them to understand why they are part of the project team, and what is required of them. If you have asked for someone to be on the project you should know why you need them. Projects are not simply an excuse to collect and stockpile people! It is amazing how often project members find themselves allocated to projects without a clear idea of the requirements being placed upon them. On the other hand, if this is done comprehensively and clearly the chance that the project will be a success is increased greatly.

Everyone on the team should therefore know:

- What their role is and what the tasks are that they are expected to perform. This should be defined clearly and succinctly. The best way to do this is not simply to list a set of tasks the individual needs to complete, but to specify the objective or goal you wish them to achieve.
- Who on the project is allowed to allocate them work, and to decide whom they will be working with or for.
- Whom they need to interact and work with to complete their tasks.
- How much time they are expected to spend on the project (in terms of both duration and percentage of time in this period to be made available to the project).
- What the measures of success for their task are.
- Why they were chosen. Even if it is true, avoid telling people that they are on the project because they were the only person available, as it is not very motivating!

For a large project this is a considerable piece of work, and arguably one of the most important tasks for the project manager. For projects with several teams this can be done as a cascade with the project manager doing this at team leader level, and the individual team leaders then breaking this down for the team members. It does not have to be done in a complex fashion, but unless every team member knows this you risk poor performance and focus on irrelevant activities. Unless you can see a direct linkage between all the activities on your project plan and the work being done by the project team, the project is unlikely to be successful.

Role assignment and allocation of tasks will not happen automatically as the people on the team may never have worked together before. It will certainly need your management.

Try to find a balance between very detailed roles and a degree of flexibility. Given that nothing is fully predictable and it is unlikely that you will foresee every eventuality, no plan will cover 100% of all tasks required. New unplanned activities will arise that need to be performed. Roles should therefore be defined so as a project progresses and new activities are discovered you can allocate them to a member of the team without causing disruption. Some of this is about writing role definitions in a way to allow this, but it is also about raising people's expectations up front that their role *may* modify as the project develops.

Once you have assigned roles and responsibilities check there are no gaps and, almost as important, no overlaps – each task requires one person or one team to be accountable for it, otherwise you will struggle to ensure it is delivered. Blurred responsibilities and accountabilities waste time, increase management overhead, and add significantly to the risk of failure to deliver. Having single points of accountability for tasks is a critical success factor in projects.

If you are working with a geographically spread or virtual team, take extra care on the role definitions. If you are all working in one room and you are alert, you will quickly identify when someone's responsibilities have not been defined clearly enough and need a bit of tweaking. If one of your team members is hundreds of miles away, you may not know about errors in role definitions for some weeks. Virtual teams can be aided by productivity tools and do not hesitate to invest in them (for example, virtual meeting rooms and online conference facilities). But technology will not completely overcome the lack of intimacy, and the foundation stone of a successful project is clear roles and objectives.

Finally, make the responsibility definitions on the project public to all project team members. This helps to avoid misunderstandings (and also can gently pressurise those who are not pulling their weight to pull their finger out rather than let the team down).

Management task 4 – Be clear about how you want people to work

In carrying out task 3 you defined what you want people to do through clear roles and responsibilities. To provide absolute clarity to the team it is helpful not only to define *what* you want each team member to do on the project, but *how* you want them to do it.

Are your team members world-renowned subject-matter experts who can get on with their work unaided, who may even resent being told how to perform the work they have been assigned? Or are your team members novices, who need clear and direct instructions to complete their assigned tasks to the necessary level of quality? In parcelling out the work on the project, be clear in telling the team members:

- How much discretion they have in defining the outcome from the task. Is the outcome precisely defined, or are there only vague instructions which you expect them to fill out?
- How much discretion they have over how the task is performed. Is there a predefined and mandatory process, or don't you care as long as it is done within the agreed time and cost constraints?
- What level of quality assurance you will have over their work. Do you simply trust them to deliver a quality piece of work, or will it be fully tested once complete?

The decision over how you want people to work, and therefore how much management control and interference you expect, is associated with the amount of learning you want team members to make and the pressure the project is under. Of course, if team members are greater experts than you then discretion in how they deliver is normally essential. But a highly pressurised project in a critical situation usually needs you to be directive, with little scope for individual exploration and learning. On the other hand, in some situations you want people to explore and learn, so they can do it by themselves next time. In the longer run it is always better to give people discretion. Occasionally, you will be let down, but motivation will tend to be higher and skills will improve greatly over time.

Management task 5 – Know when to throw people off the team

What should you do with an under-performing member of the team, especially if it adds some risk to the project? Keeping the right mix of people on the project and removing those who are not pulling their weight is essential. Hopefully it will not be something you will need to do too often, but you need to be prepared to do it. (I am talking about removal from a project, not from a company or loss of actual job role. Firing someone for poor performance is a far more complex and serious issue that needs to be handled with care and should involve specialist human resources support.)

When you become aware of poor performance, take action quickly and start by giving people an explicit chance to perform better. Ensure they are given clear feedback about how they are failing and give them a chance to turn it round. Go through the following checklist:

- Does the poorly performing individual understand what is required of him (or her)?
- Does he (or she) understand that he (or she) is performing poorly? (Will some constructive feedback resolve the issue?) It is quite common for people not to know they are performing poorly and to respond well to some constructive feedback. Most people want to do a good job.
- Do you understand what is driving the poor performance?
- Can any of these reasons be easily resolved?
- Is the individual willing and able to overcome the performance issue?
- Have you liaised with and discussed the issue with their line manager and informed human resources?

This is shown in detail in Figure 8.1.

Of course, part of this process must be to determine what your alternatives are. Sometimes, someone is better than no-one, and if you cannot change the performance but also cannot have a replacement, you will have to live with the individual. But don't assume this. There are many situations in which poor performance may be so disruptive that it is better to have no-one. One useful point is that if someone is underperforming and jeopardising a team's output, you may be surprised to find that the rest of the team support the individual's removal. There is nothing high-performing teams dislike more than an individual who is seen to be reducing their ability to deliver.

Do not leave such a review until too late. Of course, best of all is not to accept the individual onto the team in the first place. While saying no to someone is never pleasant, it is always far easier than having to remove a

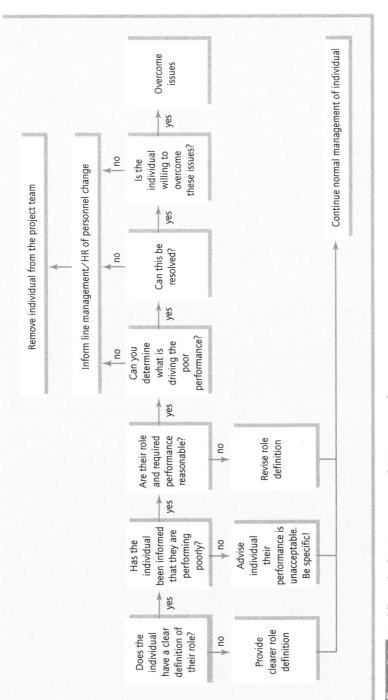

figure 8.1 Deciding whether to remove project team members

poor performer during the project. But, assuming you have not done this, do not wait until a major problem has arisen before tackling the issue. If you do this you are really shirking your responsibility as a project manager. If in doubt, pull people off the project. Your primary job is to ensure it is delivered. Developing staff is a secondary priority for you. This may seem harsh, but it is necessary. They have a line manager to worry about their development and their feelings.

This is one activity that is normally far easier for a project manager than for a line manager. Assuming the person thrown off the project will not actually lose their job, you do have the advantage over many line managers that you do not have to make them redundant or perform structured performance management activities which normally are time consuming. Advise the sponsor of the risk the person brings and get them off the project as soon as possible.

Poor performance in a project situation should not be measured in an absolute sense – as you would as a line manager – but relative to the requirements of the project. For example, someone may give you a very good but time-boxed 9 to 5 performance as these are their working hours. Sometimes on projects this is not enough, and a project requires short periods of intense working. In this situation you should consider removing your steady 9 to 5 performer. The work he is doing is not sufficient for the context of the project you are running and, equally important, others on the project who are putting in the required time will resent it if you do not remove him.

Tasks 6–10: Motivating and building the team

Management task 6 – The line management challenge – aligning objectives and motivation

The nature of most projects is that the team of people on the project will only be there for a limited period of time, and the project manager is not those people's line manager. The project manager often has limited authority or formal influence over project team members. There is a three-way relationship between the member of the project team, their normal line manager and the project manager. Project management requires the ability to matrix-manage, and although it should be minimised, in all matrix-management there is some degree of greyness. Not everything will be black and white.

The first point for any project manager is not to moan about this – it is a project manager's lot. If you want to be a line manager you should have gone into line management. (A positive feature of project management for many project managers is the fact that they do not have line management responsibility.) Most team members have a line manager who can determine things that are important to them and that will influence their performance such as pay rises, promotions and the like. The line manager may have nothing to do with the project. So if you do not have line management responsibility and the levers that go with this, how do you manage the team?

The first thing you must do is to try to align objectives:

- Agree with key individuals on the project what it is that they need to achieve for you to consider them a success. For larger projects, actually document this as if you were setting objectives for any other role. This needs to be done in conjunction with, and with the agreement of, their line manager. (See management task 3.)

- For people who are going to spend any length of time on the project, it is worth formally aligning any defined performance measures with project success. As an extreme negative example I have seen project team members who had benefits packages, including substantial bonus elements, determined by meeting their goals as set by their line managers. These people were on a project for many months and yet their annual performance objectives had nothing to do with the project. Needless to say, much of their concentration was pointed elsewhere. Discuss with their line manager, and if he or she is not responsive, with the project sponsor, whether you can have line objectives reflect the work your team member must do on the project.

- Try to pick people with a personal interest in the project. These people will often volunteer or request involvement. Excitement, drive and enthusiasm are often worth far more than apparently better skills on paper. Everyone has experienced occasions when the expert has given up but the motivated and driven non-expert has gone on to deliver. You cannot do without expertise, but do not overestimate the value of having the best experts when compared to having the most personally motivated individuals.

- Make sure people are aware that this is a visible project that more senior managers are watching. People do not respond well to having someone constantly looking over their shoulder, but people are more likely to be engaged if they know their successes (and failures) will be visible to influential people.

Most employees will do their contracted 9 to 5 hours when asked to. An issue for projects is that often at some time in the project's duration this is not enough. Secondly, the content of the work is often stretching or different from what people normally do. This will motivate some employees who like a challenge, but not all. Therefore it is often necessary to motivate people to work outside their normal expectations of work content and/or working hours.

Junior and inexperienced managers often confuse motivation with authority. As a project manager you will often have limited authority. Authority can come from position and through this the ability to control rewards and punishments (the stick and carrot). In your role as a project manager you will normally have little or no control over these, though you may be able to influence them. Authority can also come from a position of expertise, and you should ideally be respected by the team for your project management expertise, but this alone will not generate complete authority as it is only one of many types of expertise needed on a project. But do not despair: as a project manager it is still possible to motivate people once you understand what motivation is about.

The starting point for understanding motivation is the realisation that most people do not like to fail. If you and the team want to succeed, the majority of individuals will go along with this. Most people also respond to a challenge, but they must have a fundamental belief that what is required is at least possible. Motivation does not come from your ability to manage the stick and carrot. It comes from people being engaged in the work. This can be that the work is satisfying or fun in itself, it is a challenge they want, they like the team they work in, or they are getting learning or development.

Hence, having aligned objectives there are a number of actions you can take to continue to motivate the team to work towards them:

- Lead the team by example. You want each of the project team members to see success of the project as their personal goal. As the project manager, if you do not act as if your personal goals are aligned with the project goals then it will be difficult to convince a project team to align their goals.

- Motivation is about giving people a reason for wanting to be involved in the project and wanting to make the project a success. For some people being motivated is internally driven and is a normal part of their working lives whatever they are asked to do; for others motivation is driven by external factors. The most important of these external factors is usually ensuring alignment of objectives and reward with project success.

- Make sure the specific objectives and targets you have set teams and team members are possible – it's OK if they are challenging or stretching but no-one is motivated by the constant thought of missing goals.
- Keep a fair spread of work across the team. People will often work, for limited periods, very intensely without complaint. What will demotivate is half the team working hard and the other half taking it easy. Of course, there are natural results of differing skills and project needs, but try to balance the workload across the team as far as possible.
- Next you should seek to create a motivating environment. The things that make something motivating to any individual vary from person to person, but key factors include:
  - Plenty of regular informal constructive feedback. Positive reinforcement of good behaviour simply by recognition and praise is a major motivating factor for many people.
  - People work best in an environment with a combination of good support and help when they need it, but also challenge. Encourage openness and honesty when there are issues and problems.
  - Work to build a team environment that people want to be involved in and feel a part of.
  - Try to enable individual team members to achieve personal goals through working on the project.
  - Make the environment fun – encourage a positive attitude to work. This can be as trivial as building a team environment in which it is common to smile, through to organised social events. No one technique will work for everyone – having a drink or going go-karting will not suit all individuals – so you need to be creative in coming up with options that are as inclusive as you can find.
- Avoid doing things that remove people's motivation. The main things that kill motivation are uneven workloads, a lack of belonging, and lack of alignment with objectives, combined with uncertainty. Many people may say they thrive in changing environments, but typically this is because they are certain they will survive the change, or they have skills that can be readily deployed elsewhere. Clear goals and objectives combined with regular reinforcement and praise reduce uncertainty.

- Build a feeling with team members that their impact on the project is valued. Remove poor performers from the team. It is highly demotivating for most people to feel that their good work is being held back by a poor performer or that their work is carrying a 'freeloader'.

Management task 7 – Building the team

Unless you are very lucky, or working in a situation of a continuous stream of very similar projects, it is quite likely that the people in your project team will not have worked together before. You should not automatically assume that people will come together and work well as a team. You may have to work to bring them together.

There is no one right way of building a team and different sets of people will form bonds in different lengths of time. To support this as a project manager:

- Take mobilisation seriously. When the team is first mobilised make sure you communicate the purpose of the project and everyone's roles. Give some time for people to get to know one another and to question you over anything that is unclear.
- Ensure roles are clear and understood.
- Set expectations as to the working environment and culture you expect on the team. Remind everyone that a project succeeds through teamwork and regular, open communications.
- Ensure communication channels are open, not just between you and team members but across the team members.
- Bring people physically together as much as you can. When this is not possible, such as with a widely geographically dispersed team, try to find ways to encourage interaction and try to use means of communication that are as intimate as possible (e.g. phone rather than e-mail).
- Encourage activity between members of the project that you think encourages team building. Stop activity that is detrimental.
- Watch the team dynamic growing. If it is not, you will have to take action, but don't jump in every time there are minor issues. People have to learn to work together.

❝ don't take team building for granted ❞

- Don't take team building for granted. Work at it and build on tasks 3, 5, 10 and 11.

Management task 8 – Ensure there is personal development for team members

If people are on a project for any length of time, it is not unreasonable for them to expect some form of personal development out of it, and it can act as a great motivational driver for team members to feel their skills are being enhanced. One thing for project managers to watch out for is that when people are allocated to projects it is often on the promise that they will get some personal development from it. The conundrum facing the project manager is that enabling team members to develop normally means giving people the opportunity to learn or do new tasks. If you are not learning something new you are not really developing, and yet the most effective people would be thought to be those who are doing what they are very experienced at doing. If you want a brick wall built quickly, you get a great bricklayer, but generally he is not getting any personal development from building this wall, because he is already an expert.

So what should the project manager do?

- Accept the need for people's development. It is usually not a core objective for you (normally it is not a project success factor, but can occasionally be), but it may be fundamental to your success. Therefore, try to get a good trade-off between good existing expertise and learning goals. If you want to include some formal training, make sure you have the budget for it.

- Face the issue of development early on in the project, ideally when people first get involved. As part of their induction to the project, understand their needs and thoughts in this area. If their expectations are out of line or unreasonable then put them straight. It is better to take the disappointment now, when you have a chance of doing something about it, than at midnight (later in the project) when a critical task needs completing before the next day.

- Try to sell people on the idea of learning from the things that are naturally part of the project. This is a bit of a selling exercise, but often people are quite happy to learn something new in the project by actually doing things you need done anyway.

- Build any reasonable things into the project plan – whether this be training courses or getting people involved in specific activities. However, make sure development goals do not divert or alter the project in a way that adds risk.

- Make sure, in turn, you do not set any unreasonable expectations that the individual's line manager might disagree with.

■ When someone comes to you with a problem, don't always tell them the answer directly. It is far better for their development to help them work it out for themselves. With the right level of support, most people can work out many problems they think are impossible at first.

Management task 9 – Ensure people have a home to go back to

Some of the people working on your project will be full-time/professional project people. These are staff, contractors and consultants who spend their lives going from one project to another. However, many and often most of the project team have been pulled out of normal line jobs to be on the project. These line jobs had the security of having no defined end point, whereas a project has a very clear end point.

In the age of regular rounds of reorganisation and redundancies in most industries, do not be surprised that these people are concerned if they are allocated to a project team for any extended period of time. If their normal line role can do without them for several months, or even longer, do they really need them back when the work is over? Whatever the true answer, it is obviously quite reasonable for people to have this concern. Reducing concern in team members is not just a function of just 'being a nice person'; the reason this is important for the project manager is that people who are concerned for their future are at best likely to be less effective or may well not be properly motivated, or at worst may actually start looking for another job.

There are ways around this:

■ The starting point is to prepare for this issue arising before anyone is allocated to a project team.

■ Get formal and explicit commitment that their job will still be available when the project is finished.

■ If possible, have their role backfilled with another member of staff or contractor when they are on the project. In this way their job still explicitly exists.

■ For key staff an extreme method is to actually guarantee them some form of bonus or payment at the end of the project in return for taking the risk of coming on it. This is not common practice, but when I have seen it done it is effective.

The final point is that, for some people, coming onto a project is actually a deliberate way out of their current role. For these people, being on the project may be motivational in itself, and they may want to develop some transferable skills.

Management task 10 – Be aware of team dynamics and team politics

Any group of people working together will develop a style of working together. The ability to understand the dynamics of your team is crucial for project managers. The thought that you can allocate people tasks and they will gladly deliver them irrespective of the people they are working with is naive. There is no one right or wrong team style and there is no right or wrong way of responding to the dynamics of a team. You will have worked, if you are lucky, on great teams with great dynamics, and you will have worked on poor teams with poor dynamics.

- Be aware of it and monitor it – don't just ignore it as a fact of life. For long projects on which a team will be together for many months or even years, it may be worth doing some form of formal assessment of personality types. This will give you a good insight and may let you see skills or approaches you are missing in the team or over-represented with. This can help you manage rebalancing the team. Such measures, if shared with the team, can enable them each to understand how they may need to tailor their behaviour to other team members. If you do use a formal assessment (whether it is as simple as Belbin, or more complex like Myers–Briggs or OPQ), make sure you understand the results. It is easy to draw the wrong conclusions from a poor understanding of the methodology.

- Use it – it can be a positive as well as a negative force. Good team dynamics and a lack of politics should be striven for. If you have formally assessed the team members, use your understanding to help shape the team and drive individual performance.

- Don't assume it is static – it will change over time as the team changes and people get to know each other.

- Stop it if it gets in the way – if the team dynamics or politics are reducing performance it is your responsibility as the project manager to sort it out.

- Manage it when you need to bring new people on the team – this can be quite disruptive to a well-established team and can be hard for the new joiner.

- Encourage openness and honesty – successful teams tend to have few barriers to communications.

- You are part of it too, so lead by example – if you don't want politics in the team, do not politic yourself. You want to be trusted by team members; if there are problems or issues, you want to know about them as soon as possible and this is more likely if people trust you. If you politic too much you are unlikely to develop trust. Try to be consistent in your statements and actions.

- Remember that the team is more important than the individual. It is the team that delivers, not any one individual. You will have star performers who need to be looked after, but explicitly treating people to different standards will only create bad feelings and negative mutterings. Similarly, no matter how good someone's skills are, do not put up with them if they disrupt the team.
- However, even though the team is more important, you manage through individuals. Each person may need a slightly different set of interactions to keep them motivated and aligned with the project's objectives.

In many projects team members will not have met before, and even if they have met they may well not have worked together in this way before. You must use the mobilisation phase and then ongoing management to help the team form, and manage the way it interacts through the life of the project.

Tasks 11–15: Project team management challenges

Management task 11 – Physical proximity and communications channels

One of the most underestimated factors is the advantage of close physical proximity for a project team. The basic truth is that people work better when they work together. Issues are resolved more quickly, more creative solutions are designed, and conflict occurs less regularly when people have to sit together. Whenever I am starting up a new project I try to find space for the project team to be co-located. My belief is that bringing a team physically together will have dramatic effects on efficiency and effectiveness. If the project is important enough it is worth putting in the effort and living with the short-term disruption of pulling a team into one location.

In practice, bringing a team to one physical location and sitting them in close proximity is often avoided. It is put in the too-hard-to-achieve category. It is seen as a lot of effort for marginal benefit, a nice-to-have rather than an essential. Do not give up on this easily. It is worth the effort as when it is done productivity is significantly enhanced.

It is, of course, not always possible to bring a team together. The way your resources have been allocated, the nature of the organisation you are working in, or simply the size and geographic spread of the project may require a very diverse working. If possible, insist that all team members do meet physically at least once. More generally in these situations, make sure that communications chains are robust, and that people communicate in the most 'intimate' ways possible. By this I mean ideally face-to-face, next via video conference, then by phone with online conferencing facilities and, finally, by e-mail (and e-mail should be seen very much as the poorest way to communicate).

Actively discourage less intimate communications styles. Encourage plenty of continuous informal communications and use tools such as e-mail for what they are good at – and not as the sole communications channel.

Before you bring all your team together be aware that it does have some disadvantages and risks. The primary one of these is that you are more likely to be seen as cut off from the line organisation your project is delivering into. This is a particular problem for the type of projects that need constant interaction with the line organisation, or good buy-in for the results from the project. Potentially this can be overcome by strong and regular communications, but for some projects, for example business change projects, being located away from the main organisation can be a significant enough disadvantage to forgo the delivery efficiencies to be derived from having a single closely located team.

Management task 12 – Managing geographically diverse and isolated staff

If you cannot bring your team together you may have geographically diverse teams, or individually isolated members of staff. This does not need to be a problem, but it is an issue you need to manage and it will increase your management overhead. It needs careful control.

Useful tips to consider are:

- Make the relationships between teams and the way they will interact clear at mobilisation. Try, at this stage at least, to bring people together.
- Don't forget isolated staff. They may be happily and productively delivering, or they may simply be ignoring what they are meant to be doing. Unless you are managing them you will not know.
- Communicate frequently. Communications must become more deliberate. The opportunity for informal chats is reduced so you must plan your communications in a more structured way.
- Check their understanding and comprehension of the requirements on them – it is easier for them to be in error when you are not sitting next to each other all the time.

- Ensure you do not develop any location biases or tensions. These are generally unproductive.

- Communicate to your remote staff as frequently and in as timely a fashion as to local staff, especially for important news. Nothing irritates more than the feeling that head office knows something that those in the regions find out much later! It generates resentment, suspicion and rumour.

- As project manager try to travel to all locations at some time during the project if practical.

Management task 13 – Managing part-time resources

Every project manager wants a fully dedicated team who only have to think about and apply energy to the one project. In practice, on virtually every project I have been involved in, some people have other tasks to do outside the project. These other tasks may include other project work or other day-to-day operational tasks for the business.

" communicate frequently. Communications must become more deliberate "

Many smaller projects are resourced primarily with part-time staff. The 'virtual' project that has only a project manager who then must beg, steal and borrow resources to get things done is, in textbook project management, a bad thing, but in reality it happens all the time. Hence, in real life much of a project manager's time is spent in coaxing and cajoling part-time resources to focus on the particular project rather than any other task they may be doing. This can be a painful and long-winded process for the project manager, but it can often be the factor that decides whether a project is successful or not. Your ability to do this is an essential skill.

Assuming the project workload justifies it, it is worth pushing to try to get as many people as you need full time, but you will have to accept that you will get part-time resources – and you should be capable of managing in this situation.

- Make sure that you have enough resource – it is the hours people are available for that count, not simply the number of people involved in the project.

- Get fixed and measurable amounts of time from people – are they available one day a week, two days a week or for some other amount?

- Monitor them and ensure you get the time you are meant to receive. Staff under pressure on several different projects or activities may simply slip away from your work if it is easy to do so and not be noticed.

- Try to align availability times. For example, if you have two team members who work only two days a week on the project and need to work together, try at least to get them to allocate the same two days a week to the project.
- Get yourself dedicated to the project – only for small projects should the project manager not be dedicated.
- Build an 'inefficiency' buffer into your planning. Part-time staff can be very productive as they are not soon tired of focusing only on the project, though generally a number of part-time resources will be less efficient than fewer full-time staff. Even where it does not alter the number of worked hours needed to complete tasks, it can massively increase elapsed time for a project.
- Measure staff on deliverables as well as time. Time allocated should not be an excuse not to deliver.
- There will be a small number of absolutely critical people – often in expert operational roles, and sometimes quite junior in the organisation. They will be very busy and have absolutely tiny periods of time to give you, and you may feel in asking them for time that you are trying to squeeze blood from a stone. Balance your approach here, use your charm and good manners to coax them, and escalate to your sponsor to get their priorities reset to focus on your work. (If you are going to escalate to get someone focused on your work, warn them in advance. This gives them the chance to do it anyway, and also avoids it becoming a confrontation. When you escalate, advise them you are doing it not as a complaint against them, but to help them find the time to work with you. Presenting escalation as an aid and not a threat helps maintain good working relationships.)

See management tasks 14 and 15 as well.

Management task 14 – Managing upwards

Project managers manage a team of people, and these people respond to the project manager's requests, simply because that team has some reason to fulfil the project manager's needs. Often this is because there is a formal level of seniority between the project manager and the team members. However, on almost all projects there are tasks that need to be done by senior managers, and there are disciplines like law with senior professionals who will not automatically 'obey' the project manager.

How should a project manager face this task?

- Ensure the individual is pre-warned that the project may require them to do work at some time. This is easier if the senior person has a formal role on the project such as a sponsor, although I have frequently seen projects on which it is a surprise to the sponsor that he ever actually has to do some work. Tell him at the start; there will be issues escalated for resolution at the very least.

- Explain the reasons for the work clearly and simply – you must avoid patronising the person, but they should feel that it really does need someone of their seniority doing it and you are not simply being lazy!

- Explain your time frames and when you need the task done. Senior people are rarely dedicated to your work (see above), have lots of other important things to do, and regularly do not do all the things they might want to do. Tasks get de-prioritised away. You need to ensure your task does not. Constantly telling senior managers they are late for something may need doing, but it normally irritates them. If they clearly understand the implications of their work being late or sub-standard they will generally deliver.

- Be polite, clear and respectful, but be robust in making sure the task is done. Most managers are responsive to this.

Management task 15 – Managing non-dedicated specialists

Project managers will always try to get dedicated resources, sometimes for legitimate reasons and on other occasions because it just makes the management task more straightforward. But there are some specialists from whom it can almost never be justified to have full-time support. A typical example of this is lawyers. I have rarely seen projects with a dedicated lawyer. The issue when getting part-time support from a specialist is to ensure your tasks get treated appropriately; for people like lawyers your task is often one of many important tasks and giving you absolute priority may not be possible. Also, such specialists rarely understand the knock-on effect of their work being late – this is not being pig-headed, but lawyers, for example, are often worried only about legal risk and not the fact that there may be a trade-off between removing *all* legal risk and completing work on time. Generalising, most specialists are more focused on quality in their field than hitting your project timelines. The rapid progress that you need may require them to take risks, which they are uncomfortable with. You will all have come across engineers, lawyers and software specialists, for example, taking time to deliver a higher quality output than you require, or than there is time to do. As a result, you will often find lawyers and other highly paid specialist activities on the critical path even if they were not originally expected to be so. This is sometimes unavoidable, but happens regularly because no-one takes the time to really explain the context of their work in the wider project.

All you can do in this situation is to ensure that the specialist in question has actually set aside time for your task, fully understands the implication of being late (so she can make a rational trade-off between getting absolute quality in her area versus the rest of the project), has a clear understanding of the quality required and the degree of risk acceptable to the project, and, finally, understands that you are an important client who needs to be satisfied. Whatever you do, never ask specialists like this for a zero-risk solution, unless you have an infinite amount of time to wait.

Tasks 16–17: The broader context

Management task 16 – Working with the wider organisation

Projects do not exist in isolation, and the primary role of most organisations is not to deliver projects. Any project you are involved with is being done to change something within the organisation in which it is being run. And yet it is very common for projects and project teams to forget this and in so doing to forget to manage their relationship and communications with the organisation in which they are operating.

❝ projects do not exist in isolation, and the primary role of most organisations is not to deliver projects ❞

The need to manage relationships with the wider organisation varies depending on the context and content of the project. For example, on specialised technical projects it may be a small task to think about how the project stays in touch with the wider organisation. On the other hand, on a major change programme it may be one of the dominant sets of activities in your plan. Whichever, you must be conscious that the project exists only for a limited period of time, and usually only for the longer-term benefit of the wider organisational community. On the other hand, the results of the project, if successful, will live for a long time.

This community typically needs to understand what will be delivered to them, when and sometimes even why. They must be prepared to accept the deliverables and their expectations must be managed as to the general impact of the project upon them. Assessing the communications requirement to do this and implementing this as an ongoing series of interactions, whether simple and informal or as a complex set of informal and formal communications, needs to be accepted as part of the project manager's role. In special circumstances the project manager will be supported by, or may even be working for, a change management or communications specialist who will deliver much of this task. But it is a task like any other that the project manager needs to ensure is performed well and in a timely fashion.

Management task 17 – Disbanding the project team

Projects come to an end – this is part of their very nature. Therefore, unlike other organisational units there is always a known time on a project when it comes to release people, either onto the next project, or back to the line management function they came from. Don't let this just happen by accident with people drifting off as they feel appropriate. Consider:

- Preparing early for disbandment; don't just suddenly arrive there.
- Completion of a project should not simply occur when a point in time is reached – closure happens with a conscious decision that the project has been completed and the deliverables are at a standard that allows closure.
- Managing the expectations as to when people will be released. Project timelines will often flex a little and original plans to let people go on one date may move as the project shifts. Similarly, manage team members' expectations as to when they will be free to go.
- Resisting pressure to let critical resources go too early.
- Staggering the release of people – it is unusual to be able to release everyone at once, but also it is unusual to need everyone right to the end of the project.
- Explicitly thanking people – especially those who have gone the extra mile. This is not just good manners; you may need the same people later on another project, so leaving them with a good feeling is useful.
- Feedback on team members' performance to their line managers.
- Holding a wrap-up session with the project team to bring together any lessons learnt.

Ending projects is discussed more in Chapter 12.

Table 8.1 provides a team management checklist, based on the contents of this chapter. Use it to review how you go about managing your project teams, and to identify where you may be able to improve.

table 8.1　Team management checklist

Aspect of team management – do you …	Yes	No
Ensure the project team has the right capabilities and skills – managing any gap between the abilities of the project team and the needs of the project as a risk?	☐	☐
Go for quality rather than quantity – going for fewer, better people who are easier to manage and will produce more?	☐	☐
Ensure all team members have clear roles and defined objectives?	☐	☐
Provide clarity about how you want people to work?	☐	☐
Manage poor performance, giving people a chance, but not hesitating to throw people off the project team if they are adding unnecessary or unmanageable risk?	☐	☐
Align personal objectives and motivation with the needs of the project – even without direct line authority over team members?	☐	☐
Actively work to build the team?	☐	☐
Align personal development needs and opportunities for team members with project activities?	☐	☐
If possible, ensure project team members have a home to go back to once the project is complete?	☐	☐
Consciously monitor and respond to team dynamics and team politics?	☐	☐
Try to get the project team working in close physical proximity, and manage the communications channels? Where it is not possible to get people to work in close proximity, do you make sure that communications chains are robust, and that people communicate in the most 'intimate' ways possible?	☐	☐
Remember your physically remote and geographically diverse staff, and involve and inform them as much as local staff?	☐	☐
Manage part-time staff effectively – not all resources will be full time, dedicated to your project?	☐	☐
Manage upwards effectively?	☐	☐
Manage specialists who are not dedicated to the project effectively?	☐	☐
Consciously remember the wider organisation – manage your relationship and communications with them?	☐	☐
Plan for the end of the project and disbanding the project team?	☐	☐

The limits of knowledge

So you are a project manager – you know what a project manager does, and you regularly put this successfully into practice. What can limit your success? There are two traps project managers sometimes fall into that can constrain their achievements. The first is to try to apply generic project management skills to the situation in which a specialist is required. The second is to try to do things that are best done by other people. To avoid these traps you need to understand the limits of your knowledge and skills.

This chapter sets out to discuss, explain and answer two key questions related to the boundaries of project management knowledge:

1   **When do you need a specialist who can manage a project, and when do you need a professional project manager?** In many situations project managers can be caught in debates to do with the fact that on the one hand project management skills are within many people's capabilities, so the question arises 'do we really need professional project managers?', while on the other hand there is a common thought that 'isn't project management a generic skill set that can be applied to any situation?'. This leads to the subsequent thought, 'surely someone who can manage one project can manage any other?' You need to understand this argument so that you apply your skills on appropriate projects, and also so that you can respond to this debate when it occurs. (Specialist in this context relates to any particular professional or functional discipline, e.g. lawyer, accountant, engineer, HR, IT, etc.).

2 **What is it that project managers really should not do?** In any profession it is useful to be able to understand what is outside the scope of your role and what is included. In the case of a project manager this is critical because the project manager is the person responsible for delivery of a project, so you will often find yourself filling the gaps in activities or skills not covered by others. There are many tasks to be completed on a project and there is a tendency for project managers to do a range of tasks which are better done by others. This chapter outlines some specific mistakes to avoid.

The generalist vs the specialist

Key lesson

Complex projects are best managed to successful delivery by people skilled in project management. Project management is largely a generic approach to managing projects, but being a project manager is not a completely generic skill that can be applied to any project in any situation. To be successful, project managers need to understand and be able to use the language, concepts and ideas which are used within the context of the project they are managing.

Let me split the world into two categories of people. This is an artificial split, but it will help with my initial explanation. Imagine there are only two types of people: generic project managers who only know about managing projects and have no other specialist knowledge, and specialists in various functional areas who know everything about that functional area but nothing about delivering projects. Which is better, the generalist project manager or the specialist non-project manager? The answer to that question is easy. If the world really did contain only these two extremes, it is obvious that for a project to be completed we need both: one type of person to manage work, the other to do the key delivery tasks requiring the specialist skills.

In reality the question that needs to be asked is slightly more complex, as there are two types of people who can reasonably be thought to be competent to take responsibility for delivering projects – the generic project manager (or perhaps more positively put, the specialist in project management) and the specialist or expert in a specific functional discipline, like IT, HR or finance, who can also manage projects. Which is better in any one situation?

The banal answer is whoever is more likely to achieve success on the specific project in mind. I will go into a little more detail before I leave it at that, as it would be fair to say that with this answer I am sitting on the fence. In practice, it depends on the scale, complexity and content area of the project.

As I have stated earlier in the book, there are plenty of people who have experience and training in project management, who call themselves 'project managers' and who spend their lives delivering projects. There are also other people who have experience and training in project management and who spend their lives delivering projects, but for various organisational or personal reasons have a different job title. This differentiation can be ignored and, whatever the job title, both at heart are professional generalist project managers or specialists in project management rather than in the content of the project. On the other hand, there are many other types of specialists – IT systems analysts, quantity surveyors, HR professionals, etc. – who may also have project management skills in addition to their core job skills. Which type of project manager is better for which type of project?

There are no absolute rules in these situations as to who is the better choice for a project manager, but my general guidance to people is this:

- **Part-time project managers should be used on small projects only.** On small non-complex projects it is perfectly acceptable for the project manager to do other things than project management. In fact, it is very likely that the project manager's role will be contained within one of the other specialist roles on the team. This specialist will have an ability to manage projects while fulfilling his or her own specialist role, and it avoids the costly overhead of a full-time project manager.

- **Project management is a specialist skill in its own right.** Do not assume that anyone and everyone can do it, or has the time to do it. Even if someone has been trained as a project manager they may not be a *good* project manager. Except for the simplest or smallest of projects, it is generally worth having a project manager who is really competent in managing projects. The overhead of a dedicated project manager will be easily recouped on a larger project. There are lots of factors that can make a project complicated, but my rough rule of thumb would be that when there are fewer than four people to manage on a project, the project manager's role can normally be absorbed within one of the other roles (although even then it will be a significant proportion of one person's role). If there are four or more full-time people on a project it is worth considering a full-time project manager; when there are eight or more it is essential.

▩ **If you have multiple skills in addition to project management, choose which 'hat you are wearing' in any one situation.** It is true that many specialists can also manage projects, but if you are working on a large or complex piece of work you need to be clear about your role. If you are the project manager, you need to focus on managing the project and not performing your specialist role. If you want to be the specialist then you should be the specialist and leave the project management to someone else. This is simply a function of having enough time to do what on a project of any significant size is a full-time job. (If you are tempted to perform both roles, please also read the next section in this chapter.)

▩ **Project managers do not need to be experts in what they are managing.** Project managers should not seek, unless from personal interest, to be expert specialists in every single discipline required on a project. The project manager who feels he needs to know as much about the content of the project as the specialists working on it is usually not understanding, or doing, the project management tasks required. For a very complex project there may be dozens of different specialities and it is simply not possible for the project manager to be an expert in all of them. *But* ...

▩ **Project managers must have relevant contextual understanding.** The generic project manager will not be successful in delivering every project. It is true that a project manager does very similar tasks within any project and so it is easy to draw the conclusion that any project manager can manage any project. The issue is really that project managers do not operate in a vacuum; they operate within a specific organisational and project context and with people who are used to that environment. Such organisations have their own concepts, language and jargon, and methods of working, and any specific project can have its own special area of focus within an organisation. Although the project manager does not need to be an expert in any of these, she does need to be able to talk the language of the people she is managing, and without understanding the details she needs to understand the concepts and approach of the people being managed. You cannot manage people you cannot talk to and share concepts with. To put it more positively: if, in conjunction with relevant specialists, you can plan their tasks, assess risks coming from the performance of those tasks, and communicate unambiguously with them, then you probably know enough about their specialist field to manage a project in that area. On the other hand, if you do not understand the basic concepts the specialists deal with and have difficulty talking to them, or understanding what they are doing, then you cannot manage a project in that area.

To help put this more explicitly I will give simple examples. If someone can manage a software delivery project for a financial system well, then with a little contextual information they can probably manage another major software delivery project, but unless they have significant additional experience they will not be able to manage the construction of a bridge or the delivery of an HR change process confidently. On the other hand, if someone is capable of managing a project to deliver a telecoms infrastructure for a bank, they should be able to do the same for other organisations such as a manufacturing company, as the basic task being managed will require very similar contextual knowledge and almost exactly the same project management skills.

> ❝ project management is a specialist skill in its own right ❞❞

If you are not working as a project manager, but hiring one or bringing in a contractor, and you cannot find anyone without directly relevant industrial experience, you will have to take someone from a different industry. One of the things to note is how quickly they try to pick up your jargon, your organisational oddities, your ways of working and your approaches. Those who pick it up quickly and consciously really are the most likely to be the closest to your needs.

If you are a project manager and have to consider whether you are competent to manage a project in any specific situation, ask yourself:

- Are you comfortable managing this scale of project?
- Do you broadly understand the content of the project and any associate concepts?
- Are you able to operate within the organisation this project is for? Do you broadly understand any specialist language and terminology they use?
- Can you plan, direct and control the various components of the project, assuming the necessary specialists are available to do the work?
- Can you assess the quality of the deliverables, or manage a process that will assess the quality of deliverables?

- Can you challenge the specialists competently? (For example, if someone says a task will take 50 days, can you challenge them to do it in 25 and understand the implications and consequences?)
- Will the project team and customer accept you and follow your instructions? Do you have credibility with them?

If the answer to all seven of these questions is 'yes', then you have enough specialist skills to manage the project. It you answer 'no' to one or more, at the very least you will need some support or to do some research. If you answer 'no' to several questions you should seriously consider your competency to manage the project. Use Table 9.1 to assess your skills to manage a specific project and determine what action to take. The higher you score yourself on a scale of 0 to 100% the more comfortable you should be managing the project and the less action you need to take. If you score 50% or less for several questions you should be seriously concerned about your ability to deliver the project.

table 9.1　Checking your suitability to manage a project

Question	Percentage conformance with question					So the action you will take is …
	0	25	50	75	100	
Are you comfortable managing this scale of project?						
Do you broadly understand the content of the project and any associated concepts?						
Are you able to operate within the organisation this project is for? Do you broadly understand any specialist language and terminology they use?						
Can you plan, direct and control the various components of the project assuming the necessary specialists are available to do the work?						
Can you assess the quality of the deliverables, or manage a process that will assess the quality of deliverables?						
Can you challenge the specialists competently?						
Will the project team and customer accept you and follow your instructions? Do you have credibility with them?						

What should project managers not do?

Project managers must respect the need for a range of specialist disciplines on their project, and must fight for all the resources the project needs. Being a project manager on a large project is a full-time job, and even if the project manager has the skills to do other tasks he must focus his time and energy on managing the project and not doing other project tasks.

This section looks at the reasons why project managers perform activities on projects that they should not perform, what these activities to be avoided are, and the impact on projects if they are done by the project manager.

> **❝ there are a number of tasks that project managers should avoid doing ❞**

There are a number of tasks that project managers should avoid doing, but in my experience often end up doing, and in doing them increase the risk of failure for the project. The reasons why they do these activities vary, but typically the explanations include the following:

- Project managers take the overall responsibility for delivering a project. They are the only person to do so in any individual situation. Due to resource shortages the skills of project teams are rarely perfectly aligned with the needs of the project. Projects are often short of one skill or another. Frequently, especially on smaller projects, the project manager personally ends up filling the gaps between the skills of the team allocated to the project and those needed. On a small project this can work, but it needs to be managed with care. I have seen many projects fail in which the project manager is perfectly competent but overloaded because he is doing too many things other than managing the project.

- Project managers often started out in their careers in different roles and so built other specialist skills beyond their project management skills. Think of IT project managers who normally start out in programming or analysis, or technical project managers who often started their careers as engineers. Again, on small projects there is no specific reason why they should not use their original skills, but as stated in the previous section, on a big project the role of project manager is full-time. If you are finding that it is not taking up all of your time, you are probably not managing the project properly. On a big project the project manager's role is to manage, not to work on or deliver the components.

▨ Finally, and often most dangerously, there are a number of specialist disciplines that may not be recognised at all, or may erroneously be seen as synonymous with being a project manager, or are simply not thought of as difficult, complex or time consuming. In the next section I discuss seven 'culprit' skills that regularly follow this pattern. The need for these skills may have been forgotten during the planning stage, and so appropriate resources are not scoped in, or the specialist task may be underestimated. Again, what happens is that there is a gap between the skills of the project team and the skills needed to complete the project. If this is happening then my advice to any project manager is to understand your own limitations and avoid overstepping them by trying to do the tasks yourself. If you have not planned these tasks in, don't bodge them by doing them yourself. Admit the mistake and get the people you need to do them to the quality you need. This may mean you need more time or more resources for the project, which your customer may not like, but better to do this than completely fail on a project. As a project manager you have your own deliverables to produce, such as plans and progress reports, which take time and skill and for which you should be respected. As a project manager you should respect the skills and time needed to do other things.

When project managers do undertake tasks that should not really be done by them, there are two specific risks that can occur:

1 The project fails because insufficient time is being spent on managing the project.
2 The project fails because the project manager is doing a task he or she is not expert at, and an expert is required. The project manager may do the tasks, but the tasks are not completed to the quality or scope required to deliver the project.

Both of these risks need to be avoided. I next look at the nature of these disciplines that the project manager should avoid. If you find yourself spending a large percentage of your time doing such activities, you are doing the wrong job.

Specialist skills that should be recognised as not being the project manager's job

Following this introduction is a list of seven 'culprit' skills that often fall to the project manager to do, which I cannot stress highly enough need to be treated as separate activities requiring specialist skills. On small projects all of these can be done by the project manager, but on large ones they should not. Business life is littered with projects that have failed, or that struggled with great difficulty to deliver, because the following skills were forgotten or were thought to be the direct responsibility of the project manager. In some cases the project manager has this background, but as stated above, he needs to focus on managing the project, not doing these things. What is so difficult about the specific disciplines noted here is that they are all things that project managers do need to understand something about, and in restricted ways may legitimately and regularly get involved in. However, this is quite different from taking primary responsibility for them in all situations.

The seven skills I have selected are simply examples, though common ones. Understanding when you should or should not personally be responsible for or involved in a task is a matter of judgement and balanced decision making. The truth is that any situation is rarely completely black and white. So, consider the points made here to help make a decision on whether to personally perform a task or not. (See the Summary section on page 206 at the end of this chapter for the decision making criteria.)

Culprit 1 – Business analysis and requirements capture

Many projects, such as IT development activities or new product development work, require the definition and documentation of complex requirements. If the requirements are wrong, incomplete, written in an overly ambiguous fashion or otherwise faulty, the project may well fail or may eventually prove to be pointless by delivering the wrong end product or service. In building, it is accepted that you need to be a trained architect to draw up an architectural plan for a customer before building work commences. The same thought needs to apply to IT developments and other technical development projects. The skill to understand customer requirements and write them down in a coherent way is that of a business analyst, and not a project manager. Many IT project managers do have analyst skills, but don't fall into the trap of 'because you can do it you should be doing it'. Project managers need to ensure that the process for requirements capture is robust, and do need to have a good overall understanding of the requirements, but that does not mean they must collect them.

(See Chapters 2 and 3 for a discussion of the definition of scope, which is a project manager's responsibility.)

Culprit 2 – Change management

Change management is a much-abused term. It has several meanings for different audiences and it is important when using this term to understand how you are using it and to ensure that your audience is using the same meaning. The three key uses of this term are:

1 **Project change management** – probably better called change control. This is the managed process of bringing changes to requirements or scope to a project. The objective of this is to ensure that any changes required are accepted by the project team and project sponsor, and that the impact is understood before they are accepted. It is a core skill of all competent project managers and is discussed in Chapter 7.

2 **Operational change management** – this is the management of bringing in changes to live systems of some sort. (A live system in this context is any form of technical system or process that is already operational and is needed for existing work or business services – the project is simply adding to this workload. It is most often used in connection with IT systems or networks, where changes regularly need to be made to a live system.) The objective of this is to reduce the risk to current services from making a change to them. For technical projects this is often the last thing that has to be done; the project's deliverables have to be implemented in the live environment passing through the operational change management process.

3 **People and organisational change management** – this is the management of change and its effects upon people and organisations, ensuring that the change is successful in the way it is implemented and adopted by the people who will be affected.

So in the context of what is out of scope for a project manager, I do not mean change control on the requirements or scope of a project, and I am not really worried about operational change management, but I mean the actual management of change to people and organisational units. It is unfortunate that this term has these three quite distinct meanings to three groups of people, as this can cause much confusion. The skill of managing the impact of change on people is very valuable and quite specifically different from project change control. Like writing software code or doing an architectural drawing, this is a very specific skill set – which many project managers are actually quite bad at. Many projects do require specialist change managers, and experienced change managers usually have at least an appreciation of project management, or may even be expert project managers. Many project managers have little or no workable knowledge of this type of change management, and trying to do without when required will often lead to project failure.

The complexity here is that there is an overlap between change management and project management skills, and they cannot be categorised as completely distinct disciplines. All projects result in a change that affects someone and therefore are possible candidates for change management. Most changes are implemented through projects. However, a change management skill set is different from a project management one – and completing a change is more than completing a project. This is discussed more in Chapter 12.

Culprit 3 – Systems integration and testing

A project frequently has many deliverables each produced by a different person or group of people. The project manager is responsible for ensuring they are all delivered, so presumably he is responsible for ensuring that they all work together? Wrong! He is responsible for ensuring that the integration and testing tasks are done and that the results are acceptable to the customer. Again we get to the difference between managing a task and doing it. Although many organisations understand it well, it is amazing how poorly integration and testing are generally understood as concepts by senior managers, and correspondingly they often look to cut them out when a project is running too long or costing too much.

Systems integration is essentially the skill of designing and implementing a solution from an end-to-end perspective rather than from the individual components. Typically on any engineered solution there are specialist engineers who will design and implement each component. There also needs to be someone who looks at all the components and ensures they work together to achieve the overall goals of the solution. A good analogy is with building a dry stone wall: it is great to have people collecting each stone, but you need to have someone with a view of how each stone will fit the others around it or else the wall will be unstable and fall down.

Explaining why a project needs a highly paid systems integration specialist when there are already well-paid engineers and project managers on a project can often be difficult. But do not avoid having them. Push back hard on any doubting managers. These are critical stages and vital skills in many projects, and you must insist you have the necessary integration and testing skills within your team. Without them the project is at risk, and you personally are at risk, as a failed project will always reflect badly on the project manager.

Culprit 4 – Supplier negotiations

Many people think they know how to negotiate a deal with a supplier, sometimes for as little a rational reason as they get good deals every time they buy a car from a garage. Although it is true that not everyone wants to do it, as it can be confrontational and difficult (though if handled well it does not need to be), too many people treat negotiating as a straightforward task. Please do not assume you know how to handle suppliers. For many small contracts it is not worth the overhead of procurement professionals and the project manager does pick up this task. But when it gets tough, or the deal is big enough, don't avoid using them. A few project managers are trained negotiators, but except in industries such as construction or in defence procurement projects, this is comparatively uncommon.

> **many people think they know how to negotiate a deal with a supplier**

You definitely need a specialist when the contract is for something unusual or different. The way to negotiate a deal say for cement will vary hugely from the way a deal needs to be struck and structured for buying TV programmes or IT software. I have worked with very successful negotiators who were specialists in both of these areas, and their approaches and style and the types of deals they struck were completely different. If you think you know how to handle a supplier and get a good deal then next time go in with a professional negotiator who knows this sector and see the difference.

Culprit 5 – Contract and legal issues

Contract and legal support are most often used in project situations when you are involved with third-party suppliers for whom a legal contract needs to be put in place. (On the other hand, you may be a third party delivering for a customer, and then your legal people need to be involved to check your side of the contract.) Sometimes projects have to operate within legal or regulatory frameworks, especially in regulated industries such as utilities, telecommunications or government work. Legal support is normally required to confirm compliance to the necessary rules and regulations. It should not be necessary to describe why you need legal experts to be involved, but it is common on projects I have seen for a senior manager to ask the project team whether they have run the project past the lawyers and to receive an embarrassed shake of the head as a response.

Don't hesitate to involve solicitors or lawyers when appropriate, but do not underestimate how long their work takes, or how tricky they can be to manage. In fact, the length of time lawyers take to do their work is a good reason to involve them early. It is amazing how often, rightly or wrongly, the legal team is on the critical path of a project (the reasons for this and how to overcome it were described in Chapter 8).

Culprit 6 – Project office

That the project manager should avoid taking on the project office tasks will surprise many people. After all, should not all project managers be able to manage a project office? Probably, and many project managers have started their careers in or running project offices. The reason why project managers should avoid the task is partially down to the much-repeated issue here of workload and their need to focus on delivery of the project, not on doing the administrative support offered by a project office. The other issue is that I often find, rather oddly, that many project managers are not very good at project office stuff, even though most rather arrogantly think they should find it easy. Of course, many projects cannot justify the overhead of a project office and so by default the project manager must do the work. The reality is, however, that on a complex programme a project office provides invaluable support to a project manager and the overall project. Like a project manager, a project office needs to be structured in approach; in addition, the sort of administrative and frequently pedantic focus on detail and adherence to the project management process are skills that not all project managers possess.

In practice there are four types of project offices (or POs for short) that I come across. You could argue whether these all really deserve the title 'project office', but they each regularly get it:

1   **Administrative support**. Sometimes all the PO does is support some administrative functions on projects, such as distributing reports, managing documents and arranging meetings. All are important tasks, but the project manager is not an administrator. (If you find

yourself doing this, ask the person employing you to let you go and employ a more economical administrator instead.) They may also perform the task of managing a document library and, depending on the context, this may simply be a useful bit of administration or it may be a task that is core to the success of the programme.

2 **Policing function**. Checking that project managers and projects adhere to some defined process standards. This can be checking the completion of regular reports or the use of the correct document formats, or confirming that things like issues and risks logs are kept. The policing function may simply be one of process adherence (i.e. checking you follow the steps you are meant to follow) or more substantially checking quality (i.e. checking not only that you follow the steps, but that you perform them well). This is most often done in companies that have teams of project managers on different projects, with the PO supporting the project managers' line manager. It is also done in situations where adherence to standards both is mandatory and must be auditable and provable. By its very nature this task cannot be done by the project manager.

3 **Expert support**. Tasks like planning or issue management can be done by a central team partially to remove the workload on project managers, but also to ensure a high standard is maintained. As an example, all competent project managers can plan – but they may not know all the planning features of the planning tool they use and expert support can help. This type of PO is often staffed by trained project managers who like the technical rather than the people side of project management. The task can be done by a project manager, but the point of having centralised support is then removed. Centralisation ensures common minimum standards are achieved.

4 **Portfolio or programme control**. The most advanced POs are those that not only administer but manage central plans, risk and issue registers, and look for and manage common items across projects in conjunction with programme managers. They may also consolidate project plans and manage inter-project and programme dependencies and potentially do cross-project resource management. These POs may require the technical skills of a very good project manager, but the potentially valuable task they are doing really is supporting projects and programmes and not managing them. If this is achieved, the project office can provide a powerful support to management, but it is difficult to accomplish. This is discussed more in Chapter 12.

If you have a small amount of administration to do, accept that this goes with the job. If you are running a large programme or portfolio of projects, set up a separate PO.

Culprit 7 – Communications

That the project manager should not take full responsibility for all communications may surprise some people, especially as I spent the majority of Chapter 2 stating how important communication skills are to a project manager. That is not in doubt. The key person responsible for communicating core information on the project such as progress, key issues and risks, changes and so on is the project manager. However, some projects have requirements that go beyond the need to communicate well with project customers and project team members. Projects that have been set up to drive things such as large organisational change activities often need much wider communication – for example, to thousands of staff affected across a company. This type of communication is more akin to a marketing, journalistic or PR skill set than straightforward communications by a project manager to customers or team members. Underestimating the complexity and need for really strong communications planning, structuring, development and delivery skills has undermined the outcome of many substantial programmes, especially those that impact large numbers of people.

When there is a significant communications task associated with a project then employ a professional communications manager. Even if they only support you on a part-time basis their input will be valuable.

Summary

Having looked at some areas which are close to the project manager's heart, but critically not his responsibility in all but the simplest project, what actually should he do about these? For every project manager my advice on these topics is:

▪ Get a basic level of competence in all of these areas – not so you can complete complex tasks in each area but so you can actively and fully interact with professionals in each of these disciplines and so you can manage them. Each of these seven culprit areas is regularly required on many projects. You may be able and have the time to complete the most basic tasks in each area – whether it is simple or small enough is a matter for your own judgement, but if you find any of these areas absorbing significant amounts of your time you are not managing the project.

> Learn when and how to engage people in each of these areas – some of them you will normally need only for parts of a project. In fact, it is very useful to have a personal network of people skilled in these areas, both to call onto your projects but also to go to for advice.

> Learn to use their language and concepts so you can manage and challenge them without doing their job. Not being responsible for a particular specialist's work does not mean you will not be responsible for the quality of the output if it affects the success of the project.

> If you do engage them make sure your project sponsor understands why it is not your task and what the specialist brings. Some of these skill sets are in short supply and can be expensive to use. If your sponsor thinks these are your roles then, unless he or she understands the value they bring, it can cause tension between you.

Ask yourself four questions if you are unsure whether to pick up a task or not:

1 Do you understand the task well enough to be able to fully scope out what needs to be done?

❝ learn to use their language and concepts so you can manage and challenge them ❞

2 Do you have the knowledge and experience to complete the tasks to the quality required and without exposing the project to unnecessary risk?

3 Is the input of a professional in this area optional? (Some tasks have to be performed by qualified professionals for legal, audit or regulatory reasons.)

4 Do you have the time to do this work without jeopardising your project management responsibilities?

Only if you can answer 'yes' to all four of these questions should you do the task. Table 9.2 provides a summary checklist to confirm whether you should do the task. For any skill that has a single 'no' against it you should not do the tasks associated with it. (You can add further skills beyond the seven 'culprits' I have identified in the bottom rows of the table.)

table 9.2 Determining whether the project manager should be responsible for a task

Skill	Do you understand the task well enough to be able to fully scope out what needs to be done?	Do you have the knowledge and/or experience to complete the tasks to the quality required, without exposing the project to unnecessary risk?	Is the input of a professional in this area optional?	Do you have the time to do this work without jeopardising your project management responsibilities?
	Y / N	Y / N	Y / N	Y / N
Business analysis/requirements capture				
Change management				
Systems integration and testing				
Supplier negotiations				
Contract and legal issues				
Project office				
Communications				
....				
....				
....				
....				

The mechanics of project management

The project manager's toolkit

Project management methodologies contain a rich set of approaches and tools, yet project managers frequently apply only a few of these. Do not forget the other components which on complex and risky projects will be very useful. Successful project managers have a very broad toolkit which they make use of regularly.

When people perform any role they rely on a combination of the natural skills and common sense they possess, their experience, available tools, formal processes and procedures, and any relevant training they have had. This book has so far focused on improving your natural skills, strengthening your common sense, and describing experienced-based lessons.

I have largely avoided conversation on the typical project management subjects of most project management textbooks: organisations and roles, disciplines and processes, standards, templates and tools, because these are not the things that separate the great from the average project manager. But now that we have reached this late chapter it is time for reflection and discussion on these areas. This chapter is not a master class in these subjects, merely a pointer to them, and an appeal to learn the relevant techniques.

A large part of being a good project manager is about having and applying common sense, structure and logic, and normal good management disciplines. In saying this I am not belittling the core specialist skills of project managers, such as an ability to resource work, to develop a plan and maintain it through the life of a project, or to resolve issues and mitigate risks. These are fundamental things every project manager should know that will make life more structured and reliable than simply applying common sense, and will avoid some of the pitfalls that common sense alone will not navigate around. In reality, I have not focused on these because of the ongoing success of good project management discipline and training. These things are increasingly a given and therefore do not become the differentiating factor between the average and the excellent project manager. When I started in project management a formally trained project manager was a rarity; increasingly now he or she is the norm. But even with the training and accreditation there are a few core skills that are regularly documented and in which project staff are trained, but which somehow get left behind or forgotten. And we all know project managers who have done every course under the sun and have every qualification yet who are frankly useless, and others who have picked it up as they went along who are brilliant.

> **when I started in project management a formally trained project manager was a rarity; increasingly now he or she is the norm**

This chapter describes the mechanics and the toolkit of project managers. I have excluded the things that are not relevant to this book, or that are simply not differentiating factors in project managers' success. Primarily this encompasses:

- Creating standard documents, including documents such as 'project initiation documents'. It is the thinking that goes into creating these documents that matters, not the formats. The underlying principles of some were discussed in Chapters 3 and 5. Actual templates are organisation specific.

- Use of common project management software, such as planning tools like Microsoft Project. Tools are useful and can make you significantly more productive. They are not covered here, as the knowledge is specific to whichever tool you have selected. More importantly, your success is still dependent on the understanding of projects that you implement with the tool, not on the tool itself.

Additionally, I have excluded the things that are covered elsewhere in the book to a significant depth. These are essential parts of the toolkit and include:

- Planning and resourcing, including how to build a plan starting with work breakdown structures. (See Chapter 3 judgement 2, and Chapter 5.)
- Project change control procedures – how to capture, assess, choose and implement changes with controlled risk. (See Chapter 3 judgements 10, 11 and 15, and Chapter 7.)
- Decision making. (See Chapter 7.)
- Creating weekly and monthly reports to a standard format. (See Chapter 2, communication lesson 2.)
- Allocation of resources and management using tools such as timesheets and time recording systems. (See Chapters 5 and 8.)

So what is left? There are a number of other things which should lie within the standard project manager's toolkit but seem to be used inconsistently. I make no claim that these things are new or novel, although my definitions here all contain my perspective on what is practically useful. What I do see is that somehow many project managers fall into one of three traps:

1 They use some of the skills – perhaps the ones they are most familiar with or like most. But they miss others pretty regularly. It is true that many of the skills here are not critical on small projects, but on large or complex programmes they add significant value.

2 They apply the skills in an extremely complex fashion. The real talent is not to apply these tools in a highly complex fashion. It is easy to blind yourself and your team members with too much science, whereas most of these tools have their roots firmly in straightforward common sense. The great project manager therefore understands what the tool can achieve and then applies it in the simplest fashion relative to the need. This need is usually driven by the complexity and scale of the project.

3 They do not see the full toolkit as a holistic continuum, which must be adapted and used according to the situation rather than purely mechanically applied. Each of their projects has the same set of disciplines applied in exactly the same way.

To overcome these traps, project managers must see the disciplines as a toolkit to pick from, not a mandatory and rigid set of instructions. Each tool should be understood, and before each project and project issue you should assess which tools to use. Comprehending how all the tools come together into the complete framework of project management skills and then applying them appropriately is essential.

The following list is a personal view. It contains twelve skills in two groups. The first group when combined with the skills described in Chapters 5 and 7 form the core project management mechanics. The second group are supporting skills. Don't worry about the second group until you are proficient in the first.

Skills 1–7 form the core project management mechanics and as are follows:

- Management of assumptions.
- Sign-off.
- Management of external dependencies.
- The time–cost–quality–scope trade-off.
- Risk and issue management.
- Contingency planning and triggers.
- Using escalation effectively.

Skills 8–12 form the supporting mechanics and are as follows:

- Stakeholder analysis.
- Use of project office.
- Administration and management of meetings.
- Prioritisation.
- Use of project lifecycles.

Key lesson

Good project managers accept that each and every project is different, and they therefore adapt their approach accordingly – choosing which parts of the project manager's toolkit to apply in which situations – and applying them in the simplest fashion commensurate with the complexity and scale of the project.

Skills 1–7: The core project management mechanics

Skill 1 – Management of assumptions

Within every activity in everyday life we make hundreds of assumptions. Some of these are quite reasonable, and the chance of them being false is minuscule. (For example, we assume that when we wake up in the morning there will still be air to breathe; the risk of this not being true is infinitesimal so we do not worry.) Other assumptions don't matter because if they prove to be false, their impact upon us is limited. (For example, I will assume that the chair by my desk will still be there tomorrow; I do not worry about it as otherwise I will just pull up another.) But there is a third group of assumptions that need to be looked at because there actually is a risk they may not be true, and if they are not true we may be in trouble. (For example, I may assume I do not need to wear a seat belt because I will probably not crash my car – this needs more consideration, as there *is* a measurable risk of having a car crash and the consequences could be serious!)

Many risks on projects are due to the assumptions that people make. It is possible to argue that you do not need assumption management and it is just part of risk management. It is true that you can phrase all risks as assumptions, and all assumptions as risks – and equally your risk management process is quite capable of managing assumptions. However, I like the rigour of deliberately identifying and managing assumptions. I find that in practice if I don't deliberately manage assumptions, some are forgotten with regularly painful consequences.

Making assumptions is not necessarily a bad thing. There are times when we cannot know an answer to something with certainty, and we cannot progress without making an assumption. In these situations the temptation in projects is often very strong to continue working by making an assumption, as otherwise we may feel we are not making progress. When this occurs it is worth challenging the situation with the question 'do we really need to make an assumption?'

There are a couple of poor reasons for making an assumption that need to be resisted: firstly, someone may simply be too lazy to put in the effort to find the real answer, and secondly, by making caveats around assumptions people can avoid making real commitment. So when an assumption is being proposed always check that it is not just laziness or people covering themselves from personal risk. The first is relatively easy to spot, the second is harder to identify. People, especially professional specialists like engineers and lawyers, unfortunately love to give caveats and reasons, often in the form of assumptions, that although they are giving you their best advice there are several assumptions they have had to make which may mean they are wrong. Feel no qualms about challenging them and asking whether the assumptions are reasonable. Why do they have to make them, and what can they do to remove them? Specialists generally do not like this, but developing work on possibly shaky foundations needs to be challenged. You are not employing specialists to build a logically great argument from whatever set of assumptions they make. They are being paid often significant sums of money to be right.

When making an assumption for valid reasons there is normally an explicit choice between making it so you can continue to progress, or stopping your work to spend time checking the assumption. (In Chapter 4 I looked at forming a judgement of when it is valid to make an assumption.) I have been involved in situations in which the assumption was so fundamental that, if wrong, the whole project was pointless. In this position it is worth putting more work into understanding the assumption even if it delays your project. As an example, I once worked on a project to deliver a new product to a customer segment which initial market research had identified. We had to make a number of assumptions about the behaviour of this group, but we did not actually test them as we thought the cost of the necessary detailed market research was too great and it would take too long. However, our assumptions turned out to be false. Unfortunately, by the time we found out we had got a long way into developing a product based on them. Once the assumptions were shown to be false the product we were developing was largely pointless. A little more investment in market research at the start of the project would have avoided this problem.

So, it is essential to minimise the number of assumptions you make. There will be some left, and sometimes you should make assumptions, but as a major source of risk these need to be managed. The key to managing assumptions is to:

- **Identify the assumptions** – this is often the hardest step as we are completely unconscious of many of the assumptions we make.
- **Document them** – like many things, forcing yourself to write assumptions down makes you think through what the assumption really is. Seek clarity and avoid ambiguity. (See Figure 10.2 below).

▓ **Challenge them** – check they are relevant and reasonable. Do you really need to make an assumption? Is the chosen assumption actually the most reasonable?

▓ **Assess them** – prioritise action on those assumptions that are most likely to be wrong, and those that will have the most significant impact if wrong. Eliminate assumptions that are irrelevant.

▓ **Assign an owner** – the owner's role is to ensure the assumption is resolved, i.e. it is turned from an assumption to a fact during the project. When it becomes a fact the risk is removed.

▓ **Set target dates to resolve them by** – each assumption must have a clear date in the project that it has to be resolved by. This can be at any point in the project, depending on the nature of the assumption. The aim here is not just to forget them. People have a tendency to list assumptions and then to forget them, using the mentality that if they are listed that in itself solves the problem. By the time the project is finished there should be no assumptions – any that are left should not have any impact on the project and were unnecessary to log. (There are exceptions to this, and those are assumptions relating to the business case, which may be false without impacting delivery of the project. These are discussed in Chapter 12.)

▓ **Communicate them** – if you are going to have an assumption you want the whole team to know, and the whole team to be using the same assumptions! Simply doing this has significant power as it can generate a fantastic amount of clarity across the team. Regularly, when an assumption is shared, someone in the project team will challenge it, or show an alternative contradictory assumption they are making. If you do nothing else, make your assumptions explicit and shared.

▓ **Monitor them** – and be prepared to manage the consequences if the assumption turns out not to be true. Your big assumptions should appear as core items in your risk management activities.

▓ **Resolve assumptions** – especially if the assessment of an assumption shows there is both a major likelihood of it being wrong and there is a major impact on the project if it is wrong. By resolving it I mean turning it from an assumption into a fact. Sometimes with more research and analysis, assumptions can be proven one way or another. If the risk to the project is big enough, this is worth doing even if it delays the project.

This process is shown in Figure 10.1 and the typical contents of an assumption logging form are in Figure 10.2.

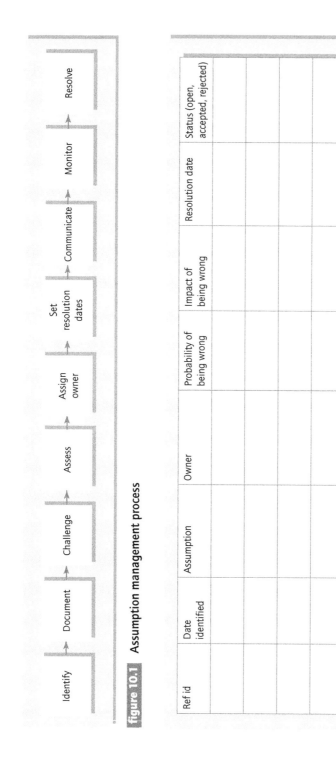

Identify → Document → Challenge → Assess → Assign owner → Set resolution dates → Communicate → Monitor → Resolve

figure 10.1 Assumption management process

Ref id	Date identified	Assumption	Owner	Probability of being wrong	Impact of being wrong	Resolution date	Status (open, accepted, rejected)

figure 10.2 Assumption logging form

Here are two examples of poor assumption management in which I was involved. The first is of a project on which we needed three days' input from an academic. The assumption was so trivial as to be missed, yet had a great impact. The academic's work was crucial to the project's success, he agreed to do it, and because it was only three days' work and we were paying well he advised us that with a couple of weeks' notice during normal working time he would be available to support us. We duly went back to him when we knew we would need his input and gave him his two weeks' notice. Unfortunately we had assumed we understood what he meant by 'normal working time'. As an academic this did not include the period from mid-June through to late September (he was working then, but abroad at summer placement in another university). We could therefore not get his input at the right time and the project was delayed as a result.

The second example was a telecommunications project I supported, which was delivering a new product which meant we had to install equipment in our customers' homes. The equipment was not attractive, but we assumed that it would be tucked away in houses and the look was unimportant. For a small fee (about £10 per home, which was not great given the equipment's cost was about £150 per home) the supplier could put a new fascia on the equipment which made it more attractive. We assumed the cost was too great for our customer, and the impact on their end customers was low. In practice, the equipment was generally placed in a visible location in the end customers' homes. It had to be re-engineered at a later date, at a much higher cost, as end customers continually complained about how it looked.

In both cases, had we identified the assumptions we were making we could have better managed the situation.

Skill 2 – Sign-off

Most good project management methodologies have the concept of getting some form of sign-off from sponsors whenever anything major changes. This could be changes to the scope, the time to deliver, or the cost to deliver. Customers never really like doing this, but it is good practice, it is important and problems can occur if it is not done. Almost all project managers understand this. A lot don't bother to do it. When was the last time you actually got your sponsor to formally sign off a change in cost or time for a project?

When discussing such a change with a customer try not to present it as a *fait accompli* – the customer should not simply be agreeing to an error in planning, he should be making a decision about whether to accept something or not. He therefore needs options. Additionally, check that the change is consistent with the customer's priorities on the time–cost–quality–scope trade-off.

Sign-off is not simply about transferring personal risk from you, the project manager, to the sponsor. This is not a constructive mindset to have. Sign-off is about ensuring that when key decisions are made the signatory is treating them as a serious issue. Without sign-off there is a higher risk that the signatory will not fully accept what is being agreed or will not put in enough effort into understanding what she is signing up to. It is also about providing a formal audit trail of decisions should you need to revisit them at any time.

Skill 3 – Management of external dependencies

Usually, complex projects have dependencies on other activities that are not within the project's scope or responsibility to deliver. This is the well-known concept of an external dependency. The questions that need to be asked in these situations are:

- What project or piece of work is delivering the dependency?
- Who is accountable for ensuring the work you are dependent upon is being delivered?

It is surprising how often project managers simply write an assumption in their scope document saying they assume that someone else is delivering it, and leave it at that. Even if the customer has accepted this point, a successful project manager does not leave it at that. If the project needs it and it is not delivered, the project may fail. Failing to deliver a project because an external dependency has not been delivered may not be the project manager's fault, but it is failure nevertheless.

The balance to find here is that, as delivering the dependency is not within the scope of the project, it really is not the responsibility of the project manager to deliver. If, as a project manager, you try to deliver every possible dependency, you may end up trying to manage too much. All you need to do is:

- Try to see if you can remove the dependency – some things that are seen as dependencies when further challenged are not. Find out precisely why the task in the project is dependent on this external activity. (If it is for a trivial reason it is often possible to sort this out within the confines of the project.)

- Ensure somebody somewhere is responsible for delivering the dependency. If no-one is, raise this with the sponsor as a significant risk you cannot resolve.
- Monitor delivery of the dependency by getting periodic updates on progress so you can assess the degree of risk on the project if it is not delivered on time.
- On critical dependencies do not simply accept statements of progress; probe the progress reports as you would any part of your own project to give yourself confidence that they are accurate.

If a dependency is crucial to the project, and you cannot identify anyone with responsibility for ensuring it is delivered, it really is a good idea at least to assess bringing it within the project's scope, even if it increases your workload.

This problem partially disappears if the project is part of a larger programme, when the management of dependencies is usually the responsibility of the programme manager. But even the largest of programmes have boundaries and resulting external dependencies.

Challenge yourself on each project: do you really understand where all your external dependencies are and who is delivering them?

Skill 4 – The time–cost–quality–scope trade-off

In Chapter 3 we discussed how important it is to understand where the customer stands on the dimensions of time, cost, quality and scope, and what can flex. While virtually all project managers understand and pay attention to this, in practice project managers are poor at turning it into a structured decision-making process and action. Understanding what the time–cost–quality–scope trade-off means in reality for the project you are currently running, rather than simply as a bit of project management theory, and then using this knowledge to structure and manage your project, is critical for success. You will use this information both in the major decisions about how you shape and plan your project, but also in the myriad of daily decisions on a project.

Do not fall into the trap of being one of those 'heroic' project managers who delivers on time at any cost, and uses delivery to time as the single measure of success. Project managers, project management literature and business culture have unconsciously conspired to build the image of time as the factor of most importance. The press hounds major projects that are late, in a way that they rarely do for budget overruns or reductions in quality. Time is sometimes the most critical factor, but not always. Don't assume you know how important time, cost or quality are. Ask your customer, explain the implications, and proactively use this knowledge in managing the project.

Skill 5 – Risk and issue management

Issue and risk management are two of the fundamental disciplines of project management. You can read huge books dedicated to these subjects, especially risk management, but for most projects complex risk management is not really required.

The first thing to understand about risks and issues is that their management is as much about attitude and proactive management as it is about formal processes and tools. The vital points to understand and apply for both risk and issue management are:

- Communicate to the project team that these are important, they will be managed, and there is a defined process. Make sure the team understand that they, as well as the project manager, should be looking out for issues and risks, and should keep themselves aware of them.

- Define how you capture them – avoiding bureaucracy. Capturing issues and risks needs to be light-touch, making sure you get the key information in a simple way. I have seen major bureaucracies being developed to capture issues and risks in which the process of capture becomes more important than their assessment. Simple forms capturing the following are sufficient in most cases:
  - Description
  - When identified
  - Owner
  - Resultant action
  - Due by
  - Probability (risk only)
  - Impact
  - Current status.

- In documenting any issue or risk be as specific as possible, and make the definition relevant. Unclear or overly broad definitions can waste significant project resource.

- What do you then do? Knowing your issues and risks, you need to assess them and determine what action to take. Once you know what action to take, it should be implemented and managed by the project manager like any other task.

- It needs to be an ongoing activity – project managers are often guilty of doing periodic exercises on risk and issue management, then forgetting them in between. These are continuous processes that should be part of your daily routine. Issues and risks should be nipped in the bud; what is a small problem that is resolvable now may grow into something unmanageable.

Figures 10.3 and 10.4 show process flows for issue and risk management. Figures 10.5 and 10.6 show the outlines of simple forms for logging issues and risks.

You need to be able to communicate the difference between an issue and a risk. An issue is something you need to resolve now to ensure progress can be made; it can usually be phrased as a question which you need to answer. A risk is a prediction of something that may potentially happen that will have an impact on the project. By understanding it in advance you have the opportunity to mitigate or remove its impact should it occur. Risk management is one way of avoiding issues arising. Understanding issues and risks is about driving management action, not simply about collecting information or assessment.

It is worth exploring risk management a little more. Good project managers have an affinity with risk. They may not like it, but they have a sense for it, and they understand that at regular intervals unexpected things will occur. You can argue that project management *is* risk management: if nothing changed and there was no risk of anything changing once a plan was complete, there would be no need to manage the project – it would just happen.

❛❛ good project managers have an affinity with risk ❜❜

Risk management processes will help you assess and manage risks, but only if you identify them in the first place. You need to develop the ability to predict issues and risks before they arise and plan what you need to be ready to do should they occur. The sources of risks will vary from project to project, but generically they come from five main sources:

1 Technical – risk that the deliverables being proposed cannot actually be delivered or will not work.

2 Management – risk that there are neither the management skills nor resources to deliver the project.

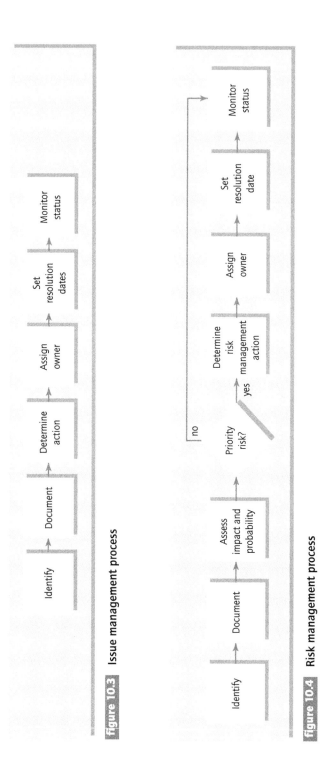

figure 10.3 Issue management process

Identify → Document → Determine action → Assign owner → Set resolution dates → Monitor status

figure 10.4 Risk management process

Identify → Document → Assess impact and probability → Priority risk? → yes → Determine risk management action → Assign owner → Set resolution date → Monitor status

no

Ref id	Date identified	Issue description	Impact	Resolution	Owner	Resolution due date	Next update due	Status (open, closed)

figure 10.5 Issue logging form

Ref id	Date identified	Risk description	Owner	Probability of occurring	Impact occurring	Overall risk rating	Risk management action	Resolution date	Status (open, resolved)

figure 10.6 Risk logging form

3 Requirement – risk that the requirements are not fully specified or not understood in the way meant by the customer.

4 Acceptance – risk that the customer will not accept the deliverables once they are complete.

5 Environment – risk that something that affects the project will change or is not understood in the environment in which the project operates.

You should be able to differentiate mentally between personal and project risks. Project risks are those things that may impact your ability to deliver; personal risks are those things that may impact your personal reputation. The reason I highlight this is that in the rush to please and be seen to be effective, project managers often hide issues and risks from their customers. You may please your customer in the short run, but if the risk actually develops and the project is delayed you have done no-one any favours, and you have essentially converted what was a project risk into a personal risk. At best you look incompetent, at worst you look like a liar.

Good project managers instinctively know about the need for options when projects go wrong. Unfortunately it is a rare project that actually gets beyond the very basic step of thinking vaguely about options. Risk management should be a continuous living process in a project, not a one-off or even periodic exercise that results in a list of things in a document. The key things to do are:

- Be clear what the risk is. Often project managers get themselves tangled in knots of defining the word risk. For example, there is a risk that the project will be late. Project managers write down the risk as 'the project may be late'. This is not a risk in project management terms – this is the effect of the risk. The risk is whatever may cause the project to be late. You must identify the root cause, as the root cause is what you can take action against.

- Where there is significant uncertainty use a phased project lifecycle that enables you to understand and manage risk as your understanding of the project expands (see skill 12, page 239).

- Ensure your project has a robust risk management approach, and regularly identify and review the risks that you have. The level of formality here does depend on the context. (For example, a business-critical project using novel technology with a fixed end date may require intense risk management. A project on a familiar subject, following an often repeated path with little impact if the end date is moved, needs only a more *ad hoc* and lighter-touch approach.) The approach that I undertake to identifying risks is to run a brainstorming session at the start of the project. I then periodically regroup throughout the life of the project to reassess this, and to accept risks from team members as they become apparent throughout the project's life. Remember, though, that the only risks you are interested in are those that can impact the project directly and that you can manage. You are not trying to create a risk management process for the whole organisation you are working in. Be careful, therefore, quite how much detail you go into in environmental risks – yes, a meteorite may hit the earth and kill everyone, stopping your project, but you cannot change this or do anything about it and adding it to your risk register adds no value.

- Assess these risks to see whether any of them results in a significant chance of something occurring with a significant impact on the project. If this is true you need to do something about the risk. You can spend a lot of time working out a scale for assessing risks and then assessing the risks against it. Almost universally I find a scale of high, medium or low for probability and impact is sufficient except on the largest of programmes.

- Plan what you can do about the risk. This essentially falls into four categories:

  - Maintain a watching brief – i.e. do nothing but monitor the situation and do something only if the risk increases or the impact increases. This is a valid option if the risk is not currently impacting your work and is monitored really regularly (and not simply written down and forgotten about).

  - Mitigate against the risk – which essentially means doing things that will reduce the chance of the risk occurring. An example is where there is a risk that your project will run out of funds, so you seek agreement to a contingency budget. The risk of your running out of money has been removed.

  - Mitigate against the impact of the risk – which essentially means doing things that will reduce the impact should the risk occur. For example, if funds are short you could look at ways a project could be done more cheaply, or even free using internal resources, should your budget run out. In this situation the risk has occurred (you have run out of money), but the impact on the project was reduced.

– Have a contingency plan – i.e. do things now on the assumption that the risk will occur. This is discussed below. You cannot have a contingency plan for every risk, but if the impact of a risk on a project is great enough and the project is important enough, you should consider having contingency plans. There is a resource–risk trade-off to be made, as even the simplest plan will absorb some additional resource. This is described more in the next sub-section, skill 6.

Modern project management practice also acknowledges the existence of positive risks, or opportunities. An opportunity is a 'risk' that something might go better rather than worse. It is definitely worth looking out continuously for better ways to manage the project and to identify improvements as you go. Whether it is formally worth managing opportunities through the risk management process is a subject of debate between project managers. It will certainly not do any harm!

Skill 6 – Contingency planning and triggers

Contingency planning is a complex subject, and good contingency plans require insight and creativity as well as structure. A contingency plan can be anything that you can implement to remove the impact of a risk when it occurs. Many project managers struggle when it comes to good contingency planning. The key points to think through with respect to contingency plans are as follows.

■ **What triggers your contingency plan?** People often assume that what will trigger a contingency plan being activated is a risk occurring. If true, this is ideal as it will avoid using up resources on something that may not be needed. Unfortunately, because of the length of time they take to implement, for many contingency plans to be useful they have to be activated before a risk has occurred. The trigger may be something as simple as a date – if activity x has not completed by time y we will implement the contingency. Activity x has not yet actually failed, but for the contingency plan to be effective it needs to be started at the latest by time y. There may alternatively be some other trigger related to the risk becoming more likely or having higher impact. Unless you understand when to implement the contingency plan, it is largely worthless. This is shown in Figure 10.7.

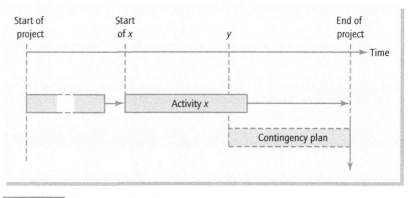

figure 10.7 Understand contingency triggers

- **Do you have the resources to implement the contingency plan?**
  Here we get to the point that undermines many projects having
  contingency plans. Implementing contingency plans increases the
  chance of success, but it will require resources. The choice a project
  manager has in this situation is to take resources from the existing
  project with obvious potential impacts, or ask the sponsor for more.
  Rare is the sponsor who happily gives up resource to cover for
  something that may not happen, remembering that in the event that
  a risk does not occur and the contingency is not needed all the work
  on the contingency is effectively thrown away. However, if the risk is
  likely enough, and if the impact on the project is significant enough,
  then the investment is worthwhile. It is somewhat analogous to an
  insurance premium – you hope you won't need it, and if you don't,
  the money can be said to be wasted, but when you do need it you will
  be very glad of it.

- **Does it actually reduce risk?** This may seem obvious, but I have
  frequently seen contingency plans that are far riskier than the original
  project. In the desperation to find a contingency I have seen people
  come up with all sorts of creative (but in reality hare-brained) ideas.
  The point is that people will often have the best solution in the
  project and if a contingency plan has a lower-risk solution this should
  have been adopted by the project in the first place. If a contingency
  plan is more risky than the original plan, it may work (as even with a
  99% chance of failure you may happen to be in the 1% that
  succeeds), though, it is not a good sign. An effective, worthwhile
  contingency needs to be significantly less risky than the original plan.
  A simple example: if you absolutely have to get somewhere and your

car is not very reliable then you may make a contingency plan based on alternative transport, but if this is even more unreliable than your car there is little reduction of risk.

■ **What can you de-scope if the choice is not delivering?** What often makes contingency plans less risky is that they rely on delivering only a subset of the full set of deliverables already planned. This may not achieve all the success factors of the project and may not be popular with your customers, who will see most of the components of the project as 'must haves'. However, if people are faced with the choice of de-scoping or having nothing at all, it is remarkable how easily they manage to reduce the list of 'must haves'.

Skill 7 – Using escalation effectively

Escalation is a core weapon in the project manager's armoury of tools to get things done. It can be used to get involvement of senior people (for example, to get more resources or decisions made), and it can also simply be used as a threat to recalcitrant team members. I do not advise too much use of the latter as it is a sign of weak management, but used occasionally and sparingly it can be very powerful. Many project managers are reluctant to escalate as they see it as failure, or, more commonly, use escalation as a dumping ground for everything they either cannot do or for some reason will not do.

Good escalation is used sparingly, but it can be valuable. Your sponsor or other senior person to whom you should escalate is a part of the project too and will have to do some work from time to time. As discussed in Chapter 4, judging the appropriate time to escalate is a fundamental understanding a project manager must develop.

> 66 good escalation is used sparingly, but it can be valuable 99

When you decide you need to escalate, put yourself in the shoes of the person to whom you are escalating. Gather the information this person will need to help you and do it at the earliest opportunity. For example, if you cannot get a person allocated to your project whom you think you need, you may escalate to a senior manager to get that person released to you. The first thing the senior manager is likely to ask you is what this person is doing now and what the impact would be of stopping that job to work on your project. To save time and appear more professional it is best to be able to answer questions like these straight away.

While it is important not to be too ready to escalate, once it is necessary it needs to be done straight away. The person you are escalating to has the right to expect some time to think things through and receive notice of problems. There is nothing that irritates senior people more than being forced into a corner at the last moment because you have sat on an issue for too long.

When you have escalated, remember you are still the project manager. Just because the item for resolution is with someone more senior does not remove your responsibility to manage the attainment of that resolution like any other task on the project.

Your attitude with regard to escalation should be to see it as a supporting aid to you and the project team and you should limit its use as a threat or weapon. For example, when someone had no time to allocate to your work, do not threaten them with escalation as if they will get hit over the head, but present it to them as an aid that will enable them legitimately to focus on your work with their manager's support.

Skills 8–12: Supporting mechanics

Skill 8 – Stakeholder analysis

Formal stakeholder analysis approaches are a useful tool for any manager, but especially for a project manager. The basic principles of assessing people's attitude towards a project (from very negative to very positive), and their power to influence the outcome can give a powerful picture of whom you need to work with and, bluntly, whom you can ignore. Successful projects need sponsors and advocates and need to ensure either either that those who oppose the outcome are brought on board or that their influence is managed away.

Many project managers have at best a limited theoretical knowledge of stakeholder analysis and at worst no knowledge of it at all. Really strong management of stakeholders is not required on all projects and on some can be pretty much ignored. However, on projects like organisational change or others that impact large numbers of people, or on those that have some faction opposed to them, assessment of the stakeholders and planning of positive actions to change their view or mitigate their actions can be essential.

The basis of stakeholder analysis is so simple as to almost make one wonder why it is so useful. Essentially, it relies on categorising stakeholders according to how much impact they can have on a project, and how favourably they view the project. (Do not fall into the trap of thinking that this conceptually simple task is easy to do – it can take real effort on a major project.) I always stick to a very simple four-way split – people fall roughly into the following four categories:

1 High impact, high support – use these people to get resources and drive support for the project. Your sponsor must be within this group; if not, the project will be problematical.

2 High impact, low support – powerful people who oppose the project are the ones you must most actively manage. Think about what you can do to get their support or, if this is not possible, mitigate against any activity they may do to oppose the project.

3 Low impact, high support – people who support the work but have little real influence on its outcome. Use these people to help you get work delivered and to support any resulting change in the organisation.

4 Low impact, low support – people who oppose the work but have little real influence on its outcome. Formal processes will indicate how you need to convince these people. My view is you need to monitor them in case their influence increases, but otherwise you can ignore them. (The main exception here is on organisational change or other programmes where people generally may need to accept the change and deliverables if it is to be a success. Then this group must be managed very carefully.)

This is shown in Figure 10.8.

Skill 9 – Use of project office

All project managers are aware of project offices, although many will have wildly different experiences of them. When do you need one, and what does it do?

Whatever the theoretical literature and methodologies may state, project offices in practice come in one of four types (which are defined in more detail in Chapter 9):

1 Administration pools

2 Process police

3 Expert support

4 Portfolio and programme control (information consolidators).

The simple answer to what it will do is that it depends on what it has been set up to do. You may set up a project office to carry out some specific tasks

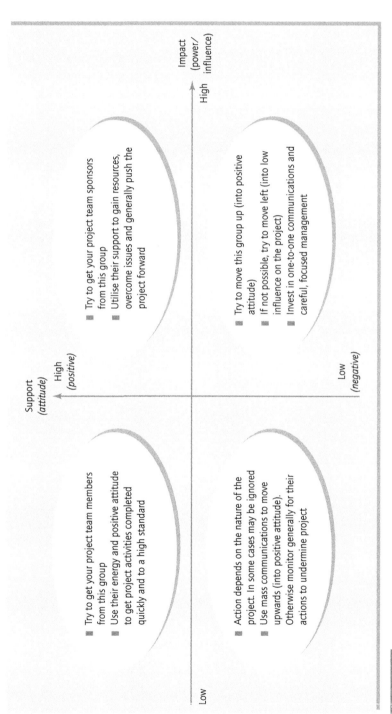

Low

Support
(attitude)

High
(positive)

- Try to get your project team members from this group
- Use their energy and positive attitude to get project activities completed quickly and to a high standard

- Try to get your project team sponsors from this group
- Utilise their support to gain resources, overcome issues and generally push the project forward

- Action depends on the nature of the project. In some cases may be ignored
- Use mass communications to move upwards (into positive attitude). Otherwise monitor generally for their actions to undermine project

- Try to move this group up (into positive attitude)
- If not possible, try to move left (into low influence on the project)
- Invest in one-to-one communications and careful, focused management

Low
(negative)

High

Impact
(power/
influence)

figure 10.8 Stakeholder analysis

for you on your project; alternatively, if you are working for a programme manager or a corporate project management function, there may be a project office already existing that performs a defined task.

The issues to think through on project offices are:

- Do you understand what you may want the project office to do? Be clear about why you need it and what it will do for you and the project. If it is just to do some administrative work for you, get an administrator or PA. You should understand how the work will split between yourself and the project office. A typical example might be:
  - Setting report formats and schedule – project office
  - Collecting and chasing reports – project office
  - Analysing of reports – project manager
  - Deciding on action – project manager
  - Managing action – project manager
  - Report quality assessments (timelines, format, etc.) – project office.
- Will this make you more efficient or effective? It may seem very obvious, but unless it actually aids you it is not worth setting up. I have seen many project offices simply blindly enforcing some project bureaucracy, to become more of a hindrance than a help to project managers.
- Who has access to the project office resource? Once a project office is set up you will be surprised how many people want it to pick up support work for them. To avoid overload you need to be clear about who can and who cannot use the project office.
- Does everyone else understand what it does? Project offices can be seen as an unnecessary overhead unless people understand the value that they bring to the project.

Skill 10 – Administration and management of meetings

Administration generally is a bit of a bugbear for project managers. Yet irrespective of whether you have a project office or not, being well organised and having good project administration is a significant factor in project success. Project managers without support often complain about the administrative burden and that they are not simply administrators. It is true that a project manager is not an administrator and it is not a good use of an experienced project manager's skills to dedicate them to administration, but you must be prepared to do some administration and do it in a well-structured way. The sorts of administrative duties that must be in place are:

- Document control and document management:
  - What information is required, in what format, and how often it is updated
  - Who owns the document and is responsible for change control
  - Where is it stored, etc.
- Schedules and formats for regular reports.
- Meeting schedules, set-up and arrangement.
- Diary management for project team members.
- Running standard business operational processes – procurement and purchase requisitions, room bookings, etc.
- Others depending on the nature of the project. Typical administrative tasks I come across regularly are access to stationery, building access and passes, arranging desk space and PCs, travel and hotel bookings, collating and analysing timesheets. Sounds trivial? These tasks can eat up a lot of project management time if they are not efficiently administered.

Although administration may not seem that glamorous to project managers, it needs to be seen as the oil that keeps the machine of a project running. Working on a poorly administered project is painful and inefficient. If the administrative overhead is large then look for support or set up a project office. Developing an understanding of the administrative requirements and therefore the administrative resource and process needs of your project will enhance your delivery.

The management of meetings is an ability most people need – you can argue whether this is a type of administration or a general management skill. As a project manager you will need to set up and run many meetings, and the better you are at it the less time you will waste. Also, you may need to develop and coach meeting management skills within the team. Meetings can be a productive and efficient way to communicate and even to develop deliverables, but if poorly managed and set up they can eat vast quantities of time for no discernible benefit. Projects can develop a culture of continuous meetings, which is rarely productive. Some simple points I try to keep to are as follows:

> ❝ meetings can be productive, but they can waste huge amounts of time ❞

- Start by thinking through why you want this meeting, and whether a meeting is the optimal way to achieve your objective. Is it to communicate, is it to generate agreed actions, or is it to develop some deliverables? Meetings can be productive, but they can waste huge amounts of time, so, before you have one, check with yourself that it is necessary. Meetings are an essential part of management, but not all meetings are essential.

- Always have an agenda – even if it is only a short meeting. A well-prepared meeting can be a pleasure. A poorly prepared meeting is usually an irritation.
- Make sure the materials and people you need are available.
- Be clear why you have invited people and what you expect of them. Do not invite people just for the sake of it. Brief them prior to coming about what is expected of them and what they are expected to bring. In general terms:
  - For information meetings – invite anyone who needs to know or who is interested. This can be a lot of people!
  - For action and decision orientated meetings – invite only those who are critical to the decision or who will make it a better decision. This should be a small group.
  - Working meetings – this depends. If it is really to do some work, keep it small and invite only those who need to be there. If it is about exploring concepts or building a team, make it more open.
- Plan for yourself what you want the outcome from the meeting to be, what you expect the outcome to be, and what actions you need to take in the meeting to get your desired outcome.
- Agree who will run the meeting and who takes the minutes – this does not need to be you. In fact, in many meetings it should not be you, as you may need to be focusing on being a contributor rather than having time to take the minutes. If the meeting is complex you should take only one role – i.e. chairperson or contributor, not both.
- Avoid continually changing diary times and locations for meetings – it can significantly disrupt the flow of work.
- Encourage plenty of regular informal communications – often this can avoid many meetings.
- Follow up on actions.
- Take a few moments at the end of every meeting to get feedback on whether it was successful or not. This can seem like overkill but if done quickly will develop your skills and understanding of and rapport with the meeting participants.

- For regular, fixed meetings have decision criteria for when they stop happening. The world of business is full of scheduled meetings that should have been stopped long ago. The criteria can be a date, when something is achieved, or when conditions change.
- Consider meetings as part of your work – if they are not contributing in some way, stop them.
- Keep them as short as possible.

Skill 11 – Prioritisation

The ability to prioritise work is a general management skill and as such is not often thought of as specifically part of the project management skill set. Project managers must have a good understanding of the principles and practice of prioritising work, as without it you cannot be sure you are actually working on the most important or urgent piece of work at any one point in time. Project managers need to be aware of prioritisation because:

- There are normally fewer resources in a project than are required to do everything possible. Project managers need to prioritise between the various tasks team members may do. If you fail to do this, team members will regularly do things that are of lesser importance – as their view of priorities may differ from yours. If you are ever on a project with more resource than you need then you may feel lucky, but you are usually not being ambitious enough in what you can complete.
- Projects themselves are normally part of a larger prioritisation of activities that goes on within organisations (see portfolio management in Chapter 12). It is of substantial value to understand this process and where the project you are running sits within the overall prioritisation system. The ability to use and manage an organisation's priority system will ease your access to resources significantly.

Prioritisation is logically very simple. Everyone understands the idea that some tasks need to be done before others and the idea of having a 'list' of activities ranked in priority order. In practice, prioritisation of complex workloads which are being done to achieve a wide variety of goals is a significant task in its own right. Factors to consider when prioritising are as follows.

- The first question you must ask yourself is on what basis are you prioritising? If the prioritisation is for a few tasks then you may not need explicit criteria, and management 'gut' reaction may be sufficient, but once prioritisation becomes complex you need to have some measure by which to form the basis of prioritisation. This may be to take on the highest 'value' tasks first, or those that deliver the most important customer requirements. Without this, prioritisation risks becoming simply a mechanism for vested interests to push their work first.

- The ideal prioritisation results in a list of each activity ranked against every other activity you may need to perform. As a result you can start by completing the task ranked at number one, then do that ranked at number two and so on until you have completed the whole list. It is a nice piece of theory, but prioritisation like planning is a tool, not an end in itself. Attempts to prioritise everything against everything else often consume so much time and resource as to make the prioritisation activity such a major piece of work in its own right that it does not get completed. The answer is to go for broad, simple categorisation of tasks that everyone understands. The categories I typically use are:

  – Must do, cannot slip – tasks that must be done and must be done on time. There should be only a few of these, around which you build your plans. If you have a large number you are normally not prioritising critically enough.

  – Must do, can allow to slip to a limited extent – tasks that must be done, and have a target time to complete, but if they slip by a few days it will not cause major problems. Many tasks normally fall into this category.

  – Must do, time can move – tasks that must be done, but which you have significant leeway over when they are done. Such tasks do need to be done so they cannot languish forever at the bottom of your priorities. These are useful items on your plans as they give you great flexibility, but in reality there are not usually too many tasks like this.

  – Optional, but important – tasks that do not absolutely need to be done, but it would be very good if they were. With normal levels of resourcing you should be able to complete these, but they may wait until the end of the project. If people are truly honest, in reality most tasks on most plans fall into this category. These are the things we really want, but the world will not stop if we do not get them.

  – Optional, not critical – nice-to-haves that will be done only if there is time and resource left. We have to be realistic; normally these do not get done unless you are running a very well-resourced project.

▦ Such a categorisation allows flexible planning of activities. I avoid prioritisations along generic, undefined categories (such as ranking projects against a simple scale of priority 1, 2 or 3). These systems often add as much confusion as help. Ask yourself, what does priority '1' mean? What you will find with systems like this is that 90% of activities end up as priority 1, which really means you have not done any prioritisation.

▦ Having made a priority list, be prepared for a reasonable degree of volatility and to respond to escalation requests. If activities can be escalated you should agree who has final say over priorities. Within a project it should be the project manager or possibly the project sponsor. If it is part of a wider prioritisation activity you may need to set up a senior steering committee to own the priorities. Senior managers should support it; after all, a key part of being a senior manager is making decisions about resource allocation, in other words prioritisation. If anyone does want to change a priority, the mindset to make sure everyone has is that anything can be prioritised higher, but something else must come lower. Pretending this is not true is kidding yourself.

▦ Make sure the prioritisation is explicit; ensure everyone is working to the same list. If you fail to do this you cannot assume everyone will intuitively work to the same set of priorities – it simply will not happen. There is no point in one half of a project team doing half a task if the other half of the project team is working on half of a different task. We all prioritise intuitively all the time, and sometimes even subconsciously, but the result is often that we do the easiest tasks first rather than those of highest priority.

▦ Be ruthless in applying priorities once they are agreed. There is always too much to do. Do not be surprised when people say they will not do a task because it has too low a priority – this is not a problem, this is the system working. Alternatively, do not be surprised if people keep working on low priority activities, ignoring the priority list because of personal interest. This needs to be rooted out and normally a bit of management direction will stop this, but in extreme cases it should result in disciplinary activity. (That sounds harsh but I have worked in many organisations where specialists like engineers love to tinker on their own pet interests at the cost of not doing what is an organisation's priority work.) The only valid exception to this rule is that people can work on lower priority work if it is the only work relevant to their skill set. For example, if you are a C++ or Java programmer and the only project requiring C++ or Java skills is a low priority one then this is obviously the one you must work on. This type of detail implication of prioritisation can make resource planning and scheduling very complex.

▪ Do not confuse how urgent a task is with how important it is. Some very important tasks can wait, while some minor tasks must be done now. Be careful, though, if your set of urgent tasks never ends and so important tasks never get started. Sooner rather than later you will need to do the important tasks even if this means dropping a less important but urgent task. This makes setting priorities intellectually harder, but you do need to be aware of the difference.

> ❝ do not confuse how urgent a task is with how important it is ❞

▪ Agree what you do with low priority tasks. Do they literally wait until all higher priority tasks are complete, or will some of them move up the priority list over time?

▪ Consider the time–cost–quality–scope trade-off when setting priorities. You do not have to perform each activity to the same level of quality or depth, so you can get through your list more quickly if you are flexible on these points. Some tasks have a high priority to be completed in a minimal sense, but completing them to the maximum possible scope is not so important.

Good prioritisation is hard work, needs critical consideration, and challenges many people's views. If you find it easy it probably means you are not being aggressive enough. It means letting go of things we may really want. It also means making tough decisions. But when prioritisation is done well it can make you significantly more efficient and effective.

Successful prioritisation results in relatively low levels of parallel activity. It is generally much more efficient and effective, if painful and politically difficult, to do a few things at any one time. You will complete them much more quickly. Once they are done, you can move on to the next group of tasks. In time, you will complete far more of your overall set of activities. If all your prioritisation does is juggle activities around, but you still do everything at once, you will remain inefficient and your output will be significantly less.

Skill 12 – Use of project lifecycles

Competent project managers understand and use various project lifecycles. I define a lifecycle as a structured definition of the sequential flow of a project through some standard stages. These lifecycles tend to vary either from industry to industry or by the type of project, but the basic principles that underlie them are the same. What you must be able to do is:

- Understand the principles of different lifecycles and apply them as appropriate.
- Be able to use the correct language on lifecycles for the context you are working in.
- Vary the lifecycle to suit the nature of the project you are running.

The advantage of utilising a standard lifecycle is that it enables you to 'quick start' your planning taking previous examples of approaches used. For example, in many organisations there are standard checklists of activities to do within different phases of a project. I am opposed to the rigid use of checklists as every project is different, but I am very keen on them as a tool to help the project manager think through what needs to be done (and have even written a book of such checklists). Lifecycles also provide a good language set to communicate to your stakeholder group and project team members about the shape and progress of the project. For example, telling someone the title of specific activities you are performing this week may not enlighten them much on project progress, but saying you are in the testing phase or doing requirements capture may help them understand better.

The classic lifecycle for projects has different terms in different situations, but taking the example of the software development project it is typically:

- Project **initiation** – which covers the activities I described in Chapters 3 and 5.
- Requirements **analysis and capture** – the detailed analysis of your customer's needs and the conversion of these into a documented requirements specification.
- **Feasibility** – a review of the requirements to determine how long the project will take and how much it will cost, and potentially whether it is possible. (This is discussed below.)
- **Solutions design** – designing the solution to the requirements.
- **Solutions build** – developing and building the solution.
- **Test** – formally testing the solution. This may cover technical testing and operational testing, as well as acceptance with the customer.
- **Implementation** – taking the developed solution and implementing it within the environment it will operate in.

- **Handover** – handing over the solution to the customer. This typically has a period of more focused support and ensures that users can utilise the deliverables while the project team is still available to help them with any problems that may arise.
- **Project closure** – includes finishing off any outstanding activities, reviewing the results to learn from the experience for the next project, and releasing resources.

This is shown in Figure 10.9.

For each project the length and complexity of each of these stages is completely dependent on its objectives and the context in which it exists. One of the skills of a good project manager is to consider what lifecycle is required in different situations. Five specific situations in which different lifecycles help are:

1 When requirements cannot be clarified or are unstable – as the customer does not have a full vision of them.

2 Where the problem is fully understood but there is no known solution to it.

3 Where there is significant risk or uncertainty about a project and it is not possible to plan accurately. Alternatively, you can plan but your customer requires more information before committing to the project.

4 Where the impact of the solution being incorrect or not working properly is very high.

5 Where you need benefits and impact quickly even though the overall project is large.

I discuss each of these in turn.

The solution to uncertain, unstable or continuously evolving requirements can be simply to spend a huge amount of time capturing the requirements. This can work, but usually it is frustrating and expensive and it can be demoralising. An alternative is to consider developing *prototypes*. This is common in the software development industry. A set of requirements is quickly captured without worrying too much whether they are complete or fully accepted by the customer. A prototype is built to expand on a concept, and to provide a basis to flesh out further requirements. It is often easier to change and expand an existing prototype than to visualise it completely in your head. Some software is effectively now developed as a continuous line of prototypes, with each iteration improving on the previous version. While no version is perfect it gives the customer a solution

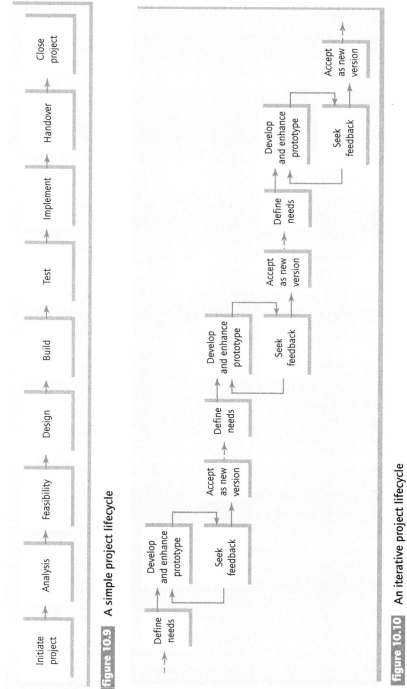

figure 10.9 A simple project lifecycle

figure 10.10 An iterative project lifecycle

quickly, which can then be improved upon. A development lifecycle can then rapidly iterate between requirements capture and development several times. In project management techniques such as Agile, such iterations may be very quick; sometimes the cycle times are as short as a few days. Figure 10.10 shows such a lifecycle.

When a customer understands a problem but has no solution to it, it is obviously not effective to start to try to deliver a solution. It may be obvious, but it is what is often proposed. Rather than doing this, split the project into two high-level stages. The first is a *solutions analysis phase*. This is really a project in its own right, the deliverable from which is a solutions concept, and potentially a more detailed design for it. Such a project typically has a lifecycle such as:

- **Problem analysis** – gaining a full understanding of the problem with the aim of being able to define it simply and comprehensively.
- **Solutions generation** – developing a set of possible solutions to the problem. There are normally many ways to solve any problem.
- **Selection criteria development** – developing a set of criteria to choose a solution against.
- **Solutions selection** – choosing the solution against the chosen criteria.

Where time is pressing, a solutions analysis phase can often be efficiently and effectively run as a series of workshops. The second phase of the project, to implement the selected solution, can be run along a more standard lifecycle as described at the start of this section.

Another reason for keeping the solutions selection and the solution implementation phases of the project separate is that it is not until the solution has been chosen that it is possible to determine confidently how long the implementation will take, nor how much it will cost.

Where there is significant risk or the customer wants to know more before committing to a project, a *feasibility phase* can be put into the lifecycle. During feasibility essentially more time is spent in deepening understanding of the project, developing more detailed plans, and potentially doing some testing to see whether the solution is actually possible. Many projects do not have a formal feasibility phase, or when it is covered the feasibility is used primarily as a planning and scoping exercise. For higher-risk projects I always insist on a formal feasibility stage with an explicit decision at the end as to whether to continue with the project.

Performing a feasibility study is essentially a risk management step. With it you can:

- Reduce uncertainty in the plans.
- Identify specific risks that need to be managed (including implementation and operational risk from the project).
- Clarify where you need contingency plans.
- Build a project plan accordingly.

You will have to do these activities anyway when you do your planning, whether or not it is explicitly called feasibility. The advantage of doing a feasibility study is that it makes this process explicit and at the end of it you can put a clear decision point for your customer to decide on the project, having much fuller information on the degree of risk and resulting time and resource requirements. You can also then build any necessary contingency plans into your schedule and resource estimates. By priming your customer up front that you will be coming to a decision point like this at the end of the feasibility phase, where estimates and approach need to be revisited, you manage expectations better. Feasibilities never give absolute certainty, but they do reduce risk. The length and depth of the feasibility is a function of how risky the situation is or how much appetite for risk your customer has, hence the lower the risk and the higher the level of risk your customer is willing to take, the shorter the feasibility can be.

Where the impact of the solution being incorrect or not working properly is very high, you should look at the *testing lifecycle* you have implemented. Testing may be a short and simple activity, but where testng is essential it has a complex lifecycle of its own. Preparing for testing can start very early in a project. A typical testing lifecycle may be:

- Development of test acceptance criteria – what needs to happen for the solution to pass the tests. An example of acceptance criteria for software may be that the software has to pass 100% of the mandatory tests and 90% of the optional tests and have fewer than ten minor bugs in it.
- Development of detailed test scripts – defining the detailed actions that will happen in the test.
- Optionally – factory acceptance tests (FAT), and site acceptance tests (SAT) when you have equipment or supplies being produced in a third-party location.
- Unit test – testing each component of the solution separately.

- Integration test – testing all the components of the solution together.

- User acceptance test – getting users to use the solution and checking that they accept that it meets their needs.

- Operational testing – a final phase when the solution is integrated into the wider environment to see that it can, in practice, work with all other activities required.

In each of the test phases a solution can fail, which means further development work is required. Additionally, for projects involving things like the launch of a new product it is usually sensible to include a trial phase. Trialling of products is a skill in which marketing professionals have developed detailed expertise. In essence, in this phase the product is actually taken out to prospective customers who can trial it. In this way you gain feedback as to product acceptability. Potentially this can include charging a customer for the product to understand pricing acceptance and sensitivities.

Finally, where you need rapid feedback or knowledge of benefits or impact from what is a very large project, consider breaking the project, down into many smaller *phases*. Each phase is a complete project in its own right. Alternatively, plan regular milestones on the project, at which point you should be delivering something that has external value to the customers. This often seems quite hard, but with some creative thinking it is normally achievable in practice. Analyse the development process to identify partial deliverables of use to the customer. Brainstorming 'quick wins' can form the basis of this approach. Usually based on good experience, customers often will not trust the mega-project that delivers nothing of value to them for eighteen months. They will be far happier with a series of incremental value-adding deliverables at regular intervals. It develops trust with your customer group if you can do this, and it returns value to the business you are operating in more quickly. These interim deliverables do not need to be huge, but must explicitly be valued by the customer.

What more can you learn?

I have presented a broad body of knowledge you can build up to enhance your ability to deliver projects. Good project managers are constantly expanding their skills and learning from experience. This is beneficial, but in enhancing your knowledge do not lose sight of common sense and judgement, the bedrocks of project management.

> ❝ good project managers are constantly expanding their skills ❞

To learn you must be open to learning and be honest with yourself when things have gone wrong or could have gone better. This personal honesty and ability to understand what has happened, not to look for external reasons, but to question yourself about what you could have done differently, lies at the bottom of true personal growth.

If you do want to expand your skills, think in terms of the following categories in which to seek knowledge, training and exposure:

- The human and 'soft' skills identified specifically in this book. While these are called 'soft' they are often the hardest to master. Focus on communication and relationship building skills.

- Enhanced technical project management skills beyond those in this chapter. Your skills need to be sufficient for the complexity and scale of projects you are running. If you are running larger and larger programmes then it is worth looking at more in-depth training in areas such as risk management, estimating and powerful approaches such as the critical chain method. (Remember the lesson from the start of this chapter, though – keep the processes you implement as simple as you can for the scale of project you are running.)

- Supporting skills. There are a host of supporting skills which will enhance your ability to work as a project manager. In this I include financial awareness, business case development, negotiation and presentation skills.

- Tools. Understand the full capabilities of the software tools available and what specific processes and algorithms they implement.

- General management and leadership skills. Project management is a very specific way of managing, but many of the requirements – setting up teams, allocating work, motivating individuals and driving performance – are the core parts of any manager's role.

- Contextual knowledge. Many industries require significant contextual knowledge. As I discussed in Chapter 9 you do not need to be an expert in all the areas you are managing, but you do have to be able to understand the concepts and use the language and jargon of the industry you are working in. There are many advantages to good contextual knowledge. The better you understand the context, the more likely you are to develop good plans; relationships with your project team will be better, you will find it easier to judge the quality of deliverables, and you will more proactively identify issues, risks and assumptions.

Table 10.1 lists a variety of more advanced project management tools that can be researched when the basics in this book are not enough.

table 10.1 Advanced project management tools and techniques

Advanced project management techniques and tools	Circumstances in which they may be of use
Alternative lifecycles and rapid development approaches (e.g. iterative approaches, Agile, concurrent engineering, critical chain, goal-directed project management)	When you are looking for ways to reduce project duration, or generally to explore ways to increase the levels of project success. (Different techniques suit different situations, and therefore there is no single best technique for all occasions)
Benefits management/realisation	See Chapter 12
Bodies of Knowledge (e.g. APM BoK, PM BoK)	When you require a reference source for project management standards
Change management	See Chapter 12
Control and progress assessment techniques (e.g. Earned Value Analysis or EVA)	To track project progress combining both progress to schedule and progress against budget
Critical chain	When you are applying the Critical Chain method or CCPM
Critical path	To identity the set of tasks that create the length of a project and which, if delayed, will increase the project's duration
Estimation techniques (e.g. PERT)	When you want to include more accurate contingency in your project plans
Financial formulae (e.g. NPV, IRR, etc.) and data (e.g. discount rates)	Used in business case development and prioritisation
Governance (project/programme/portfolio governance)	(See Chapter 12)
Maturity models (e.g. OPM3, CMMI, P2MM, etc.)	When you are looking to benchmark or improve your project management capability. This is less about project management directly and more relevant to people managing project managers
Network diagrams	A powerful way to present project plans used by some professional project managers
Portfolio management	See Chapter 12
Programme management	See Chapter 12
Project management software tools	Once you know the basics, invest in tools – at least buy some planning software. For more complex situations consider investing in software for online reporting, issue and risk management, document management, and activities like time recording (time sheets)

Advanced project management techniques and tools	Circumstances in which they may be of use
Proprietary and standard project/ programme management approaches (e.g. Prince 2, MSP, etc.)	In specific environments in which these methodologies are mandated (such as public sector), or where you do not have existing project management standards
Quantitative risk assessment techniques (e.g. sensitivity analysis, and probabilistic techniques such as Monte Carlo assessments)	When qualitative risk assessment (as described in this chapter) is not sufficient. You may need to understand absolute risk levels (qualitative risk assessments provide only relative risk levels), or you need to add up the individual risks to determine cumulative risk levels
Requirements collection and business analysis techniques	When you are faced with complex and non-trivial requirements in a project, and when there are uncertainty and ambiguity in requirements
Resource management techniques (e.g. resource levelling, resource smoothing).	When you want to level the rate of resource use within a project, or to manage resources across multiple projects
Testing and trialling techniques	To improve the quality of deliverables
Value engineering and value management	To improve the design and maximise the value of deliverables; to maximise the value an organisation receives from a project investment

My final advice is to develop trust in your own judgement. As I have stressed on many occasions in this book, every situation is different. If the specific situation you are working in has unique characteristics and needs alternative approaches – trust yourself, decide on an approach, use it, and learn from the results.

Knowing when to say 'no'

Having spent the previous ten chapters outlining some hints, tips, lessons and general advice on how to get into the master class of project management, it may seem odd to be approaching the end of the book with a chapter on when you should avoid a project altogether. But some things are just not meant to happen. No matter how well the work is planned, how well structured the team is, or how inspirational the sponsor, some projects are just never going to come to a successful conclusion. As a project manager these are the times to keep your head low and avoid the work, or speak up firmly against it – for project management is about ensuring delivery, not about pointless heroics against unassailable odds.

When things are not going to happen it is best to avoid them, or better still, and perhaps more constructively, ensure they are killed off before they get anywhere. There is no shame in constructively stopping bad ideas, or ensuring that unimplementable good ideas are killed off. Strong and successful organisations will regularly generate more creative ideas than they can implement, some of which will not work in practice. Rejecting ideas and killing projects is not weakness but a sign of organisational strength. But, no matter how well you do it, you will not get to be a great or successful project manager by spending your whole life brilliantly failing to deliver impossible projects. A useful skill is therefore knowing when to say 'no', and equally important how to say 'no'. This chapter looks at those tell-tale signs that should make you at least think of whether the project is a flier or should be grounded for good.

When do you actually need a project manager?

Just because someone thinks they need a project manager, it does not mean that they really do, nor that it is actually the best use of your time.

Before having a discussion about when projects should not be recommended to proceed, it is worth reflecting on the situations in which you actually do not need a project manager in the first place. Is it, in fact, your problem to solve? Project managers get asked to do all sorts of work, some of which is not really an appropriate use of their skills or time. This classically happens with in-house project management teams within companies that get a reputation as reliable sets of hands to sort things out. My argument is that unless those 'things' are really projects, and relevant prioritised projects, a project manager is not really the best person to solve the issue or be put in charge of the work. Before accepting project work it is worth considering:

- **Is this the best use of the project manager?** Project management is a skill set in short supply in many situations, so project managers should be used only on the highest priority projects. If you compare the other possible projects you could be working on with the one on offer, would any of the others be more important?

- **Does this project manager have the right sort of skills?** A specific project manager may be a great project manager, but may have no relevant experience in the subject being delivered. As discussed earlier, an IT project manager would probably be a high-risk option for managing the delivery of a major road construction programme!

- **Is this really a project-based activity?** Project managers often give people a feeling of comfort that someone is managing the work, especially if no-one else has that direct responsibility. If it is not actually a project, however, this is not a good use of project manager skills. A typical example of misuse of project managers I have regularly seen is for fault and complaint resolution. Organisations start getting faults from customers, or complaints, and the nature of the resolution crosses many departmental boundaries. They have no formal fault and complaint mechanisms, or such mechanisms are not working properly. The only people who regularly work across departmental boundaries are project managers, hence the logic is 'let's use a project manager to resolve the issues'. These cross-departmental 'business as usual' activities often get pushed in the project manager's way. Of course, you can think of a complaint as a mini-project to resolve, but it is far better for a business to have a defined complaint handling process. If as a project manager you accept this type of work, do so because you feel it is important and not because you are delivering a project. (There is a valid potential project in these situations, such as *develop a new or improved complaints handling process and system*, and if that is how the work is scoped then it is a good, challenging project to be responsible for.)

Knowing the danger signals

Key lesson

There are many clear indications when a project is likely to fail. Look for these and assess whether you are able to manage the risks or not.

If you have got through the first section let us assume the activity you are working on is legitimately a project you should be managing. Is it still sensible to accept the work? There are a number of danger signals that should make your ears prick up and start your mental risk management process firing. There are no absolute rules or algorithms that can be applied to find out deterministically whether these factors are so bad as to kill the project off, or whether they are simply factors that need to be managed through your risk management approach. The only way to really tell is to use your judgement. Don't rely on gut feel as it can be wrong, but use it to trigger more analysis, and don't ignore it altogether as it normally has some reason for being there.

> ❝ don't rely on gut feel as it can be wrong ❞

In no priority or order of importance, the danger signs I look for are:

- **No energy.** The team and the sponsor seem apathetic towards the end goal. No matter how important something is, if no-one cares it is unlikely to be successfully completed.
- **No real drive or sponsorship.** The project seems a low-priority afterthought to the sponsor. Any significant project either using a

large amount of resources or resulting in a significant change on a company needs senior sponsorship and support throughout the project. Alarm bells should ring if the main sponsor treats the role of being sponsor like an honorary degree – as a symbol of seniority rather than having to do anything on the project.

■ **No willingness to free up the right resources.** How many times have I seen senior managers, on one hand, excitedly banging on about how important a project is, only to be giving, a few minutes later, reasons why good people or money cannot be allocated? If it is important, the resources need to be freed up; if they are not, then the project is not important! It really is that simple. Of course, managers must prioritise their demands, but if your project is so low priority that you cannot get access to the right resources, suggest it is put on hold until the resources are available.

■ **Overly demanding customers with unreasonable expectations.** Check out your customers' expectations at the beginning of the project. If they expect to achieve significantly more than you think is possible, or do it in less time or with fewer resources, then you need to challenge them. It is worth understanding the rationale for their beliefs, as sometimes there can be new and innovative ways of doing things that achieve substantially more than traditional methods. Also, a challenge is often a good thing, and some managers will challenge simply to test how robust the thinking and planning behind the project are. But there are limits. More often than not, the driver for unreasonable expectations is simply that the customer needs a huge amount and has only limited resources. I'm afraid that in this situation you need to get your head clearly accepting the fact that just because they want a miracle does not mean it will happen (even if you don't put it quite so bluntly to your customer). Try to manage expectations to a more sensible place.

■ **Customers with fixed ideas and a lack of listening skills.** Customers regularly have ideas and views about how a project should be run. Your role as the project manager includes determining how to deliver the project. In doing this, listen to your customers; sometimes their ideas can be helpful and provide creative help to you as the project manager. On other occasions they can be wrong or unworkable. If poor ideas come from customers who are rigidly fixated on them or seem incapable of listening to your input, then tread carefully.

■ **Conflicting goals** – or too many goals. An example could be to achieve a cost saving by reducing staff numbers and at the same time improve staff morale. As a project manager you not only need to understand the goals, but also need to have belief that they are achievable. At the very least, conflicting goals need to be challenged, and if you cannot remove the conflict at least try to have the goals prioritised. In the example stated, ask the customer which is more important, the cost saving or the staff morale? You need to know which one is more important in case the conflict between the goals becomes real and it is not possible to achieve both. If you cannot do this you are dealing with an unreasonable customer.

- **Conflicting customers.** Many projects do not have a single customer but a group of people who act as a sponsoring board. If this team seems to want very different things from the project and spends more time arguing between themselves than helping the project to progress, this is a bad sign. If the conflict results from differing opinions and it can be worked through then that is fine. If the conflict arises because the project will impact vested interests, you will need to find powerful support.

- **Poor understanding of requirements.** To deliver, a customer must understand what he wants. It is perfectly acceptable for the requirements to be hazy if the customer is willing to invest in real analysis of requirements, or in activities such as prototyping which can drive out a better understanding of needs. However, if the poor understanding of requirements is combined with a 'just get on and do it' attitude then there is a significant risk of failure to deliver against expectations.

- **Lack of flexibility to plan.** You will not be able to estimate how long a project will take and how much it will cost until you have scoped and planned the work (and even then it still remains an estimate subject to risk). In many situations customers have real or perceived constraints on time and cost – the project must be complete in six months or less, it cannot cost more than £250k. This is the real world and as a project manager you must learn to work within these types of constraints; however, you are not a miracle worker. Working within such constraints is possible only if they are reasonable or you have the opportunity to flex scope and deliverable quality.

- **Not enough time to test.** The project's customer accepts the need to develop things but will not accept time for steps like testing that are there to ensure the quality of the output. Without testing the end results will often be very flaky. Testing time, as it usually sits at the end of a project, often gets compressed as a way of shortening delivery times. Also, it is not always intuitively obvious why you need testing. If you have an engineering background, the need for testing is so inbuilt as to be unquestioned. If your customer has a background like accounting or marketing, to them it is not so obvious. (For example, when an accountant or marketer has done some work it may be discussed or checked by their line manager, but it is not normally formally tested.) It is not only technical testing that is critical. User acceptance testing and operational readiness testing are critical tasks. Your customer may think, 'if you developed it properly in the first place, why do you need to test?'. If you cannot convince them then the project is likely to be very problematic.

- **Too many parallel activities and too short a time for key tasks.** Timescales on projects are often shortened for a variety of reasons. A method of coping with this is to take sequential activities and try to do them in parallel. There is nothing wrong with parallel tasks, and all plans will have some degree of parallel working. Although it depends on the specific situation, in general the more parallel tasking you have the more complex and risky management becomes. Where a plan is compressed so that more and more tasks become parallel and finishing tasks such as testing and training become shortened then risk increases, sometimes dramatically. It also means you must have more resource available at any point in time.

- **High risk with tight deadlines and no contingency plans.** High risk can be handled by a good project manager. In fact, some great project managers thrive on running high-risk projects. But if high risk is combined with tight and fixed deadlines, limited budgets and no contingency possible, you should really think through whether this lack of opportunity to manoeuvre is not simply magnifying the risk to unmanageable proportions.

- **Unknown technology or solutions for a demanding high-through-put situation.** Applying new or novel technology always has some risk, but it needs to be done sometimes or we would never implement anything new. The track record for delivering high-technology projects to time and budget is poor. However, the combination of completely novel technology and a mission- and time-critical project is particularly dangerous. We can all think of projects on which it has worked (the NASA moon shots, for example) but there are hundreds more examples where it has turned out disastrously wrong. Unless new technology offers significant benefits, stick with the tried and tested or use it first in a situation which is not mission critical.

■ **The project that has been kicking around for years.** There are activities that seem to be around for ages and ages without ever progressing. Often they are renamed several times, in an attempt to inject energy or to hide the fact that they are the same project that was tried a few months ago. It may be that you can find a new way to deliver them, but often there are very good reasons why such a project has not got far in its many previous incarnations. Accept responsibility for them with care!

No single issue here need sound the death knell for a project, but any can be, and a combination of them should really make you concerned. In the end this will have to come down to a judgement based on your experience. If you are not sure, talk it through with a more experienced colleague. The best and most highly sought-after project managers are the ones who can handle high-risk projects that exhibit these characteristics, but much of their skill is not that they can perform miracles that you cannot; it is at least partially due to the fact that they are good at removing the risks, and will convince sponsors to change something so that some of the characteristics in the above list are no longer exhibited by the project.

Constructively killing projects off

Key lesson

It is far better to kill off bad ideas, or impractical good ideas, than to try to run an impossible project.

You have assessed a project as having very high risk with limited chance of success or limited chance that the benefits will be achieved. So what can you do in this situation? Essentially there are two options you can consider:

1　Seek to change some features of the project to move it from the walking dead to simply a project with risks. It is unlikely that you will ever be able to change such a project to a low-risk one without it changing so much as to have little in common with the original concept. But you may be able to change it into an achievable project, in which case all well and good. If not, you need to consider the next option.

2 Kill it off. Stopping work that is never going to complete should not be seen as a defeat or negative. We should positively encourage the killing off of bad ideas. We cannot avoid bad ideas, as it is a simple truth that if you allow creativity some of the resulting ideas will be no good. Strong organisations have two main strengths: firstly, they generate lots of ideas; and, secondly, they ruthlessly kill off the ones that will not work and only focus on a few good ideas.

In some organisations or some project management processes there are formal mechanisms for filtering out the weaker or riskier projects in the first place. The whole point of doing activities such as concept reviews and feasibility studies is not only to manage risk by scoping out the work more and to understand what must be done to deliver it, but also to stop some of the projects. If you have a concept review and feasibility process in your organisation and every single project is passed through, you are almost certainly not being critical enough (or possibly not creative enough). Stopping poorly thought-through, inappropriate or impractical ideas is a successful application of a filtering process and not a failure.

It is worth preparing yourself for some bad feeling coming back to you if you do kill off a project in mid-flight. No matter how suicidal a project was and no matter how sensible it was to stop it, there may be members of the project team who have put in significant effort getting it to the state it was in. In fact, on very high-risk projects people often work insanely hard because of the challenge of overcoming the problems or because they get emotionally attached to the work. These people will feel at least a degree of disappointment when the project is stopped. Don't be hard on them. This is human nature and these are the people with the right attitude to getting work delivered; it's just that it was wrongly placed this time. You may need to work with these people again so it is worth trying to manage feelings with sensitivity. I have seen major morale problems occurring in teams when a project has been killed. I clearly remember one specific situation – everyone logically agreed with the project being stopped, but people had put in extra effort trying to get the project to work, and their emotions really felt the disappointment of stopping it. One person even resigned soon afterwards.

The other group which may exhibit bad feelings comprises those with significant vested interests in the project coming off for one reason or another. Two things to realise here are that strong interests can make people blind to risk and having an absolute need for a project can remove any concern about risk, even if it is seen. Manage people who wanted or needed the project with care. Be clear in your mind that wants and needs do not make the impossible possible.

Just say 'no'

Key lesson

If you can, walk away from impossible projects. Gallantly failing to deliver is still failure.

If you do get to the point of needing to kill a project off, my tips are:

- Do not assume that everyone understands why you think the project is a bad idea. It may be completely obvious to you, but simply stating that it is a bad idea, or that it is obvious it is a bad idea, will just irritate people, especially those who came up with the idea in the first place. You will need to explain it to people in a way that they understand.

- Structure a clear and brief presentation of why the project is a bad idea. Try to find at least some positives for the project so that you do not come across as just a negative sort of person. Put these into the language of your customer. Avoid or explain complex technical or specialist technology. Specialist reasons which cannot be explained to a non-specialist audience smack of a lack of desire to do a project rather than a lack of ability.

- Include constructive comments on how the project could be made feasible from your viewpoint. (You are doing this partially to provide a real alternative, but also partially to show that you are not inflexible or unreasonable. In this case, even if you know your alternatives will be unacceptable, it is worth including them in your response.)

- Prepare yourself to push against someone who may have emotional attachment to the idea. Emotion is a great thing when driving for success, but it can be very difficult when someone is attached to what is fundamentally unachievable. Do not assume they will always argue rationally or will not be willing to indulge in political tricks.

- Do not get emotionally involved – argue rationally from simple facts. If you are arguing from emotion you may, of course, be wrong and it will tend to come across in your communications.

- Listen and be open to counter-arguments and analyse them properly, but avoid making so many compromises that the project is pointless even if it now becomes achievable.

- Let the final choice be your customer's; give her the advice she needs to make a rational decision. If she understands the risk but still wants to proceed, this is her legitimate right. You may also legitimately question whether the project risk may reflect on you and become a personal risk to your own reputation. No-one succeeds by failing.

- Should the decision not be in your favour, decide on the degree of personal risk and, if it is higher than you want, back out of the project (if possible).

So what do you do in the worst case? if you get to this part of the chapter, let's assume you have done these things. You have assessed the project and it is a disaster waiting to happen; your constructive approach to killing the project has failed. Someone still wants to move it on, and that someone is going to see that it happens. All your judgement and assessments continue to tell you it will be a failure. You have tried to get the work changed or stopped. You have used all your communication skills to say why it is a bad idea.

But no-one is listening to you.

This is the time to pack your bags and say 'no'. You are the professional in these matters and if your customer or sponsor is not going to listen to this, they probably will not listen to anything else you say, which will make your working relationship difficult. I know you cannot always do it, but you will be amazed at the power of simply standing up and moving away from someone, having said something like 'well, I have given my advice to the best of my professional ability, and I respect the fact that you wish to ignore it. I don't have all the answers and it may well be that someone else can deliver this project. I cannot. Good luck and I honestly hope that I am wrong.'

> ❝❝ do not get emotionally involved – argue rationally from simple facts ❞❞

Thank them politely for the opportunity, say 'no' and leave. You owe it to yourself. I am not saying everyone will like you, or many people will thank you, but that is not always what being a consistently successful professional project manager is about.

12

The wider context

Project management does not work in isolation. There are a number of other management disciplines that create the right environment for projects and which work alongside project management to deliver value to an organisation.

Project management is a useful and powerful tool that enables organisations to successfully complete a wide range of endeavours, but getting the most from projects needs more than project management. Projects thrive in organisations in which the environment is conducive to projects, with clear direction, rapid decisions and sufficient authorisations. The creation of this environment is outside the remit of project management and is dependent on activities such as strategy, portfolio management and governance. Additionally, projects aim to deliver value in the form of benefits to the organisation they are run in. The benefits are the return for the investment made in projects. Reliably delivering benefits sometimes takes more than pure project management offers, and consideration has to be given to topics like change management and benefits management, as well as the relationship between projects and business operations.

This chapter is a high-level introduction to a number of areas that are important for the project manager to understand. Key issues are raised, and although this is a brief summary it does contain the critical and most important concepts in each area.

Strategy and projects

Projects are one of the main ways of implementing strategy. Unfortunately for project managers, it is inherent in a modern business for strategy to be vaguer and more volatile than often suits effective project delivery.

Don't we love the word *strategy* in business? Project management is no different. Project managers talk about *project strategies* (the overall approach to achieving a project's objectives) and *project management strategies* (the project management approach that will be used on a project), and endlessly discuss the link between projects and business strategy. It is this link that I want to briefly explore.

This is not a general management book, so I am going to avoid the debate about whether a business strategy is even a meaningful concept in the modern world, and assume it is. This is a reasonable assumption, as the majority of management thinkers still value the idea of business strategy and chide organisations for not having one. Unfortunately, they often disagree on what a useful strategy is. Most project managers accept the need for strategy, and generally spend a lot of time moaning that one does not exist or it is not clear.

The truth is that a lack of an absolutely explicit strategy is the norm for many businesses nowadays, and project managers really ought to just get used to it. The other factor in the modern world is that strategy, if it is to be worthwhile, changes quite rapidly. Unfortunately, for project managers, this is often more rapidly than projects can be completed. Hence the increasing demands for faster and faster projects. This is not simply unreasonable of senior management as it often seems to the project community, but is a reflection of the modern business world. If a strategy radically changes every six months, there is little value in 24-month projects, which may well become irrelevant while they are still being planned in detail. The important point for project managers to remember is that strategy is not created to help project managers – projects exist as one way of implementing strategy. Projects have to be designed to work at the speed of the strategy.

Read most strategy books and they pay little or no attention to projects. This is a shame as projects are one of the main ways of implementing strategy. An understanding of the strengths and weaknesses of project management could help in devising more easily implementable strategies. Strategy should influence the selection of projects by determining organisational priorities (described below in the section on portfolio management). Project objectives and priorities (such as the balance of the iron triangle) should be aligned with strategy, and ideally even day-to-day decision making should be consistent with a business's strategy.

So what can project managers do? It is simply this. Try to seek as much clarity as possible in what the strategy is. Work with project sponsors to interpret the strategy in the context of the project they are responsible for. Align objectives, scope and requirements with the strategy. Make day-to-day decisions on projects that are consistent with strategy. Be prepared for it to be updated, and don't get depressed if half-way through a project the strategy changes to such an extent as to require major modifications to the project. Provide feedback to those responsible for strategy as to whether it is clear, meaningful and deliverable with the available resources. Finally, take every opportunity to educate those who set organisational priorities and strategies about the reality of projects, what will work and what will not. As project managers, we can't really complain about the lack of strategy if we have never told anyone what we need.

Operations and projects

Key lesson

Projects provide benefits to operations, but also create a variety of problems. It is worth understanding these problems from the perspective of operational managers to be able to gain their support.

A strategy is helpful for setting the direction an organisation will go in and for guiding the allocation of resources. But the real day-to-day effort of an organisation, and where all the value is created in a business, is in operations. I use the word *operations* in the broadest way to mean all those things a business does day in and day out to achieve whatever is the rationale for the organisation. So in a typical business this includes procuring inputs, turning those inputs into whatever product or service the business sells, selling them, providing service to customers and all the supporting activities.

The relationship between projects and operations is interesting, and conflicted. A large proportion of projects are involved with making improvements to business operations. Operational managers are the sponsors of and customers for a huge range of projects. Today's operations will not be good enough for tomorrow, and probably already suffer from a number of problems. Projects can be the saviour of operations, offering all sorts of enhancements and improvements to make the job of operational management easier.

It might therefore be thought that operational managers open their arms wide and welcome project managers in to run any and all projects they want. In truth, operational managers are often adverse to projects and sceptical about their benefits. There are a number of reasons for this, and they are reasons the project manager should understand if he or she is to work successfully with operational managers. Common reasons are:

- **Projects require resources**. In a modern business, with years of cost cutting and efficiency drives, operational departments are often stretched thin. The operational manager does not then welcome it when a project manager comes along and asks for staff to come and work on his project – and not any old staff, but often the operational manager's best. This is a reasonable request from the project manager, but it is also perfectly reasonable for the operational manager to be unhappy about it.

- **Projects result in disruption, risking operational performance**. Operational managers will be targeted to achieve all sorts of KPIs and output volumes. Every project results in some degree of change, and it is probably impossible to implement this sort of change without creating disruption. Therefore, whilst in the longer run the operational manager may benefit from the project, in the short run she will often suffer.

- **Past history of projects**. Operational managers have been promised every conceivable benefit in the past and have enthusiastically supported projects. Unfortunately, they have often been disappointed by projects that under-achieve. Every time you ask for an operational manager's support you are fighting against this history.

- **The need to deliver benefits**. Project investments have to be justified, and they are justified by benefits – some cost cutting here, an increase of output there, and numerous performance targets improved. Generally, it is not the project manager who has to deliver these benefits, but the operational manager. Next time you are looking for support at least have some sympathy for the operational manager. What you are actually saying is that in return for something which she has to have faith will be delivered, you are going to ask her to cut her budget or increase targets – in other words make her life harder. Would you trust someone with that bargain, or be happy about it?

- **The number of hours in the day**. The final reason why operational managers may not exactly be over-enthusiastic about your project is that it will mean some work for them – sponsoring or supporting the project. Operational managers are generally already 100% busy and a little extra work may be the last thing they need.

All of these issues can be overcome. Projects are successfully delivered all the time with the proactive and strong support of operational managers, but don't blindly think that they will automatically support you. If you understand where they are coming from, you will have a much better chance of gaining their support.

Programme management

> **Key lesson**
>
> A programme is not simply a name for a large project, but includes endeavours that go beyond projects. Programme management is based on project management, but extends beyond it.

I have not spent much time in this book discussing programmes or programme management. The words crop up occasionally in the text. One reason is that many of the factors that make great project managers will also make great programme managers. But it is overly simplistic to consider programmes as just projects under another name.

There are many different definitions of a programme, and hence of programme management. Sometimes, people apply the term programme simply to denote a large or complex project. We should ignore this definition as it is irrelevant and unnecessary. A big project is just that – a big project. The word programme, if it is to be useful, refers to something slightly different. To me a programme is a series of different projects that are being commonly managed to achieve a common objective. So there may be a customer services programme of several projects all improving customer services. There could be a cost reduction programme, made up of a wide variety of initiatives which contribute towards reducing costs.

Many of the skills of a programme manager are equivalent to those of a project manager. Programme management approaches are essentially an extension of project management, and have developed from project management. Good project managers will easily understand the work of a programme manager. In fact, project managers will in some way do most of the tasks a programme manager does. However, the scale and complexity of the work and the focus of management time can be significantly different.

Where does programme management go beyond project management? There is no single universally accepted definition, but to me a programme manager faces the following challenges in addition to all of those faced by a project manager:

- **Multiple project management.** A project manager sometimes has responsibility for more than one project at a time, especially if the projects are small. Programme managers are always dealing with multiple projects, some of which individually may be large.

- **Managing common risks and issues across projects.** Project managers have to deal with the issues and risks within their projects. Programme managers often have to look for and resolve issues and risks across several projects.

- **Inter-project dependencies.** If a programme is made up of projects, and each project has a competent project manager, one of the most important tasks for the programme manager is to identify and manage inter-project dependencies between those projects.

- **Resource balancing – and prioritisation relative to an outcome and a resource constraint or budget.** Project managers tend to be focused on deliverables. Programme managers' roles are more usually outcomes – to achieve an $x\%$ improvement or a $y\%$ cost reduction. To achieve this they need to consider how the resources allocated to the programme are best balanced across the projects that are being run. Hence some projects can be made faster, and some slower.

- **Deciding on the phasing of projects.** This is related to the resource balancing work a programme manager does. Often the flow of benefits relative to resources available can be maximised by phasing projects differently. A project manager just delivers his or her project. The programme manager has some options over which projects to deliver, and critically in what order.

- **Managing senior stakeholders.** Simply due to the scale of programmes, programme managers are usually dealing with more senior stakeholders. This does not just mean that programme managers need to be better at stakeholder management and communications; it typically means they spend a far higher percentage of their lives dealing with these issues. (If you don't like this side of project management it's probably best to avoid programme management.)

- **Change and benefits management.** Most programme managers take a larger responsibility, even accountability sometimes, for the delivery of business change and the realisation of benefits. (Change and benefits management are discussed below.)

This list gives a flavour of the programme manager's role. If you want to move on from managing projects to programmes, these are the areas of competency you will need to develop.

Portfolio management

> **Key lesson**
>
> Portfolio management is concerned with the selection of the optimal set of projects to achieve organisational goals, relative to the available resources.

Portfolio management is a phrase that is used more and more often in project management circles. It does not have a universal definition. Sometimes the title portfolio manager is used in a similar way to programme managers to denote someone who manages a collection of projects, with portfolio management being the skill set they apply. For me, the term denotes something quite different from project and programme management, and whilst a portfolio manager may once have been a project or programme manager the role they perform is dissimilar.

At their hearts project and programme management are about delivery. Portfolio management is about control and decision making. Whereas project and programme managers seek to optimise the way they manage any project, a portfolio manager seeks to optimise the set of projects and programmes that are being run. To do this there are three main activities within portfolio management:

- **Determining portfolio objectives.** A portfolio is a selection of projects and programmes. Making a selection needs some basis, and the basis is the portfolio objectives. If a company has one portfolio, these objectives should be the subset of the overall organisational goals which are to be achieved through projects. For example, consider a company that wants to reduce its cost base by £100m. The company may task line managers with cutting their budgets through business-as-usual activities by £50m. The other £50m of savings will be delivered through project-based activities. Hence one portfolio objective is to deliver a total of £50m of savings from projects. There will normally be a range of objectives. One of the goals of the portfolio manager is to balance the range of projects across what may be non-complementary objectives such as increasing levels of customer service, reduced costs, increased health and safety, regulatory compliance and so on.

■ **Selecting the optimal set of projects to achieve these objectives relative to the resources available.** The next and perhaps the core task of the portfolio manager is to manage the process by which the projects that are to be delivered are selected. This requires maintaining an inventory of existing and future projects, with sufficient information that they can be compared. Relevant information includes costs, benefits, dependencies, resources required, risks and impacts. This is a non-trivial task. Once there is an inventory, it is possible to select the set of projects that best meet the portfolio objectives and to prioritise between them. This is a simple concept but incredibly hard to do well in practice. The principles of prioritisation were discussed in Chapter 10. Prioritisation is more complex on a portfolio than on a project, but the principles are the same.

■ **Managing the in-life portfolio.** The in-life portfolio is the set of live projects. The portfolio manager is not responsible for project delivery; this lies with the individual project managers. But the portfolio manager needs to track progress, which will rarely be exactly according to original plans or expectations, identify risks to achieving portfolio objectives, and so make regular changes to the portfolio. The portfolio manager, by looking across all projects, is also in a good position to judge the scale of change by department or function of the business and plan implementations so there is no overload in any one area. The complexity of portfolio management is increased by the fact that this is always highly dynamic. New project ideas arise all the time, existing projects over- or under-deliver and take different times than expected, and business priorities and hence portfolio objectives regularly change. A delay in one project impacts other projects because of dependencies, but also because it means resources will be tied up for longer. Portfolio management must deal with challenges like this on a regular basis.

There are many tools and complex techniques for portfolio management. Success is often about managing at a sensible level of detail and accepting that portfolio management can never perfect the selection of projects. Information is never complete and 100% accurate. Additionally, what is the optimal set of projects will change all the time. The portfolio manager needs to respond by adapting the selected projects, but if this is done too often nothing ever gets delivered. One important success factor in portfolio management is the number of projects selected. There is always pressure to add more projects to the portfolio of live projects. It is better to stick to a small set of projects and to deliver them rapidly. Don't clog up the whole business with too many projects, spreading resources too thinly and never getting anything delivered. Taking the hard decisions and doing a few things well, rather than having resources constantly jumping between projects, always ends up with a better result.

Change management

Key lesson

Change management provides a set of theories and tools that extend beyond project management, and which are essential for delivering the sustained change that many projects require.

Like most of the other terms in this chapter, there is no single and universally agreed definition of the term 'change management'. What is important is that any project results in some form of change. If there is no change then the project has delivered nothing. Change management has been developed as a way to ensure the required change occurs, but project and change management are not the same thing. Some project management books present change management as if that is project management. Change management books, in contrast, often do not mention project management. (For a full discussion of the similarities and differences between project and change management, see Chapter 9 of my book: *The practice and theory of project management: creating value through change*.)

The most productive way to consider project and change management is as useful toolkits, and the best project managers (and most programme managers) need to be able to pull from both of these toolkits according to their specific endeavour. Some business changes are implemented without projects (for example, continuous improvement activities), some projects result in very limited business change (for example, many purely technical deliverables), but many projects require significant business change to deliver results. This encompasses all sorts of projects such as organisational redesign activities, IT systems implementations, process enhancements, and building moves.

As I stated in Chapter 9, do not dabble in change management, at least where any significant change is occurring if you don't understand it. Get trained or get specialist help.

So what is the difference between project and change management? That is a long discussion, but it can be summarised as primarily an issue of timing and scope. Change management extends before and after a project's completion. Change management is concerned with developing an environment within a business in which change is possible. This is something that needs to be in place before any projects begin. Change management is also concerned with delivering sustained change. A project creates deliverables and starts a process of change. But it is no good to a business if the organisation reverts to its original status soon after the project has completed. Change management is therefore focused on making sure the change sticks. Whereas project management looks at completing activities and making deliverables, change management is all about the transition of an organisation from one state to another.

There is a close relationship between project and change management. Activities such as stakeholder management are a core part of project management, but are arguably also part of change management. Good project managers plan for the handover of deliverables and the closing down of the project. Most of the handover activities are as much about organisations accepting change as they are about pure project management. Also selecting the most appropriate implementation strategy, from phased roll-outs to 'big bang' implementations, is as relevant to change management as it is project management. A good way for project managers to consider change management is as a set of tools which maximise the likelihood of project success by answering two questions:

- What will facilitate this change – and how can we make use of this?
- What will block this change – and how can we remove or mitigate this?

Change management brings tools in addition to those typically considered as project management. I cannot in the space of a few pages cover all the richness of change management, but there are two aspects of change management which are crucial for the project manager to understand to deliver any kind of change:

▦ From the perspective of individuals in the organisation affected by change. The individual will be asking 'how does this change impact me?' and the project manager wants to know 'how can we persuade this individual to support the change?'.

▦ From the perspective of overall business operations. Operational managers want to know 'how will this change impact the business?', and the project manager wants to know 'how can we ensure we maximise the positive aspects of this change, and minimise the negative?'.

To achieve change at an individual level we must enable individuals to:

▦ Understand the change. This comes about by:

- Repeated communication – why the change is needed, what it is, and how it impacts them personally. Simple, clear and consistent communications are key.

- Providing an opportunity to discuss the change and if possible having an involvement in change design. Involvement is a powerful way of developing understanding and acceptance for the change.

▦ Have the capability to perform in the changed way. If we want someone to use new processes or tools, or to work in a new way, they must have the skills and competencies required to work in this way. Components of providing this capability include:

- Role definitions, process and procedures, tools and systems.

- Providing any necessary training and development.

- Not overloading people with too much change at any one time. It is easy to swamp people with change. It takes time to adapt to any change. Too much change at any one time is always highly risky.

▦ Be motivated to work in a changed way. Unless you have complete control over your staff you cannot force them to work in a changed way. People participate in change rather than have it done to them. For the change to succeed there needs to be some level of motivation to accept the change. Factors in developing this motivation include:

- Ideally, some involvement in the change design. This develops enthusiasm and a sense of ownership.

- Belief in the change. This can be achieved by seeing quick wins and critically the consistent behaviour of their managers, especially senior ones. The first time a senior manager acts in a way that is contrary to the change, you have a major problem on your hands. Consistent behaviour of managers is never easy, but it is important in delivering successful change.

– Performance management and rewards being consistent with the change. There is no point in bonusing staff in one way when your change is trying to do something different. Consistency of rewards with change objectives is essential.

To prepare business operations for change we must do the following:

- Provide quality deliverables that provide the full capability to make the change. It is at the point of implementation into business operations that any compromises on quality to meet project time and cost deadlines will become apparent. Unless the deliverables are fit for purpose the change will not work.

- Provide adequate, trained and motivated human resources (including managers). If people cannot or will not work in the changed way, the operations will not operate in the changed way. It really is that simple.

- Choose the best timing for change. There are good and bad times to make change in businesses. Most businesses have an annual cycle of peaks are troughs in work. Making significant change at a peak time is generally a mistake. Also any other changes that are happening in parallel need to be considered. Like individuals, business operations can only adopt so many changes at once. It is often the capacity to absorb change in operations that finally determines project timelines. On the other hand, when there are dependencies between projects, they all need to be delivered to create the necessary change. For example, if a new IT system requires new PCs to access it, there is little point in rolling out the system in one project until the project implementing the new PCs is also complete.

- Put the correct management processes in place. This includes management roles and responsibilities and defined organisational boundaries, as well as making the necessary management information available to support appropriate management decision making.

Benefits management

Key lesson

Benefits management ensures that value is achieved from projects. Projects should be selected, designed and managed to optimise the flow of benefits relevant to an organisation.

Benefits management or *benefits realisation* is the process used to ensure a project (or other investment) achieves a return in the form of value. Value is often associated with financial factors (reduced costs, increased margins and so on), but value can be in a non-financial but measurable form (such as increased customer satisfaction or improvement in operational KPIs), and can be in intangible form (for example, improved strategic alignment). However value is to be returned to a business, if possible it should be measured or confirmed after a project. This activity of measuring benefits after a project is normally known as *benefits tracking*. It is the fact that a project delivers benefits that is the rationale for doing the project in the first place.

The benefits management process starts with the development of a business case. The business case formally defines the costs and benefits of the projects and generally lays out a rationale for doing the project. The business case should be one of the key considerations in selecting and prioritising projects. It is common to come up with project ideas and then search around for benefits to justify them, but this is not ideal. Ideally you start by identifying what benefits you want to achieve in your business, based on strategic priorities, and then designing projects to achieve them.

Business cases are often overly biased to purely financial measures, and it is generally easier to justify a project with a strong financial benefits case than one with good intangible benefits. This is a mistake. Obviously, financial benefits are critically important and a good proportion of projects should deliver good financial returns, but any organisation, even a business, is more than finances, and other projects that strongly benefit the business but cannot simply be put in financial terms should also be pursued.

It is not simply the scale of benefits that is important, but also their timing. Earlier benefits are disproportionately more valuable than later benefits. This is partially due to factors such as the time value of money, and achieving objectives within accounting years. It is also because strategy changes rapidly. A benefit that is important to a business now may be less critical in a year's time when the strategic focus is elsewhere. If benefits delivery is slow it will always lag behind strategic priorities.

Normally, having developed a business case, the benefits are then forgotten until the end of the project when they may be tracked. Again this is a mistake. Projects are volatile things. The benefits to be achieved will vary throughout the project as assumptions change, because real life turns out to be different from plans, and because of risks and issues. Benefits have to be assessed during project progress and regularly updated. Sometimes benefits increase, sometimes they decrease – occasionally to such an extent that the project is no longer worth continuing. Benefits should be at the forefront of the project manager's mind, as projects can be designed and actively managed to optimise benefits. Factors like the scope, the requirements that are included and the phasing of projects directly impact the scale and timing of benefits. When issues, risks and changes occur, project managers often think only about managing the impact on time or cost of the project. The paramount consideration should be the impact on the benefits. Worry a little less about 'how does this impact time, cost or quality?' and a little more about 'how does this impact the achievement, timing and scale of benefits?'.

Assuming the project is completed and benefits were optimised, it is time to track benefits. This is not as easy as it sounds. There are several problems with being sure that benefits have been achieved, and formally measuring them in some form of benefits tracking approach, including the following:

1 Benefits are often simply difficult to measure. For example, incremental operational efficiency improvements in a complex organisation that are due to a project may be very hard to track. How would you measure the 1.3% efficiency improvement I saw in one project's business case, in your own work?

2 It is usually difficult to be sure that it was the project that delivered the benefits and not some other change elsewhere. In most organisations there are hundreds or even thousands of small changes being implemented all the time. How can you be sure that the benefits achieved are due to your project and not one of the other changes occurring in parallel?

3 Benefits typically arise only after the project has been completed. If a project will deliver cost savings over three years, then you can only be sure that the benefits have been achieved three years later. By this time the project manager and the project team members are probably dispersed, doing work on something else, somewhere else.

4 Benefits are generally only roughly estimated at the start of a project. Even if a full and detailed business case has been developed it is usually riddled with untested assumptions. These sorts of assumptions are often not validated as the project progresses, and may be found out to be wrong only when benefits are not delivered. Initial estimated benefits are good for providing guidance, but poor for

providing an accurate target – they can equally well underestimate benefits as well as overestimate them. (I find that often in the drive to get pet projects approved a sponsor may be over-optimistic when judging benefits, and then commit the project team to delivering them. This can create significant problems for operational managers who have to find the benefits one way or another).

Additionally, measuring benefits can unfortunately drive as much bad behaviour as good if the measures and incentives to hit them are poorly thought through. For example, if your project is to deliver a headcount reduction in a company, and you are measuring and rewarding people based on achieving this, they may focus only on the headcount reduction at the cost of everything else. The answer here is to apply a balanced set of benefit measures, but this takes time and effort.

If well thought through and with sufficient effort, benefits realisation can be achieved, and can be a very positive force driving success on a project. The activities to perform if you are going to manage benefits are:

- Design the project for benefits, not the other way around.
- Define well-estimated benefits at the start of the project. If you are going to track them and measure success against them, it is worth really putting in effort to get the benefits reasonable and clear in the first place. Any assumptions made should be tracked through the project assumption management process.
- Ensure it is possible to measure at least some of these benefits. Projects can be done to achieve intangible benefits, but you cannot track them. A benefit such as a cost saving is conceptually easy to track, something like staff satisfaction is somewhat harder, and incremental improvements in things like company reputation are almost impossible to measure.
- Agree who is responsible for achieving the benefit at the start of the project. This is a source of much contention – it is usually an operational manager who must live with the results of the project once it is completed. By signing up to achieving the benefits, the operational manager is taking a risk that the project will be successfully delivered.
- Constantly manage the project with benefits in mind. Daily decisions can increase or reduce benefits. The project manager should always strive to optimise them.
- Assign resources and responsibility for measuring the benefits. It is a task that will take some time and will not happen unless someone is assigned to doing it.

▨ Set expectations about how much benefit will be achieved during the lifetime of the project and agree with the project sponsor how benefits will be tracked after the project has been completed.

Behaviour on projects will frequently improve when people know the end results will be robustly and formally measured and tracked. Do it, but do not fall into the trap of underestimating the effort required to do this properly.

Governance

Governance provides the overall framework and controls that guide the selection and delivery of projects.

Corporate governance ensures that a company has objectives in line with various stakeholder needs (especially those of shareholders), that achievement of those objectives is monitored, and that action is taken to see that those objectives are attained. Corporate governance is the responsibility of a companies' board of directors. As a significant part of many companies investments are in projects and one of the main ways to achieve strategic goals is through projects, it is logical that projects should also be considered within corporate governance. In reality, many of the issues to do with projects are too detailed to be included within corporate governance, which works at a high level across the whole business. Hence the project management community has developed the concept of project governance (or programme governance or portfolio governance).

Like many words within project management, the term governance has been seized upon and used in a variety of contexts. To me project governance is concerned with the overall framework that is put in place to control and direct projects. It is the responsibility of the board of a company, but in practice is usually delegated and managed quite effectively at a senior operational level. Some of the most important objectives of project governance are to:

▨ Put an adequate portfolio management system in place to optimise the selection of projects.

▨ Ensure alignment of portfolio objectives with strategic goals and ensure that the right projects are being selected.

- Provide a decision-making and authorisation process that facilitates rather than hinders the delivery of projects.
- Provide general oversight and direction.
- Ensure development of an appropriate project and programme management capability within the organisation.
- Insist on the use of robust benefits management and tracking.
- Encourage an environment and culture in which successful project delivery thrives.

Closing thoughts

This book provides guidance for project managers on making the step from basic project management to more advanced skills. It is intended to sit alongside the formal knowledge you have developed and training you have had in project management mechanics.

The irony is that most of the things in this book are intuitively more obvious than many advanced project management processes. That does not mean you should ignore them. When you go and see a great speaker making a presentation, you will often find that when you analyse what he or she has said, those brilliant points rang true and added tremendous value mainly because they were easy to understand and self-evidently correct. It is no different for project managers, as project management is an applied rather than an abstract discipline. It has been interesting for me to note that feedback on earlier editions of this book from students and new project managers has been positive, but with the caveat that 'it's obvious really'. The feedback from more experienced project and programme managers has been consistently along the lines of 'this is truly helpful and has improved the way I deliver projects'. Sometimes we all need a little experience to see the value of the obvious that we never really knew.

I agree with the need for good project management process. You should go away and learn your project management processes, but learn the practical rather than the theoretical way of using them. When you are in action as the project manager no one cares how well you apply the accepted processes and tools – they only care whether the project is delivered or not. If you want to be really good, the processes are not enough.

You need to apply common sense and use the skills referenced in this book. Build up your experience in using the lessons here so they become automatic and intuitive.

Project management can be a boom-to-bust business. When businesses are thriving they absorb huge numbers of project managers. When business is in a downturn and costs are being looked at then project managers are an obvious target. It can be hard working in a profession that tends to be first in and first out, especially in situations where firms often find the only way to cut costs is to stop projects and the only way to stop projects is to fire the project managers. Don't despair, as the very best project managers remain in demand even in the most vicious downturn. Even cost-cutting projects require project managers! In the boom times being a great project manager will drive your success, and in the downturns it will help to maintain your success.

The standards of project management will keep on rising as the occupation continues to become more professional. The days when people became project managers simply because they had nothing else to do are over. The challenge for you as a professional project manager is therefore to learn the lessons and to continue to improve.

Observe other project managers. I have learnt many great lessons from watching other project managers, some of whom have never had a day's formal project management training in their lives. All the advice in this book I have used successfully in practice, but much of it originated from other better project managers. Seek out good project managers and try to work alongside them, or try to work for them as part of a bigger programme and learn their lessons. Learn from yourself as well. When you find a technique that works well, remember it and apply it again.

Every time a project completes, do perform a review of it and think about what went well and what went badly. If it all went wrong, work out why, and be honest with yourself if it was your own fault. Work out what you would do differently next time. You must at least be truthful with yourself. Don't hide behind the fact that there were too many changes, too many risks, too few resources. What did you do about it? You were the project manager! All great project managers have made mistakes at one time or other, but they have survived and learnt from the experience.

Good luck.

Quick reference guide – summary contents

This section provides a quick reference summary to the core contents of the book. It is intended as a rapid *aide-mémoire* which you can call on in your everyday application of the lessons from the book. If you need more detail do refer to the original chapter.

Chapter 1 – Some basics

Key lesson

You must understand and be able to define the key terms used within your project. This must include a clear definition of your role as the project manager, a definition of the customer, and a common understanding of success for your project.

A **project** is essentially a way of working, a way of organising people, and a way to manage tasks. It is a style of coordinating and managing work. What differentiates it from other styles of management is that it is totally focused on a specific outcome, and when this outcome is achieved the project ceases to be necessary and the project is stopped. A project starts at a defined point of time, ends at a specific point in time, and is complete when the outcome (normally as agreed at the beginning of the project, and normally defined in terms of specific tangible deliverables) is complete. It typically has some limited amount of resources, most commonly money and people's time, to deliver the outcome. When the outcome is delivered something will have changed. Although different projects may have some common features, each project is unique, with a specific one-off set of activities. Projects are almost always subject to risk.

Project management is a formal approach to managing projects. It is made up of a defined set of processes, tools and methods.

A **project manager** is someone who is accountable for the delivery of a project (or a specific component of a project if working as part of a hierarchy of project managers).

You must be able to define your role in any specific project. A good way to do this is to be able to identify which components of the project plan and which set of deliverables you are accountable for.

Projects are done for **customers**, where a customer is someone who has any of the following three characteristics:

1   She will legitimately put objectives or requirements upon the project.

2   She will enjoy the benefits of the project once it is complete.

3   She has a formal role in judging the success of a project once it is complete.

Success in a project can be measured against three criteria:

1   Delivery of the deliverables.

2   Achievement of associated benefits.

3   Customer satisfaction.

Chapter 2 – Listening and talking

> **Key lesson**
>
> Think about, plan and execute your communications with care, effort and impact. Your communications must be based on an understanding of your customer that goes beyond the requirements specification and sharing periodic reports. Your communications with the project team must go beyond sharing the project plan and having sporadic updates.

Communication skills are the core differentiator between average and great project managers. If you need to focus on enhancing your skills in any area, start by working on your communication skills. Many points about communication can seem self-evident or obvious, but they are still important. Start by thinking about who you must listen and talk to – this is your 'audience'.

> **Key lesson**
>
> Identify and assess your audience's information needs. Identify who is your customer and plan your interaction with them.

Your 'audience' can be split into three broad categories:

1   **People directly involved in the project** – this can be the project team, but will also include suppliers and other third parties responsible for delivery and delivery-related activities.

2   **Customers of the project** – the person or group of people for whom a project is being delivered. The customer can be broken down into several distinct categories:

    – The sponsor

    – The financer

    – The beneficiary

    – The end user

    – The end customer.

    The project manager has to:

    – Identify who the customers are

    – Identify relative cricticality and importance

    – Determine what information is relevant to them

    – Determine what is the best timing, media and approach to use in passing this information

    – Determine what they need in return from the customer.

3   **Other stakeholders** – a broad group that may include anyone else impacted by, or able to impact the outcome of the project. As far as the stakeholders are concerned the project manager needs to:

    – Identify who the stakeholders are

    – Assess their relevance to the project

    – Target those with significant impact on the project's success

    – Target those significantly impacted by the project's outcome

    – Determine appropriate communication.

Key lesson

There is much more to understanding your customers needs than is written in the requirement specification. As project manager you must understand all the requirements at a high level, and specifically understand fully the scope of the project. Real understanding requires a constant two-way dialogue.

There are several things the project manager always needs to know before she can say she understands what the customer wants. They are:

- The objectives of the project
- The scope of the project

- The measures of success
- The detailed requirements.

There are seven key lessons for the project manager when it comes to understanding customer needs:

1 Make assumptions explicit – minimise the number of assumptions, and if you must assume, get the assumptions clear and shared.

2 Understand the scope – and make sure you can write down the answers and express them in words meaningful to both you and your customer.

3 Make sure you understand the customer requirements and how they relate to the project you are running. Expect differences of opinion and put in place some mechanism for resolving them. The test for you is:

   – Do you have an overall grasp of the customer requirements, and how they relate together to give the overall customer solution?

   – Do you understand why the customer has included these requirements?

   – Has the customer included only requirements which relate to achieving the agreed scope and objectives of the project?

   – Do you understand how these requirements will translate into blocks of work that the project will deliver?

   – Do you understand how these blocks of work hang together?

   – Can you visualise and explain this?

   – Will the combined set of requirements achieve the customer's desired outcome and expectations?

   – Is each requirement clear, unambiguous, traceable (i.e. do you know its source?) and testable (i.e. do you have a way of being certain you have achieved it?)

The answer to all of these questions must be 'yes'. This is not a demand that you understand and memorise each and every line of the requirements specification, and each and every line of every plan within your project. It is a demand that you have a logical understanding of how it all comes together and when you look at every major activity within the project you know why it is being done and what the impact of its failure will be. Without this knowledge you cannot plan, manage or deliver the project. If you are on a project and you cannot answer 'yes' to each of these questions, do some more work so you can answer 'yes' (or find someone else to run it).

4 Keep checking and enhancing your understanding. Being sure last week is not the same as being sure today.

5 Customer needs go beyond the requirements specification – you must also understand how your customer wants to work with you.

6 It's not your project – remember you are working for your customer!

7 Listening is probably your biggest task.

Talk, talk and talk again – the weekly report will not do it all. Practise and learn the eighteen communication lessons to ensure you communicate fully and continuously with your customer and project team.

The basic mechanism for a project manager's communications via is usually some form of regular reporting, be it weekly or monthly (and in some cases daily or quarterly). Also, there are eighteen additional communication capabilities required of project managers. They are as follows.

Lessons 1–4: Your planning and approach to communications

1 Plan your schedule of communications.

2 Accept regular reporting as part of the job.

3 Use formal presentations appropriately.

4 Use informal communications spontaneously and continuously.

Lessons 5–13: The style and method of communications

5 Use your audience's specialist language where appropriate.

6 Avoid too much project management jargon.

7 Clarify what you mean by risks.

8 Present complex information in a clear way.

9 Tailor communications to the audience.

10 Effectively communicate with senior audiences.

11 Do not rely on e-mails.

12 Be specific.

13 Present key factual information in whole messages at discrete time intervals.

Lessons 14–18: Rules to underpin all communications

14 Tell the truth.

15 Maintain only one version of the truth.

16 Obsessively manage expectations.

17 Communicate to deliver (don't deliver to communicate).

18 Remember that you are the role model.

Chapter 3 – What actually is your project?

Key lesson

The foundation on which all good projects are built is a clear understanding of the scope. Without it a project maïnager will struggle to deliver successfully.

Scope is the foundation stone upon which all further project management activities are performed. The scope defines what is in and what is out of the project. Before you understand the scope you must not start to develop your project in any detail. Do not rush into developing solutions until you understand the scope.

Key lesson

The scope of a project can best be understood by going through a set of structured questions with your customer.

A good set of scoping questions are:

1 What is the overall objective of the project?

2 What are the deliverables?
   - Are there are deliverables required by the project which it is explicitly not responsible for?
   - Are you working to deliver a finite set of deliverables or to provide some business capability?
   - Are you working to deliver a set of independent deliverables or an integrated end-to-end solution?
   - How will the quality of deliverables be determined?

3 Are you working to implement a specific solution or to solve a problem?

   – Are you responsible for the delivery of deliverables or for achieving the business benefits?

4 How is the customer going to measure success at the end of the project?

5 What, from the customer's viewpoint, can flex?

   – Do you want predictability or speed?

6 Are there any other constraints on the project?

   – Are there any currently known issues, risks or opportunities?

   – Are there any external considerations?

7 How does your customer want to work with you?

   – How will decisions be made on the project?

   – Can your sponsor allocate all the resources the project requires or do other stakeholders need to be involved?

   – How high is the project in your customer's overall priorities?

   – Who can legitimately put requirements upon the project?

8 Does the customer have any implicit requirements, assumptions or needs that are not defined in the scope or requirements documents?

Chapter 4 – Some key traits

There are three key personality traits required by project managers:

1 A sense of ownership for what they do

2 Good judgement

3 The ability to be creative.

> **Key lesson**
>
> To be the most successful project manager, you must feel and externally display a sense of complete ownership for the project and its outcome.

> **Key lesson**
>
> Each and every project is different and a project manager needs to adapt to each one. Although tools and processes will help, the basis for this adaptation must be the project manager's judgement.

Fifteen sample areas where a project manager regularly needs to apply judgement are:

1 What is in scope? Ensuring the scope is broad enough to achieve value, yet narrow enough to be achievable.

2 What should be in the plan? Making your plan detailed enough to achieve what you need to achieve with it, and yet to be manageable.

3 Which bits of the project management process to apply and which to ignore? If you try to apply every project manager discipline in every situation, you will spend your whole life managing and nothing will actually be delivered.

4 When to escalate? Finding the balance between escalating too soon and too late.

5 When to get into the detail and when to skim?

6 When to do and when to delegate?

7 Who can you trust in your project team?

8 What is an acceptable level of risk? The things to think about when assessing whether the level of risk is acceptable are:
   – Do you fully understand the risk or is it just the tip of an iceberg?
   – Are the risks independent issues or are they interrelated and cumulative?
   – Have you got a way around this risk – can it be reduced, can you mitigate it happening, or do you have a contingency plan should it happen? (Is the plan viable and are there resources to implement it?)
   – How risk-averse or risk-favouring is the organisation you are working in?
   – How critical is it that the project is delivered? If the risk derails the project, will that have a significant impact on your customer or will they cope easily?
   – How good is your project team? A strong team is usually better able to handle and resolve risks.

9 What is an acceptable level of parallel activity? The questions you need to ask yourself are:
   – Do you have sufficient resources to do the work in parallel?
   – Are any of the tasks now in parallel logically only possible sequentially?

   – What is the impact on testing and training?

   – Can you as the project manager actually manage this?

   – What is the impact on individual team members?

   – What is the impact on benefits delivery?

10 What is an acceptable level of change? The key things to do are:

   – Ensure there is a robust change control process.

   – Develop an ability to explain the impact of change unemotionally.

   – Determine how important the change is.

   – Determine what the impact of the change on the project is.

   – Assess how the project team members are handling it.

11 When should you enforce the change management process?

12 When is it reasonable to progress based on an assumption?

   – What is the impact of not making an assumption? (Will your work be delayed, cost added, etc.?)

   – What is the risk of making an assumption? (How likely is it that it will be wrong, and what will be the impact if it is?)

   – How easy or difficult would it be to confirm the assumption you want to make?

13 How many levels of project management organisation do you need? One simple way of looking at it is how many people do you have managing work as opposed to doing work? If your number of managers is not a small percentage (less than 25%, perhaps as low as 10%) of the doers then you have too many layers of management. I have seen projects where 40–50% of the team seem to be managing rather than delivering – this is too high. Countering this, if you have significantly less than a 10% management overhead you probably have too few managers.

14 When to consider broader stakeholder groups?

15 When is the project complete?

Key lesson

Never be creative with your customer's requirements, but always look for creative ways to deliver those requirements.

Creativity has its roots in many places. In practice the main sources of creativity are:

- Yourself and the project team
- Other people
- Formal processes.

Chapter 5 – Getting your project started

> **Key lesson**
>
> The way you plan and resource your project will set the framework and constraints within which you will operate through the project. Take the time and make the effort to do it properly.

The following points should be considered in planning:

1 What your plan is for:

- Forming a view of what tasks there are in a project and thus how long it will take, and from this be able to derive what resources will be required.
- Explaining to senior managers and other stakeholders how a project will be delivered.
- Enabling people involved in the project to be allocated to work and for them to understand how their work fits within the project.

2 Therefore you should consider in every situation in which you are using a plan:

- The level of detail required in this situation
- The presentation format
- The degree of 'specificity' – for example, is it generic about resources and resource type, or is it specific and names a particular individual?

3 The basic planning process is:

- Build a work breakdown structure.
- Identify and build in the dependencies between the tasks.
- Add the lengths of time each task will take.
- Determine the resource types and quantities you need to meet this plan.

- Add in your resource availability – and update the plan.
- Add in appropriate levels of contingency.
4 The factors to consider in building your plan are:
    - Who helps you develop the plan?
    - Milestones
    - How many plans?
    - The level of detail in your plan, both overall and at the different stages
    - Task size
    - The types of dependencies
    - How much parallel activity you will allow
    - What consideration you will give to risk.

Key lesson

Be prepared to change your plan – the measure of success is not an unchanging plan, but meeting the end goals within the reality of continuous change.

The following points should be considered in estimating task duration and resources:

- Estimate task length for tasks you understand.
- Make sure the requirements are clear.
- Look for someone with experience to help you.
- Break a task down into smaller known tasks if possible and if this helps.
- Look for similar activities to model on.
- In the worst case – make an assumption.

Key lesson

When presenting time, cost or resource estimates, correlate the detail and precision of your estimate with the level of certainty associated with it.

The following points should be considered in resourcing:

1 The key questions resourcing will resolve are:
    - Where are you going to get resources from?

– How are the people allocated to the project going to interact with the organisation in which they work?

– How are you going to organise the project team members within the project?

2   The basic points to resource allocation are:

– To determine from the plan what skills you require, and how many people with those skills you need for how long.

– To work with resource owners (generally line managers), to get the necessary people allocated to the project.

– To reflect on the degree of risk and contingency required the project.

– To aggregate resources to understand points of over- and under-usage.

– To avoid thinking that the solution to every problem is to add more resources.

– To reiterate the plan taking account of the actual resources available, which may be different from those you originally requested. You may reiterate between planning and resourcing several times. (In fact, to some extent this is a continuous interplay for the life of the project.)

3   The organisation of the project team. Take account of:

– Size of project

– Stage of a project

– Complexity of the work

– Type of staffing

– Relationship to end users.

It's not just people we have to resource a project with! You must also budget for:

▨ Items the project must buy as components of deliverables.

▨ Items the project must pay for as they are required to do the work in the project.

▨ External resource costs – contractors and consultants.

▨ Internal resource costs – staff from your own organisation.

Key lesson

Having contingency built into a plan is essential and is not a sign of poor project management. The critical factor is how much contingency, and how you allocate and manage this. This should be related to the degree of risk of your specific project.

The basic process for including contingency in your plan is:

- Avoid building contingency into every activity.
- Hold your contingency pot centrally.
- Manage people to hit the plan – but release contingency when required.
- Manage and monitor your contingency pot. If it is disappearing faster than progress on the project, you have a problem looming.

The following points should be considered with regard to mobilisation. Mobilisation is to:

- Energise and align the project team. If it is a large project team this may take some considerable effort (see also Chapter 8).
- Ensure the broader stakeholder community is supportive of the project and ready for it (or you have activities planned to overcome resistance where necessary).
- Ensure project team members understand the objectives of their involvement, the specific work tasks that have been allocated to them, and how they fit within the overall plan.

Key lesson

Project management theory often defines the ideal environment to set up and run a project in. In practice, not all ideal environmental conditions will be achieved, and as a project manager you must learn to deliver in sub-optimal situations, managing a variety of constraints and compromises.

When you have to work within constraints:

- See the constraint as a constructive challenge.
- Plan your project without the constraint at first.
- Assess the impact of the constraint.
- Then review your approach to your project.
- Look at the project lifecycle you are implementing and see if additional stages need to be added.
- Are there mitigating actions you can take?
- Talk to your customer and explore options.
- In doing this, present them with options.

- Make an explicit decision on how you will manage this constraint.
- Having decided which path you are taking, re-plan the project accordingly and communicate the changes.

Chapter 6 – Personal styles

> **Key lesson**
>
> There is no right interpersonal style for a project manager; successful project managers have a variety of styles. But there are certain approaches to avoid, and some key attributes of style to develop.

> **Key lesson**
>
> Certain interpersonal styles will limit your success as a project manager.

Styles to avoid:

1 Bully boys

2 Process nuts, compulsive planners and detail obsessives

3 The 'Teflon man'

4 The panicking manager.

> **Key lesson**
>
> Choose the personal style that best develops your personal brand. Build the attributes of good style to help you succeed.

What are the attributes of personal style that have the largest impact on people's perception of you? There are eleven factors:

1 Having empathy with your customer

2 Displaying both management and leadership skills

3 The ability to handle stress

4 Respect for people

5 Dynamism and positivism

6 Networking skills

7 Political sensitivity

8 Having sufficient presence

9 A sense of humour

10 Being sensitive to your environment

11 Adapting your style to the situation.

Chapter 7 – Managing your project

> **Key lesson**
>
> To manage projects a project manager must understand what she should be managing, have a mechanism to provide information to understand when management action is required, and finally implement action when the information tells her it is necessary.

> **Key lesson**
>
> The degree of difficulty in managing a project is closely related to how well you have set the foundations (in terms of expectations, scope, plan and resources) in place.

1 What should you manage?
   – The time the project is taking to deliver
   – The resources you are using to deliver
   – The quality of the work done and the deliverables produced
   – The scope and outcome
   – Your customer's expectations.

2 How do you know to take management action?
   – Formal progress reporting and progress monitoring:
      – Progress reports and other formal inputs from the project team
      – Ongoing planning and monitoring
      – Budget and spend tracking
      – Project team meetings.
   – Use and assessment of outputs from project management tools, e.g.:
      – Risk management
      – Issue management
      – Assumption management
      – Change control.

 – Quality control and quality audits of deliverables
 – Informal day-to-day conversations and communications
 – Direct feedback from the customer.

3 How should you manage?

 – Change the way the team are working
 – Change resources on a project
 – Change the scope of a project
 – Add tasks to the project
 – Change the plan or approach
 – Change the quality
 – Make decisions and escalate to senior managers where necessary, for them to make decisions
 – Terminate the project.

Key lesson

The success of a project manager depends on an understanding of what can be managed and the sources of information to trigger management action. The measure of success depends only on the taking of the action and its result.

Key lesson

Change control provides a mechanism for a project manager to respond to changes in a project's scope and requirements in a controlled fashion. It is essential to successful project management to have a robust change control process supported by ongoing expectation setting.

Change control and management

▨ Capture and log any changes that are proposed.

▨ Understand and assess the change.

▨ Determine viable options for responding to the change and determine the resulting impact upon the project.

▨ Discuss with the sponsor and agree whether to accept the change, and if so which approach to take to it.

▨ Adapt your plans accordingly.

Decision making

The key points about decision making are that it is a constant trade-off between the following:

■ How critical is the decision and what is the impact if it is wrong?

■ How critical is the decision and what is the impact if you take too much time to make it? (The most difficult to make are those that must be made quickly but that also need lots of information and have a big impact if wrong.)

■ Understanding who can and who should make the decision. Can you do it? Do you need an expert specialist? Is it something for your sponsor to decide?

■ What is the culture of your organisation? Some companies value considered decision making, others value speed and pace over accuracy.

Chapter 8 – The team

> **Key lesson**
>
> One of the main tasks for a project manager is to manage and motivate the project team to deliver all that is required for the project. Pure project management process and methodologies will not achieve this. A project manager above all else is a people manager.

To get the best from the project team, the project manager should follow seventeen people management tasks.

Getting the basics right – right people, right skills, right tasks (management tasks 1–5)

1　Ensure the project team has the right capabilities and skills – managing any gap between the abilities of the project team and the needs of the project as a risk.

2　Go for quality rather than quantity. When in doubt always go for fewer, better people – they will be easier to manage and will produce more.

3　Ensure all team members have clear roles and defined objectives. Everyone on the team should therefore know:

– What their role is and what the tasks are that they are expected to perform. This should be defined clearly and succinctly.

- Who on the project is allowed to allocate them work, and to decide whom they will be working with or for.
- Whom they need to interact and work with to complete their tasks.
- How much time they are expected to spend on the project (in terms of both duration and percentage of time in this period to be made available to the project).
- What the measures of success for their task are.
- Why they were chosen. Even if it is true, avoid telling people that they are on the project because they were the only person available, as it is not very motivating!

4 Be clear about *how* you want people to work.

5 Manage poor performance, give people a chance, but do not hesitate to throw people off the project team if they are adding unnecessary or unmanageable risk.

Motivating and building the team (management tasks 6–10)

6 Align personal objectives and motivation with the needs of the project – even without direct line authority over team members.

7 Actively work to build the team.

8 Align personal development needs and opportunities for team members with project activities.

9 If possible, ensure project team members have a home to go back to once the project is complete.

10 Be aware of team dynamics and team politics.

Project team management challenges (management tasks 11–15)

11 Try to get the project team working in close physical proximity, and manage the communications channels. Where it is not possible to make people work in close proximity make sure that communications chains are robust, and that people communicate in the most 'intimate' ways possible. By this I mean ideally face-to-face, next via video conference, then by phone and, finally, by e-mail (and e-mail should be seen very much as the poorest way to communicate).

12 Do not forget your physically remote and geographically diverse staff.

13 Learn to manage part-time staff – not all resources will be full time, dedicated to your project.

14 Learn to manage upwards.

15 Learn to manage specialists who are not dedicated to the project.
Ensure that the specialist in question has actually set aside time for
your task, fully understands the implication of being late, has a clear
understanding of the quality required and the degree of risk
acceptable to the project; and finally understands that you are an
important client who needs to be satisfied.

The broader context (management tasks 16–17)

16 Don't forget the wider organisation – manage your relationship and
communications with them.

17 Plan for the end of the project and disbanding the project team.

Chapter 9 – The limits of knowledge

There are two traps project managers sometimes fall into. The first is to
try to apply generic project management skills to the situation in which
a specialist is required. The second is to try to do things that are best
done by other people.

> **Key lesson**
>
> Complex projects are best managed to successful delivery by people skilled in
> project management. Project management is largely a generic approach to
> managing projects, but being a project manager is not a completely generic skill
> that can be applied to any project in any situation. To be successful, project
> managers need to understand and be able to use the language, concepts and
> ideas which are used within the context of the project they are managing.

If you are a project manager and are having to consider whether you are
competent to manage a project in any specific situation, ask yourself:

1 Are you comfortable managing this scale of project?

2 Do you broadly understand the content of the project and any
associated concepts?

3 Are you able to operate within the organisation this project is for? Do
you generally understand any specialist language and terminology
they use?

4 Can you plan, direct and control the various components of the
project, assuming the necessary specialists are available to do the work?

5   Can you assess the quality of the deliverables?

6   Can you challenge the specialists competently?

7   Will the project team and customer accept you and follow your
    instructions?

If the answer to all seven of these questions is 'yes', then you have
enough specialist skills to manage the project.

Key lesson

Project managers must respect the need for a range of specialist disciplines on
their project, and must fight for all the resources the project needs. Being a project
manager on a large project is a full-time job, and even if the project manager has
the skills to do other tasks he must focus his time and energy on managing the
project and not doing other project tasks.

There are seven regular culprit areas of work that project managers often
try to do themselves when they are usually better off using a specialist
expert in the area. The culprits are:

1   Business analysis and requirements capture

2   Change management. The three key uses of this term are:
    - Project change management – legitimately part of a project
      manager's role.
    - Operational change management – typically the responsibility of
      an operational manager, but needs to be understood by the project
      manager.
    - People and organisational change management – to be done by
      specialists in change management.

3   Systems integration and testing

4   Supplier negotiations

5   Contract and legal issues

6   Project office

7   Communications. Projects that have been set up to drive things such
    as large organisational change activities often need much wider
    communication – for example, to thousands of staff impacted across a
    company. This type of communication is more akin to a marketing,
    journalistic or PR skill set than straightforward communications by a
    project manager to customers or team members.

Having looked at some areas which are close to the project manager's heart, but critically not his responsibility in all but the simplest project, what actually should he do about these?

1 Get a basic level of competence in all of these areas – not to complete complex tasks in each area but so you can actively and fully interact with professionals in each of these disciplines and so you can manage them.

2 Learn when and how to engage people in each of these areas.

3 Learn to use their language and concepts so you can manage and challenge them without doing their job.

4 If you do engage them make sure your project sponsor understands why it is not your task and what the specialist brings.

Ask yourself four questions if you are unsure whether to pick up a task or not:

1 Do you understand the task well enough to be able to fully scope out what needs to be done?

2 Do you have the knowledge and experience to complete the tasks to the quality required and without exposing the project to unnecessary risk?

3 Is the input of a professional in this area optional?

4 Do you have the time to do this work without jeopardising your project management responsibilities?

Only if you can answer 'yes' to all four of these questions should you do the task.

Chapter 10 – The mechanics of project management

> **Key lesson**
>
> Project management methodologies contain a rich set of approaches and tools, yet project managers frequently apply only a few of these. Do not forget the other components which on complex and risky projects will be very useful. Successful project managers have a very broad toolkit which they make use of regularly.

Excluded because they are covered elsewhere in the book, or are not relevant to the book:

1 Planning (Chapter 5)

2 Project change control procedures (Chapter 7)

3 Decision making (Chapter 7)

4 Creating standard forms and documents

5 Creating weekly and monthly reports to a standard format

6 Allocation of resources and management using tools such as timesheets and time recording systems

7 Use of common project management software.

Good project managers accept that each and every project is different, and they therefore adapt their approach accordingly – choosing which parts of the project manager's toolkit to apply in which situations – and applying them in the simplest fashion commensurate with the complexity and scale of the project.

Thirteen skills to ensure you understand and apply as required are as follows.

Skills 1–7: The core project management mechanics

1 Management of assumptions:
   - Identify them
   - Document them
   - Challenge them
   - Assess them
   - Assign an owner
   - Set target dates to resolve them by
   - Communicate them
   - Monitor them
   - Resolve them.
2 Sign off – do it.
3 Management of external dependencies:
   - Ensure you understand what project or piece of work is delivering the dependency, and who is responsible for ensuring it is being delivered.
   - Try to see if you can remove the dependency.
   - Ensure somebody somewhere is responsible for delivering the dependency.

- Get periodic updates on progress.
- Probe the progress reports to give confidence that they are accurate.

4 The time–cost–quality–scope trade-off – understand it fully and apply it in day-to-day decision making.

5 Understand and apply risk and issue management proactively. Risk management tips:

- Make sure you understand what the risk really is.
- Use a phased project approach that enables you to understand and manage risk. Performing a feasibility study is essentially a risk management step – with it you can:
  - reduce uncertainty in the plans
  - identify specific risks that need to be managed
  - clarify where you need contingency plans
  - build a project plan accordingly.
- Ensure your project has a robust risk management approach, and regularly identify and review the risks that you have.
- Assess these risks to see whether any of them results in a significant chance of something occurring with a significant impact on the project. If this is true you need to do something about the risk.
- Plan what you can do about the risk. This essentially falls into four categories:
  - Maintain a watching brief.
  - Mitigate against the risk.
  - Mitigate against the impact of the risk.
  - Have a contingency plan.

6 Contingency planning and triggers. The key points to think through with respect to contingency plans are:

- What triggers your contingency plan?
- Do you have the resources to implement the contingency plan?
- Does it actually reduce risk?
- What can you de-scope if the choice is not delivering?

7 Using escalation effectively.

Skills 8–12: Supporting mechanics

8 Stakeholder analysis:

- High impact, high support

- High impact, low support
- Low impact, high support
- Low impact, low support.

9 Use of project office:
- Do you understand what you may want the project office to do?
- Will this make you more efficient or effective?
- Who has access to the project office resource?
- Does everyone else understand what it does?

10 Administration and management of meetings.

11 Prioritisation:
- On what basis are you prioritising? You need to have some measure by which to form the basis of prioritisation.
- Go for broad, simple categorisation of tasks that everyone understands, such as:
  - Must do, cannot slip
  - Must do, can allow to slip to a limited extent
  - Must do, time can move
  - Optional, but important
  - Optional, not critical.
- Be prepared for a reasonable degree of volatility and to respond to escalation requests.
- Make sure the prioritisation is explicit.
- Be ruthless in applying priorities once they are agreed.
- Do not confuse how urgent a task is with how important it is.
- Agree what you do with low priority tasks.
- Consider the time–cost–quality–scope trade-off when setting priorities.

12 Use of project lifecycles:
- Understand the principles of different lifecycles and apply them as appropriate.
- Be able to use the correct language on lifecycles for the context you are working in.
- Vary the lifecycle to suit the type of problem you are trying to resolve.

Chapter 11 – Knowing when to say 'no'

Project management is about ensuring delivery, not about pointless hero-ics against unassailable odds. When things are not going to happen it is best to avoid them, or better still, ensure they are killed off before they get anywhere. No matter how well you do it, you will not get to be a great or successful project manager by spending your whole life bril-liantly failing to deliver impossible projects. A useful skill is therefore knowing when to say 'no', and equally important how to say 'no'.

> **Key lesson**
>
> Just because someone thinks they need a project manager, it does not mean that they really do, nor that it is actually the best use of your time.

Before accepting project work it is worth considering:

- Is this the best use of the project manager?
- Does this project manager have the right sort of skills?
- Is this really a project-based activity?

> **Key lesson**
>
> There are many clear indications when a project is likely to fail. Look for these and assess whether you are able to manage the risks or not.

Danger signs to look for are:

- No energy
- No real drive or sponsorship
- No willingness to free up the right resources
- Overly demanding customers with unreasonable expectations
- Customers with fixed ideas and a lack of listening skills
- Conflicting goals, or too many goals
- Conflicting customers
- Poor understanding of requirements or scope
- Lack of flexibility to plan
- Not enough time to test

- Too many parallel activities and too short a time for key tasks, including testing or training, in the plan
- High risk with tight deadlines and no contingency plans
- Unknown technology or solutions for a demanding high-throughput situation
- The project that has been kicking around for years.

> **Key lesson**
>
> It is far better to kill off bad ideas, or impractical good ideas, than to try to run an impossible project.

> **Key lesson**
>
> If you can, walk away from impossible projects. Gallantly failing to deliver is still failure.

Chapter 12 – The wider context

> **Key lesson**
>
> Project management does not work in isolation. There are a number of other management disciplines that create the right environment for projects and which work alongside project management to deliver value to an organisation.

Strategy and projects

> **Key lesson**
>
> Projects are one of the main ways of implementing strategy. Unfortunately for project managers, it is inherent in a modern business for strategy to be vaguer and more volatile than often suits effective project delivery.

- Try to seek as much clarity as is possible in what the strategy is.
- Work with project sponsors to interpret the strategy in the context of the project they are responsible for.
- Align objectives, scope and requirements with the strategy.
- Make day-to-day decisions on projects that are consistent with the strategy.

- Be prepared for it to be updated, and don't get depressed if half-way through a project the strategy changes to such an extent as to require major modifications to the project.
- Provide feedback to those responsible for strategy as to whether it is clear, meaningful and deliverable with the available resources.
- Take every opportunity to educate those who set organisational priorities and strategies about the reality of projects, what will work and what will not.

Operations and projects

Key lesson

Projects provide benefits to operations, but also create a variety of problems. It is worth understanding these problems from the perspective of operational managers to be able to gain their support.

To gain operational support for a project, the project manager should understand the operational manager's issues, for example:

- Projects require resources.
- Projects result in disruption, risking operational performance.
- Past history of projects.
- The need to deliver benefits.
- The number of hours in the day.

Programme management

Key lesson

A programme is not simply a name for a large project, but includes endeavours that go beyond projects. Programme management is based on project management, but extends beyond it.

Where programme management goes beyond project management:

- Multiple project management.
- Managing common risks and issues across projects.
- Inter-project dependencies.

- Resource balancing – and prioritisation relative to an outcome and a resource constraint or budget.
- Deciding on the phasing of projects.
- Managing senior stakeholders.
- Change and benefits management.

Portfolio management

Key lesson

Portfolio management is concerned with the selection of the optimal set of projects to achieve organisational goals, relative to the available resources.

The three main activities within portfolio management:

- Determining portfolio objectives.
- Selecting the optimal set of projects to achieve these objectives relative to the resources available.
- Managing the in-life portfolio.

Change management

Key lesson

Change managemenrt provides a set of theories and tools that extend beyond project management, and which are essential for delivering the sustained change that many projects require.

A good way for project managers to consider change management is as a set of tools which maximise the likelihood of project success by answering two questions:

- What will facilitate this change – and how can we make use of this?
- What will block this change – and how can we remove or mitigate this?

Two crucial aspects of change management for project managers:

- From the perspective of individuals in the organisation affected by change. The individual will be asking 'how does this change impact me?' and the project manager wants to know 'how can we persuade this individual to support the change?'.

- From the perspective of overall business operations. Operational managers want to know 'how will this change impact the business?', and the project manager wants to know 'how can we ensure we maximise the positive aspects of this change, and minimise the negative?'.

To achieve change at an individual level we must enable individuals to:

- Understand the change. This comes about by:
  - Repeated communication
  - Providing an opportunity to discuss the change and if possible having an involvement in change design
- Have the capability to perform in the changed way:
  - Role definitions, process and procedures, tools and systems
  - Providing any necessary training and development
  - Not overloading people with too much change at any one time.
- Be motivated to work in a changed way. Factors in developing this motivation include:
  - Ideally, some involvement in the change design
  - Belief in the change
  - Performance management and rewards being consistent with the change.

To prepare business operations for change we must:

- Provide quality deliverables that provide the full capability to make the change.
- Provide adequate, trained and motivated human resources (including managers).
- Choose the best timing for change.
- Put the correct management processes in place.

Benefits management

Key lesson

Benefits management ensures that value is achieved from projects. Projects should be selected, designed and managed to optimise the flow of benefits relevant to an organisation.

The activities to perform if you are going to manage benefits are:

- Design the project for benefits, not the other way around.
- Define well-estimated benefits at the start of the project.
- Ensure it is possible to measure at least some of these benefits.
- Agree who is responsible for achieving the benefit at the start of the project.
- Constantly manage the project with benefits in mind.
- Assign resources and responsibility for measuring the benefits.
- Set expectations about how much benefit will be achieved during the lifetime of the project and agree with the project sponsor how benefits will be tracked after the project has been completed.

Governance

Key lesson

Governance provides the overall framework and controls that guide the selection and delivery of projects.

Some of the most important objectives of project governance are to:

- Put an adequate portfolio management system in place to optimise the selection of projects.
- Ensure alignment of portfolio objectives with strategic goals and ensure that the right projects are being selected.
- Provide a decision making and authorisation process that facilitates rather than hinders the delivery of projects.
- Provide general oversight and direction.
- Ensure development of an appropriate project and programme management capability within the organisation.
- Insist on the use of robust benefits management and tracking.
- Encourage an environment and culture in which successful project delivery thrives.

Index

Page numbers in **bold** indicate **chapters**
Pages in *italic* indicate chapter *summaries*

FINANCIAL TIMES

Think big for less